The media's watc
Here's a sampling

VAULT GUIDE TO THE
TOP 25 TECHNOLOGY CONSULTING FIRMS

VAULT GUIDE TO THE
TOP 25 TECHNOLOGY CONSULTING FIRMS

**NAOMI NEWMAN
AND THE STAFF OF VAULT**

Library of Congress CIP Data is available.

ISBN 13: 978-1-58131-417-5

ISBN 10: 1-58131-417-5

Printed in the United States of America

ACKNOWLEDGMENTS

We are extremely grateful to Vault's entire staff of writers, editors and interns for all their help in the editorial and production processes.

In order to ensure that our research was thorough and accurate, we relied on a number of people within the consulting firms that we profiled. A special thanks to all of the recruiting managers, public relations executives, marketing professionals and consultants who graciously provided feedback whenever we needed it.

To the consultants who took the time to be interviewed or to complete our survey, we could never thank you enough. Your insights about life inside the top consulting firms are invaluable, and your willingness to speak candidly will be a great service to job seekers and career changers for years to come.

Table of Contents

INTRODUCTION   1

A Guide to This Guide 2

THE VAULT PRESTIGE RANKINGS   5

Ranking Methodology 7

The Vault 25 9

OVERVIEW OF THE TECHNOLOGY CONSULTING
INTERVIEW   11

The State of Technology Consulting 13

Practice Areas 16

THE VAULT 25   21

1. Booz Allen Hamilton 22

2. Deloitte Consulting LLP 36

3. IBM Global Services 44

4. Cisco Systems, Inc. 58

5. Accenture 66

6. Lockheed Martin Corporation 80

7. Oracle Consulting 90

8. Capgemini 96

9. HP Services 104

10. BearingPoint 114

11. Computer Sciences Corporation 130

12. EDS 140

13. Unisys 150

14. Sapient 160

15. DiamondCluster International Inc. 168

16. Keane 180

17. Perot Systems 188

18. Infosys Technologies Ltd. 198

19. Getronics NV 206

20. Wipro Ltd. 212

21. CGI Group Inc. 218

22. Tata Consultancy Services 226

23. Fujitsu Consulting 236

24. PA Consulting Group 242

25. BT 248

THE BEST OF THE REST   253

Affiliated Computer Services, Inc. 254

Ajilon Consulting 262

Alliance Consulting Group 270

Appian Corporation 276

Aquent 282

Atos Origin 288

Bull 294

CIBER Inc. 298

Covansys Corporation 304

CTG 310

Financial Insights, an IDC Company 314

GFI Informatique 318

Interactive Business Systems, Inc. 322

LogicaCMG 326

Satyam Computer Services Ltd. 334

T-Systems 340

Technology Solutions Company 346

Telcordia Technologies 350

TIAX LLC 356

Xansa 362

APPENDIX   367

Index of Firms 368

About the Editor 372

Visit the Vault Consulting Career Channel at www.**vault.com/consulting** — with
insider firm profiles, message boards, the Vault Consulting Job Board and more.

V/\ULT CAREER
LIBRARY   **xi**

Introduction

Welcome to the third edition of the *Vault Guide to the Top 25 Technology Consulting Firms*. This is the third year we've published our guide to the technology consulting firms—everything from tech strategy stars to top implementors. The 25 top technology consulting firms were chosen and ranked by 741 practicing technology consultants though an exclusive Vault survey. In total, you'll find 45 technology consulting firms in this guide.

The technology consultants in this book range from gigantic powerhouses like Booz Allen Hamilton and IBM Global Services to specialized boutiques, and are headquartered all over the world. One thing's for certain, though—they're all top, desirable technology consulting employers.

Technology—and technology consulting—is a key factor in the workplace of the 21st century. Do your research. Take a look at the firms in our guide—you might be choosing your next employer.

Good luck with your technology consulting career!

The Editors

Vault, Inc.

A Guide to this Guide

If you're wondering how our entries are organized, read on. Here's a handy guide to the information you'll find packed into each firm profile in this book.

Firm facts

• **Locations:** A listing of the firm's offices, with the city of its headquarters bolded. For firms with a relatively small number of offices, all cities are included. Countries for international offices are typically not specified unless the location is uncommon.

• **Practice Areas:** Official departments that employ a significant portion of the firm's consultants. Practice areas are listed in alphabetical order regardless of their size and prominence.

• **Uppers and Downers:** Good points and, shall we say, less positive points of the firm, as derived from consultant interviews and surveys, as well as other research. Uppers and downers are perceptions based on surveys, research and interviews and are not based on statistics.

• **Employment Contact:** The person, address or web site that the firm identifies as the best place to send resumes, or the appropriate contact to answer questions about the recruitment process. Sometimes more than one contact is given.

The Buzz

When it comes to other consulting firms, our respondents are full of opinions! We asked them to detail their opinions and observations about firms other than their own, and collected a sampling of these comments in The Buzz.

When selecting The Buzz, we included quotes most representative of the common outside perceptions of the firms, even if in our opinion the quotes did not accurately or completely describe the firm. Please keep in mind when reading The Buzz that it's often more fun for outsiders to trash than praise a competing consulting firm. Nonetheless, The Buzz can be a valuable means to gauge a firm's reputation in the consulting industry, or at least to detect common misperceptions. We typically included two to four Buzz comments. In some instances we opted not to include The Buzz if we did not receive a representative array of comments.

The Stats

• **Employer Type:** The firm's classification as a publicly traded company, privately held company or subsidiary.

• **Ticker Symbol:** The stock ticker symbol for a public company, as well as the exchange on which the company's stock is traded.

• **Chairman, CEO, etc.:** The name and title of the leader(s) of the firm or of the firm's consulting business.

• **Employees:** When disclosed, the total number of employees, including consultants and other staff, at a firm in all offices (unless otherwise specified). Some firms do not disclose this information; figures from the most recent year the information is available (if at all) are included.

• **Revenues:** The gross sales the firm generated in the specified fiscal year(s). Some firms do not disclose this information; numbers from the most recent year the information is available (if at all) are included. In some cases, revenues are given in Euros.

The Profiles

The profiles are divided into three sections: The Scoop, Getting Hired and Our Survey Says.

• **The Scoop:** The firm's history, clients, recent firm developments and other points of interest.

• **Getting Hired:** Qualifications the firm looks for in new associates, tips on getting hired and other notable aspects of the hiring process.

• **Our Survey Says:** Actual quotes from surveys and interviews with current consultants of the firm on topics such as firm culture, feedback, hours, travel requirements, pay, training and more. Profiles of some firms do not include an Our Survey Says section.

The Best of the Rest

Even though the name of this book is the *Vault Guide to the Top 25 Technology Consulting Firms*, we didn't stop there, adding 20 other firms we thought notable and/or interesting enough for inclusion. These firms are listed alphabetically.

THE VAULT
PRESTIGE
RANKINGS

Ranking Methodology

For the 2007 edition of the *Vault Guide to the Top 25 Technology Consulting Firms*, we selected a list of top technology consulting firms to include on the Vault survey. These firms were selected because of their prominence in the technology consulting industry and their interest to job seekers.

The Vault survey was distributed to the firms on Vault's list in the summer and fall of 2005. In some cases, Vault contacted practicing consultants directly. Survey respondents were asked to do several things. They were asked to rate each consulting firm on the survey on a scale of 1 to 10 based on prestige, with 10 being the most prestigious. (Consultants were unable to rate their own firm and were asked only to rate firms with which they were familiar.)

Vault collected 741 survey results and averaged the score for each company. The firms were then ranked, with the highest score being No. 1, all the way down to No. 25.

We also asked survey respondents to give their perceptions of other consulting firms besides their own. A selection of those comments is featured on each firm profile as The Buzz. We typically included two to four Buzz comments. In some cases, we opted not to include The Buzz on a profile.

Remember that Vault's Top 25 Technology Consulting Firms are chosen by practicing consultants at top consulting firms. Vault does not choose or influence the rankings. The rankings measure determined prestige (as judged by consulting professionals) and not revenues, size or lifestyle.

The Vault 25 • 2007

[The 25 most prestigious technology firms]

RANK	FIRM	SCORE	PREVIOUS RANK*	HEADQUARTERS/ LARGEST OFFICE
1	Booz Allen Hamilton	6.970	1	McLean, VA
2	Deloitte Consulting LLP	6.450	2	New York, NY
3	IBM Global Services	6.391	3	Armonk, NY
4	Cisco Systems, Inc.	6.249	NR	San Jose, CA
5	Accenture	6.096	4	New York, NY
6	Lockheed Martin Corporation	5.765	NR	Bethesda, MD
7	Oracle Consulting	5.685	NR	Redwood Shores, CA
8	Capgemini	5.459	6	New York, NY/Paris
9	HP Services	5.280	7	Palo Alto, CA
10	BearingPoint	5.266	5	McLean, VA
11	Computer Sciences Corporation	5.150	11	El Segundo, CA
12	EDS	5.020	15	Plano, TX
13	Unisys	4.939	13	Blue Bell, PA
14	Sapient	4.762	12	Cambridge, MA
15	DiamondCluster International Inc.	4.627	8	Chicago, IL
16	Keane	4.619	10	Boston, MA
17	Perot Systems	4.365	16	Plano, TX
18	Infosys Technologies Ltd.	4.224	14	Fremont, CA/Bangalore
19	Getronics NV	4.171	24	Billerica, MA/Amsterdam
20	Wipro Ltd.	4.088	17	Bangalore
21	CGI Group Inc.	4.013	20	Montreal
22	Tata Consultancy Services	3.855	19	New York, NY/Mumbai
23	Fujitsu Consulting	3.712	21	Edison, NJ
24	PA Consulting Group	3.585	25	London
25	BT	3.581	NR	Arden Hills, MN/Fleet, UK

* Previous rankings refer to the rankings published in the 2006 edition of the Vault Guide to the Top 25 Technology Consulting Firms, published in June 2005.

OVERVIEW OF THE
TECHNOLOGY CONSULTING INDUSTRY

The State of Technology Consulting

The IT factor

After sizable industry gains in the 1990s, consulting firms—especially in the technology sector—suffered crushing blows in the stock market bust of 2000-2001 and the ensuing recession and corporate cutbacks that persisted through 2003. IT spending, viewed by many corporations as a luxury, not a necessity, was often the first item slashed from budgets. Since 2004, though, as businesses recovered from the downturn and revenues started climbing, companies unfroze their hold on IT improvements and turned to tech consultants to bolster their performance and efficiency.

While things are now heading in the right direction for IT consulting firms, they're not out of the woods yet. Lower-than-expected earnings in early 2005 sparked worries in the industry regarding the pace of technology spending. In 2004, Forrester Research predicted that IT consulting will grow at a 5 percent annual rate from 2003 through 2008, and *Management Consultant International*, a newsletter produced by Kennedy Information, forecasts that the consulting industry will experience only modest growth through 2007 due to the conservative pace of spending on IT consulting.

A nip and a tuck

The slow rebound in IT spending since 2004 has forced tech consulting firms to rethink their service offerings and innovation strategies. One way some have adapted to the market is by muscling their way into the arena of management consulting, bringing the two disciplines together under one roof. EDS was one of the pioneers of this approach, acquiring A.T. Kearney in 1995 (though A.T. Kearney completed a management buyout from EDS in January 2006), followed by the 2002 acquisition of KMPG Consulting by Atos Origin and PwC Consulting by IBM in 2003. These firms maintain that the convergence trend reflects today's business environment in which technology and business strategy are inherently linked. They claim that businesses are looking for firms that can identify client needs, execute a particular IT strategy, install the system and then stay on board to provide turnkey services that include day-to-day management of the client's computer department and/or other departments. Others contend that some

Visit the Vault Consulting Career Channel at **www.vault.com/consulting** — with insider firm profiles, message boards, the Vault Consulting Job Board and more.

VAULT CAREER LIBRARY   **13**

clients are wary of awarding an entire project to a specific firm and prefer to use separate vendors for business strategy and IT implementation.

Shoring up revenues

Another way companies are coping with reduced tech spending is by taking advantage of offshoring opportunities. While companies have been outsourcing technical work to India for nearly two generations, the practice really took off during the recession of the early 21st century, when companies were determined to cut costs. Indeed, offshoring has become just another business strategy for profitability and growth, rendering it a necessity for maintaining a company's competitive advantage in the market. A January 2006 article in *BusinessWeek* magazine cites McKinsey Global Institute in estimating that, to date, $18.4 billion in global IT work and $11.4 billion in business process services have been shifted abroad. The latest Quarterly Index from sourcing advisory firm TPI reports that although the average value of outsourcing contracts in 2005 was 24 percent lower than those in 2004, the number of outsourcing contracts continues to rise—up 11 percent from 2004—reflecting increased competition and expansion in the marketplace. In addition, a considerable number of first-generation offshoring contracts, awarded in the last seven to 10 years, are now up for renewal. Of these, TPI notes that there were $43.8 billion in renewals in 2005, and expects to see $49 billion in 2007.

Dissenting opinions

Although offshoring has proven to be a viable force in generating financial returns to U.S. companies, it has also been a frequent subject of hot debate. Some industry observers are concerned with offshoring's impact on traditional consulting, saying that the prevalent outsourcing model—which groups consulting services into larger outsourcing engagements—has depressed the prices of traditional consulting services and, in a sense, commoditized the business. The main concern becomes cost-savings, as opposed to selling value that can differentiate one provider from the next. Another major concern for those opposed to offshoring is that outsourcing jobs will hold down IT job growth and salaries; Forrester Research projects that IT jobs will grow slowly, at an annual rate of 3 percent through 2008, with salaries growing only 6 percent during that period.

Those in the pro camp suggest that offshoring is a win-win game. It frees up resources that can be used to generate high value, and companies can invest their savings from offshoring into new, more productive initiatives at home. For American IT consulting outfits, the rush to open offshore facilities has emerged as a competitive necessity, reducing IT spending and improving the overall corporate bottom line. As for the loss of jobs, any turnover generated by outsourcing is viewed as part of the natural flow of economic activity. These jobs will be replaced by others that will emerge when companies invest their savings from offshoring into new ventures.

Regional palates

Until recently, India has been the primary receptacle for U.S. offshoring pursuits. The country's large talent pool boasts a heavy concentration of IT consultants and an ever-ready supply of Indian recruits waving MBAs. Billing rates for skilled IT consultants are among the lowest in the world, and competition has grown rampant within the country as the leading outsourcers—Infosys, Tata, Wipro—compete head-to-head with big-league American consulting firms like IBM and Accenture for local IT development centers employing Indian engineers. Consequently, wages for mid-level employees are on the rise, and companies are offering attractive incentive plans to boost retention. With these increased wages and geographic diversification away from India, the nation's IT outsourcers have been forced to focus on emerging markets to capture cost efficiencies and market share.

Rising costs in India have encouraged consulting firms to look elsewhere for cut-rate offshoring opportunities. Countries such as China, Malaysia, Australia and New Zealand are becoming attractive locations for cost-efficient IT development centers. In fact, Kennedy Information predicts that the Chinese consulting market will prove to be heady competition for India, growing at a compound annual rate of 32 percent from 2005 to 2008, with India lagging behind at 24 percent. Demand for consultants in China is now on the rise, though the biggest challenge to growth in the country is the difficulty of training and retaining skilled labor. There are far fewer Chinese recruits wielding MBAs than there are in India. It can take up to 10 years to train a consultant and, once trained, many talented Chinese consultants opt for more lucrative positions with Western consulting firms.

Seeking specialists

With corporate America spending money on technology again, the IT job market has sprung back to life. According to Moody's Economy.com, some 125,000 tech jobs were created in 2005, with 217,000 jobs predicted for 2006—what promises to be the industry's best year since 2000. Technology consultants comprised 34,000 of those positions, a number that's expected to grow in 2006. The job market for consultants is now candidate-driven: Recruiters are having difficulty attracting enough talent to meet their hiring targets, putting candidates in advantageous negotiating positions when faced with competing job offers. The health of the industry is also evident in the upturn in voluntary turnover, which, according to *Consultants News*, reached 25 percent in 2005.

Now more than ever, clients are demanding expertise in a particular industry or functional area, and the need for generalist consultants is in decline—a trend that has taken hold in the past few years. The small size of the talent pool for specific operational issues, such as Sarbanes-Oxley regulation and national defense, coupled with heightened demand from consulting firms has caused salaries for specialists to spike.

Practice Areas

Systems integration

This is one of the traditional jobs of tech consultants, and a growth area today as companies augment their business processes with complex IT systems. When two companies merge, or a single company wants to implement new hardware or software, they turn to consultants to make all of the technology compatible. Sometimes this is a simple matter of installing upgrades or changing settings; more often, it's a long and arduous process of writing new code to allow hardware and existing software to co-exist and operate efficiently together.

Outsourcing

Another long-time area of tech consulting expertise, business process outsourcing (BPO) is the bread and butter of many firms. Some companies find it easier and more cost-effective to pay somebody else to manage their technology for them, positioning consultants, in effect, as the client's IT department. Consultants handle everything from help desk and call center operations to server maintenance and passkey and ID tag issuance. Even governments and armies outsource nowadays; CIBER has a number of contracts with the U.S. Army Reserve's Regional Support Commands and the U.S. Marine Corps and Navy, while Computer Sciences Corporation has outsourcing deals with the UK, Germany's armed forces and Australia.

Enterprise solutions

A major impact of the Enron (2001) and Worldcom (2002) accounting scandals was the summer 2002 passage of the Sarbanes-Oxley Act. SOX mandates that companies publicly listed in the U.S. market conduct internal audits, provide more detailed financial information to investors, and store financial data for a specific period of time. Many companies initially thought they could manage the IT implications of SOX on their own, and it has taken a couple of years for huge SOX-compliance IT contracts to become commonplace. Companies have found that they need vastly improved data storage, records management and security systems to maintain confidentiality of their newly prodigious amounts of financial information, in addition to process management software systems to facilitate audit, tracking and reporting requirements.

SOX compliance is just one of the major types of consulting that is generally bundled into the "enterprise solutions" category. Supply chain consulting, for example, is an even larger piece of the pie. Supply chain consultants help client companies streamline parts and materials ordering processes and reduce manufacturing input costs. Supply chain projects can focus on inventory reduction, throughput enhancement and manufacturing cost containment. Enterprise resource planning (ERP) is an extension of supply chain management that further integrates product planning, customer service, order tracking, finance and HR processes.

Customer relationship management (CRM) systems received a lot of hype in the late 1990s, only to be hit hard by an economic downturn that meant that even the most sophisticated CRM system wasn't going to grow in sales. CRM consulting engagements involve developing organized and efficient ways for clients to manage relationships, usually through a complex software solution that facilitates storing and mining large amounts of customer data.

IT strategy

IT consulting engagements that involve a broad view of the client's business or high-level tech decisions are often simply referred to as "consulting" or "strategy" projects. These engagements often entail aligning a client's IT infrastructure with its overall business strategy. Most of the large, brand-name management consulting firms have IT strategy practices, including Booz Allen's technology strategy group and Accenture's Strategic IT Effectiveness (SITE) group, which resides within its business consulting division. These IT strategy consulting groups are often managed by industry specialists (e.g., utilities, financial services) who are deeply familiar with the specific information challenges faced by potential clients.

Many IT strategy engagements fall into the category of business process reengineering (BPR). When a company decides to purchase a new software package, or simply to improve its business processes, the result is not simply a new IT system, but usually a dramatic shift in the way employees interact. BPR assignments involve rewriting work rules and shaping communication paths, calling upon consultants' general business know-how over technical computer knowledge.

Web services

Long the domain of design and hosting companies based in Silicon Alley (New York's tech center), Web services include e-commerce implementation and other secure-transaction work, though consultancies do some page design and site hosting as part of their overall deliverables as well. This specialty is receiving a lot of attention from major technology players such as IBM, HP and Accenture. Gartner predicts that Web services spending will reach $14.3 billion in 2006.

Security

Five years after the September 11 terrorist attacks and the resulting heightened awareness of security threats to U.S. residents and businesses, information security consulting work is still a hot area. IT businesses have realized there's money to be made in designing and implementing better security and identification methods. The industry has seen progress in biometrics (the science of identifying a person via retina patterns, voice, fingerprints and other unique biological characteristics), contraband detection and secure communications.

Research and development

Some consultants spend their time in the lab developing new hardware and software. Often, this work is geared toward creating new products (such as servers and analysis software) that will help companies sell work and accomplish engagements.

How many consulting job boards have you visited lately?

(Thought so.)

Use the Internet's most targeted job search tools for consulting professionals.

Vault Consulting Job Board

The most comprehensive and convenient job board for consulting professionals. Target your search by area of consulting, function, and experience level, and find the job openings that you want. No surfing required.

VaultMatch Resume Database

Vault takes match-making to the next level: post your resume and customize your search by area of consulting, experience and more. We'll match job listings with your interests and criteria and e-mail them directly to your inbox.

THE VAULT 25

1

Booz Allen Hamilton

8283 Greensboro Drive
McLean, VA 22102
Phone: (703) 902-5000
Fax: (703) 902-3333
www.boozallen.com

LOCATIONS

McLean, VA (HQ)
More than 100 offices worldwide

PRACTICE AREAS

Design and engineering
Enterprise resource management
Imagery analysis
IT architecture and design
IT implementation
IT strategy and transformation
Systems engineering and integration
Technology transfer
Telecom and network

THE STATS

Employer Type: Private Company
Chairman and CEO: Dr. Ralph W. Shrader
2005 Employees: 17,000
2004 Employees: 16,000
FY 2005 Sales: $3.3 billion
FY 2004 Sales: $2.7 billion

UPPERS

- "The firm's core values"
- "Flexible hours and advancement programs"
- "Prestige and brand recognition"
- "The opportunities are endless"

DOWNERS

- "Lack of clear lines of reporting, aloof partners"
- "No bonuses unless you're a level 4, 5 or partner"
- "Working remotely can place you on the fringe of the culture"
- "The government side does not pay well enough"

EMPLOYMENT CONTACT

E-mail: Recruiting_Feedback@bah.com

THE BUZZ
WHAT CONSULTANTS AT OTHER FIRMS ARE SAYING

- "Diverse and huge"
- "Well respected in the government sector"
- "Headstrong"
- "Pay's not great"

THE SCOOP

From classic strategy to tech savvy

Booz Allen Hamilton was founded in 1914, but don't let its antique origins fool you —the firm has carved a nice niche for itself in the 21st century world of tech consulting. Founded by Edwin Booz as a classic management consultancy, Booz maintains a solid presence in the strategy consulting arena, serving the world's leading corporations, governments and other public agencies, emerging growth companies and institutions. But its broad consulting services also include IT strategy and systems; encompassing IT implementation; architecture and design; design and engineering; systems engineering and integration; technology transfer; telecom and network services; imagery analysis; and enterprise resource management.

The firm, which raked in $3.3 billion in fiscal year 2005 (up from $2.7 billion a year earlier), employs 17,000 people in more than 100 offices worldwide. The firm's global expansion got a boost in the 1990s, when it moved its headquarters to McLean, Va., (just outside of Washington, DC) and began opening new offices overseas, from Abu Dhabi to Shanghai. The firm most recently expanded its facilities in Fairfax, Va., in late 2004, investing $133 million; Booz Allen expects to create 3,700 new jobs in Virginia over the next decade.

The public and private sides of Booz

Booz Allen's headquarters, in the high-tech corridor of McLean, Va., represents the sweet spot of the firm's business model, allowing it to court both corporations and public sector clients. Until recently, the firm's broad client base was served by its two business units, the Worldwide Commercial Business (WCB) and the Worldwide Technology Business (WTB). The former, as the name suggests, worked mainly with corporations, operating as a classic strategy and operations consultancy. WTB worked with government agencies, institutions and infrastructure organizations worldwide, offering those clients an array of management consulting, engineering, information technology and systems development/integration services. Each sector had its own culture, including separate recruiting and hiring practices.

The line between these two businesses has grown increasingly fluid in recent years and officially disappeared on April 1, 2006, when Booz Allen's new worldwide organization debuted. In its reorganization, the firm no longer operates through two separate business units, but presents itself as one firm with three market focuses:

Global Commercial Markets, Global Government Markets and Global Integrated Markets. This is in keeping with what Booz Allen chairman and CEO Ralph Shrader told *The Economist* in September 2005: As the public sector was becoming increasingly interested in borrowing the best business ideas from the private sector, the firm was reviewing its bifurcated model. In that interview, Shrader reported, about 10 percent of the firm's work was located in the "joint arena," meaning that both WCB and WTB consultants worked together in mixed project teams. "This is putting pressure on the firm to come up with a new single career path that combines the two types of work," *The Economist* reported.

The feds pony up

A new enthusiasm among government agencies toward private sector consulting expertise also means they are willing to pay rates that are closer to those of their corporate counterparts, *The Economist* added. Certainly, the feds haven't been stingy when it comes to Booz Allen. In 2005, about $1.8 billion of the firm's sales came from federal prime contracts, according to *Washington Technology*, which placed the firm at No. 9 on its annual Top 100 Federal Prime IT Contractor's list. Company execs told the publication that the firm's legacy in management consulting helps it approach projects in a "mission-oriented" manner, giving it the ability to "recognize and separate the people problems from the technology problems."

Where the (DC) elite meet

A number of Washington's elite have made Booz Allen the site of their post-public-sector careers. Former CIA director James Woolsey is a vice president of the firm, and former Navy Chief Information Officer Ron Turner, former associated director for the CIA's homeland security division Winston P. Wiley, former Army deputy chief of staff for intelligence Lt. Gen. Robert W. Noonan, and former Department of Health and Human Services CIO Melissa Chapman also joined Booz Allen after leaving their federal positions. As for chairman and CEO Shrader, Booz Allen officers voted in late 2004 to extend his tenure until 2009.

September 11's effects

Booz Allen's location in the DC corridor makes it a natural candidate for federal contracts. It also brought the events of September 11, 2001, close to home, when three Booz Allen staffers working on a U.S. Army project were killed in the attack on the Pentagon. As the government scrambled to retool and strengthen key departments, Booz Allen was there to lend a hand, quickly jumping into action with projects for the Federal Transportation Authority and the newly formed Department of Homeland Security. The firm also developed its Analytical Risk Methodology, an innovative tool designed to help government clients evaluate threats and institute risk-mitigation programs.

The contracts keep coming

Booz Allen has maintained its strong ties to the Department of Homeland Security (DHS). In September 2005, the Department's Science and Technology Directorate awarded Booz Allen a five-year, $250 million contract for various forms of support for DHS technology programs. Other federal contracts have continued to roll in. In June 2005, the firm announced that it had developed and deployed a new system for the FBI, known as the Regional Data Exchange (R-DEx) system, which provides agents with sophisticated search, retrieval and analytical tools. The system, deployed in the St. Louis region, is part of a larger justice system strategy to share federal, state, tribal and local law enforcement information on all crimes.

The firm scored a contract renewal from the Department of Defense (DoD) in September 2005 for continued information management support to the Joint Requirements and Integration office, including developing the DoD's architecture for human resource systems. And in April 2005, the firm landed a 10-year, $550 million IT services contract with the Federal Deposit Insurance Corporation (FDIC), along with IBM, Lockheed Martin and Pragmatics. Other major government clients include the Internal Revenue Service, the Air Force and the National Institute of Child Health and Human Development.

On a roll with transportation

There doesn't seem to be any limit to the sectors Booz Allen can serve with its IT know-how. According to a September 2004 article in *Forbes*, the firm's transportation business has grown at a rate of 17 percent over five years, largely due to increased demand by transit agencies for updated technology. In fact, the article notes, half of the firm's mass transit consulting revenues stem from tech-related engagements. Big-name Booz Allen projects in the transportation arena include the Gold Line, a new trolley route connecting Los Angeles and Pasadena, and IT systems work for the Washington Metropolitan Area Transit Authority.

Covering the tech biz

Amidst all of its tech consulting, Booz Allen still manages to churn out volumes of studies and surveys, many of which focus on the tech sector. In July 2005, for instance, the firm published research on the viability of using mobile phones on commercial airlines (Booz Allen predicts this will happen in 2006) and m-payment, cashless payment transactions that can be accomplished using mobile phones.

Quality assured

Booz Allen reached a significant technical milestone in June 2005, when two of its project teams successfully passed the ISO 9001:2000 Quality Management System (QMS) audit performed by the British Standards Institute, the latest in a series of annual audits since the firm was first certified in 1999. Compliance with ISO standards has contributed to higher quality work products and helps Booz Allen achieve cost savings, according to the firm.

"Best-of" Booz

Booz Allen regularly lands on best-of lists for its philanthropy, its standing among consultancies and its employee-friendly working environment. The firm has placed among *Working Mother* magazine's list of top 100 mom-friendly companies for seven years running. It was also among *Consulting Magazine*'s top 10 consulting firms in 2005. In June 2005, Booz Allen was named one of the top companies to work for in an inaugural award by the *Washington Business Journal*, which looked at factors such as company culture, employees' relationship with supervisors and the company's core values.

Golf, giving and more

Thanks, in part, to its high-profile Booz Allen Classic golf tournament, the largest charitable sporting event in the DC area, the Booz Allen name has become synonymous with corporate giving. In fact, the firm, which has held itself to a high standard of community service since its founding, has developed an entire philosophy oriented toward corporate citizenship—the "spirit of service." With an "employee-centered approach," the firm aligns its own financial, in-kind and pro bono resources with the charitable giving and volunteering interests of its officers, staff and their families, and gives out annual "Involvement and Impact" awards to recognize Booz Allen staffers' charitable efforts.

The firm's work on behalf of ALS, or Lou Gehrig's disease, earned it the first-ever Corporate Philanthropy Award from the ALS Association's DC/MD/VA chapter. Booz Allen's contributions to the association include volunteer, financial, pro bono and in-kind support, mostly jump-started by Booz Allen employees in honor of a colleague who was diagnosed with the disease in 1999. The firm has also kicked in to help with recent high-profile disasters, including the South Asian tsunami of December 2004—it matched employee contributions up to $50,000 and undertook rigorous pro bono efforts to boost relief efforts in the area—and the aftermath of Hurricane Katrina in 2005. Pro bono clients have included The Nature Conservancy, the Children's Defense Fund, Lincoln University, Charity Skills (in the UK), the Texas Ballet Theater, Special Olympics International and the United Negro College Fund.

GETTING HIRED

Bring it to Booz

Booz Allen's extensive career site lists available positions divided into "cleared-intelligence opportunities," "college opportunities," "European opportunities," "experienced professional" and "MBA opportunities." Candidates must set up a profile and all candidates must apply online through the site. The firm also offers interviewing tips and a case primer for those interested in consulting for commercial clients.

It's who you know—40 percent of the time

Tech consulting insiders put a lot of stock in the power of networking—according to one source, "The firm encourages employees to submit acquaintances' resumes." Internal referrals make up 40 percent of all hires for government-focused projects, according to our sources. The interview process varies according to position and experience. Says a Booz Allen insider, "Hiring of professionals is informal and left to the judgment of mid-level managers. Hiring of new college grads is more structured." The process also differs depending on business area. "In the commercial side of the business, we rely on traditional business school recruiting. In the federal space, we generally hire more experienced staff," an insider reports.

Visit the Vault Consulting Career Channel at www.vault.com/consulting —with
insider firm profiles, message boards, the Vault Consulting Job Board and more.

VAULT CAREER LIBRARY   27

"Easygoing" or "rigorous"?

One consultant describes the hiring process as "the most rigorous I've ever encountered—I had maybe two phone interviews, followed by a timed, written assignment, followed by an in-person interview, where I was interviewed by four separate people." An insider, hired into the firm's government business right out of school, explains, "For me, the hiring consisted of a telephone conversation, and then I interviewed at the campus. No case interviews; I met with three managers for about half an hour each. They were really easygoing." Another consultant says, "I had a four-hour interview with five different people asking a variety of different questions after going through two levels of phone interviews." "Others have had a simple phone interview, though." Yet another insider reports being "picked up" from an online job site and invited to "an invite-only 'job fair.' Twenty or so teams from Booz Allen attended and talked with over 300 potential employees. [It was] very informal and let you see what the company was up to." According to another consultant, "They don't drag the hiring process over weeks like some firms."

When recruiting MBA prospects to work with commercial clients, Booz Allen tends to skim from the top—sources suggest the firm goes after the top 10 percent at the top 15 business schools in the world. And with regard to selecting undergraduates for work with government clients, one consultant reports, "Many engineers are solicited from Virginia Tech and UVA. I recently met an MIT grad. I also know of annual job fairs in Virginia, DC, Maryland, Southern Pennsylvania and New Jersey where we have booths" to recruit for the headquarters location.

Getting an early start

College students with GPAs of 3.0 or higher can apply for Booz Allen's government business or administrative internships, available during the summer months and the academic year to those who have declared a major and completed 30 hours of coursework. One former intern describes the experience as valuable, noting that "I was able to try numerous different IT areas." Another former intern elaborates: "I found that in order to get very valuable work I had to be very aggressive. During my first term, I kept getting passed around because no one 'had time for' an intern; my first few days were pretty much a flop. I nearly left the job. I 'happened' to meet someone who needed help with something, and once I was able to complete the task I was finally noticed as being, well...alive." Summer associates for the commercial side are recruited from the elite business schools worldwide.

OUR SURVEY SAYS

Sticking to the core

Booz Allen gets exceptionally high marks from its consultants for its corporate culture. "I know of no other consulting firm with a better culture," one insider raves. "I can honestly say that I work with the smartest yet the most fun people in the [consulting] business," another source notes. As a worldwide organization, Booz Allen doesn't boast an entirely consistent culture, one insider notes: "McLean's corporate culture is more involved but that is due to the fact that that is Booz Allen's headquarters. San Diego is the fastest growing [office] outside of Virginia, but there is still a way to go before company culture is as good as the mothership."

Most sources are quick to point out the firm's commitment to its "core values." This commitment, a consultant notes, "informs and influences everything we do—from interactions with colleagues to service to our clients." One insider even provides an anecdote to illustrate this commitment in action. Right after being hired, this commercially-focused consultant was assigned to an overseas engagement: "I arrived at the firm with 48 hours to complete all the administrative paperwork, apply for a corporate credit card and order a stack of business cards. There is no way this could have been completed anywhere else but [Booz Allen]. Yet, from the moment I arrived to the moment my plane departed from JFK my 'New Hire Buddy' was there to guide me through each step and pressure those who needed to be pressured to get the job done. And upon arrival...my New Hire Buddy had already made introductions on my behalf. This is the difference in front of the client—when the team works as a team. Thus far, I have been enormously impressed by the reality of an organization that actually does operate in line with its core values."

Diverse, but not cutthroat

According to another insider, diversity strengthens the firm: "Booz Allen leverages diversity in its widest possible sense to bring the best results to clients. This is the first place I have worked that realized diversity was much more than race or gender, but was really about diversity of background, experience, ways of thinking, etc." Despite their differences, Booz Allen consultants are able to work together comfortably. While some consultants say they work alongside "moderately competitive younger people," according to another source, they generally find Booz Allen to be "without the cutthroat antics typical of the bigger firms."

Hassle-free travel

Insiders report few complaints about the firm's travel requirements. "Booz Allen really goes out of [its] way to make traveling easy and hassle free," says a WCB source, adding, "I travel every Monday, [and] work either in my home office or at home on Fridays. [It's a] much better arrangement compared to the daily 9 to 5 grind." Generally, those who work on the WTB side travel much less than their WCB counterparts. "Travel is about 25 percent of my time, and that was made clear at hiring. In fact, it was one of the attractions for me," says a WTB source. "Travel depends on the project and client requirements. In my case, this varies year to year, but it's never excessive," another WTB insider reports.

In fact, Booz Allen consultants generally seem happy with their schedules, though there are always a few exceptions. As one consultant puts it, "The firm whole-heartedly embraces a work/life balance, however there are managers here and there who are still adjusting to the concept." "The firm's programs and incentives are unbelievably great. However, the work ethic is so strong among peers and expectations sometimes so great by our clients, it is often difficult to take advantage of at an individual level," says another source.

A flexible firm

Flexibility is a primary draw for many Booz Allen consultants. "My firm has allowed me to work from home while I attend school. The firm has exhibited confidence in my ability to work from home, which is a big confidence boost for me," says one insider. According to another government-side source, "Booz Allen Hamilton lets us decide if we want to put our family first or the firm and any combination depending on the circumstances. We are not penalized for having a family, which is not always the case [at other firms]." "My former consulting firm created work 'crises' when they didn't have to [do] so; Booz Allen equally respects clients and staff," an insider adds.

It's your prerogative

Work hours generally are as intense—or as easygoing—as consultants want them to be. "For the projects I've been on, I've rarely experienced an intense spike in my workload; however, I know some folks who put in 60-plus hour weeks. Overall, this is pretty rare on the WTB side, as the government schedule is the norm," one consultant says. And during these spikes, says a colleague, "we share the load and back each other up." A colleague agrees: "The firm is very supportive of the individual—if [you are] a contributor, the firm will bend over backwards to accommodate [you]. It's a great place to work!" According to another insider, "You work until you get the job done. That doesn't entail 14-hour days. If it involves five hours one day, 10 hours the next, three hours the third, and 15 hours the fourth day, that is your prerogative."

Performance-based promotion

Flexibility is also the name of the game when it comes to advancement at Booz Allen, though the firm notes that flexibility in this area generally holds true only for those working in the government sector, or WTB. "The [WTB] promotion policy is flexible based on an individual's desired path. Competitive, fast-paced people can work alongside those who prefer more stability and/or longevity in a position," a source says. Agrees a colleague, "[In WTB] the rate of advancement is really up to the person. Advancement will come sooner to those who work hard and contribute to the organization." In addition, a source maintains, "Since the company is performance-based, someone [in WTB] with no degree may progress just as fast, or faster, with someone who has a bachelor's, a graduate degree, an MBA, or X number of years in a service." Another insider explains, "[In WTB], people can stay in a functional role as long as they are productive. Promotion to the more senior positions requires a business case and serious due diligence. Consultants with undergrad degrees are encouraged to get grad degrees. The firm offers programs to assist. Consultants with undergrad degrees can move into more senior positions by providing quality client service and developing strong client relationships."

Although WTB consultants are not on a strict timetable for promotion, they still are subject to a rigorous "perform or go" philosophy, according to a consultant. As one WTB insider states, "Advancement is predicated solely on your performance and contribution to firm goals."Another WTB source sheds more light on this: "If you are producing to your level, you do not have to advance. Consultants can expect to advance after about two years, but it's all capability based, not time based. Experience can be 'traded' for education." In contrast with the flexible career progression for government consultants, their commercial counterparts adhere to a strict up-or-on promotion model.

Cashing in

One incentive to advance is the scaled compensation package offered to government market consultants, a source suggests. "Starting salaries may be low [on the WTB side], however, once a person establishes [himself] and proves his worth, compensation follows." As one insider tells us, "Sure, I could get paid better somewhere else. But would I have a boss that I learn from, clients I have great respect for, and co-workers who set the bar high and challenge me to be my best?"

Salary and bonuses do vary according to which side of the business consultants work in, insiders report. "There are no bonuses on the WTB side of the firm until you reach a higher level in status…It makes it frustrating since [all] individuals on the WCB side of the firm have bonuses, as well the opportunity for greater tuition reimbursement. WTB only allows for $5,000 per calendar year on tuition reimbursement," says one source. For all consultants, however, Booz Allen provides a 401(k) contribution which has been at least "10 percent of your annual salary," according to a source.

"Much more than the money"

According to another source, Booz Allen offers "some of the best traditional benefit packages for a company its size that I have heard about, including family leave; personal development and education; medical and dental; wellness programs; onsite day care (location dependent); robust 401(k); private company with bonus and profit sharing; a wide range of philanthropic and community service events and programs; holiday celebrations and family outings; and interaction with state-of-the-art hardware and software in most IT fields." Another insider praises the "wonderful HR department," noting that "benefits are explained in depth so that informed decisions can be made." A colleague appreciates the firm's "tremendous support to the National Guard and Reserve in terms of pay differential, as well as [the encouragement] to support my country. It's the encouragement that means much more than the money." Offices are described as "not over-luxurious," but "five-star" compared to some government clients' facilities. "Offices are fairly standard. Associates and below share an office with an officemate, while senior associates and above get their own office. Office furniture is standard modular furniture," a source reports. An additional perk offered to the McLean office is the "spectacular" annual holiday party.

Training perks

Many insiders also see Booz Allen's commitment to training as a key benefit. "Unless you work for IBM, which spends astronomical amounts of money, you won't beat Booz Allen for training," a source says. In fact, in March 2006, the firm was ranked No. 1 for employee-sponsored workforce training and development by *Training* magazine. A consultant raves about the "excellent training opportunities both within and outside of the firm. They have teamed with many top colleges and graduate programs to offer in-house degrees after work and on the weekends." "The management of our team expects us to use all of our training money for certifications or degrees each year. The money is not just for show, to bring in hires," says a colleague. However, one insider grumbles that there are "not enough training courses available internally, [and therefore some individuals are] always wait-listed. Training is level-based and seems incorrect. You are not trained for a level until you are [at] that level and then you have to wait until you can get into a class, leaving a gap of time when you are untrained, yet expected to perform at the new level."

Few bad apples

As for management, one consultant sums it up: "All companies have bad apples, micro-managers and lazy bums. Booz Allen is no exception, but the percentage is lethally low." According to another source, "Mid-level management has a better reputation than highest-level management." "Overall, my supervisors are great," says an insider, "although the hierarchy and nature of how we work sometimes makes an actual chain of command unclear." "For the most part my supervisors have almost always been top-notch," a consultant adds. "However, people are people—but it seems that Booz Allen has recognized this and has a multi-level accountability established where even a less than exemplary manager's influence can be counteracted by other managers and supervisors."

Women at work

Consultants praise Booz Allen's "strong emphasis on providing opportunities for women and encouraging growth to senior levels within the firm." However, one source laments, "The firm has a hard time attracting female applicants." While there are "many women," another insider says, there are "not many in management positions. The firm has not resolved how women's nonlinear career paths can fit into a linear development model." Still, according to another consultant, "There's a diversity forum and Booz Allen has its own professional women's networking group. While I would say that I work mainly with married men and ambitious, single women, I think that may be par for the course. Booz Allen is great at advancing women fairly and I see a lot of equal promotions."

As for racial diversity, an insider says, "The firm seeks quality irrespective of culture or background. Our active diversity forums are a result of the firm's commitment to evolving a diverse staff." "I work with an abundance of people of different races, creeds, ethnicities, etc. And I love it," another source reports. "The firm speaks a lot about diversity, although it is defined in many different ways, not just [by] race," a consultant notes.

Sexual orientation is generally a non-issue at Booz Allen, but it may depend on location. "As a lesbian, I am proud to work for a company that does as much as Booz Allen. I have always felt supported and welcomed—which is a huge change from my last consulting experience," one consultant says. "The company overall is very diverse with respect to gays, but not in the upper bible belt of Omaha. That would not be considered OK," another insider comments. "We have a very active chapter of GLOBE, the firm's LGBT diversity forum. We also have partner benefits which is surprising," a Washington source says. And another insider tells us, "It's never an issue, really. I've worked with several gays, bisexuals and lesbians...more than I have with any other company."

Saving the world

It might be easier to name community and advocacy groups with which Booz Allen is not affiliated, rather than those with which it is—this do-gooder firm supports a host of causes. One consultant reports, "The firm is involved in numerous charities including American Red Cross disaster relief, Cabrini Mission Foundation, National Action Council for Minorities in Engineering, Building Together (Christmas in April), National Organization on Disability, Metro TeenAIDS, Wolf Trap, Fire Department—City of New York, Smithsonian Early Enrichment Center, Dance Theater of Harlem, Special Olympics International, Chesapeake Bay Foundation, Volunteer Fairfax, Children's Hospital & Research Center at Oakland, Children's Defense Fund and Birdies for Charity." "The firm is very active in the community. I find this to be one of the things I love about working here," a source agrees.

"Booz Allen leverages diversity in its widest possible sense to bring the best results to clients."

— *Booz Allen consultant*

Visit the Vault Consulting Career Channel at **www.vault.com/consulting** — with
insider firm profiles, message boards, the Vault Consulting Job Board and more.

VAULT CAREER LIBRARY

35

Deloitte Consulting LLP

1633 Broadway, 35th Floor
New York, NY 10019
Phone: (212) 492-4500
Fax: (212) 492-4743
www.deloitte.com

LOCATIONS

New York, NY (HQ)
Offices in more than 40 countries

PRACTICE AREAS

Technology Integration
Architecture and Network Services
CIO Advisory Services
Development Services
Enterprise Connection Services
Enterprise Systems Management
Information Dynamics

THE STATS

Employer Type: Subsidiary of
Deloitte & Touche USA LLP; U.S.
Member Firm of Deloitte Touche
Tohmatsu
CEO: Paul Robinson
2004 Employees: 21,000 (consulting
practice only)
2004 Revenues: $5.9 billion
(consulting and advisory services
only)

UPPERS

- "Emphasizes work/life balance"
- "Level of learning on the job is very good"
- "People who grew up within the Deloitte firm are generally very good people"

DOWNERS

- "Travel is harsh"
- "Industry hires are not valued as much as recent grads"
- "Raises are not very good at all for the ridiculous amount of hours people put in"

EMPLOYMENT CONTACT

careers.deloitte.com

THE BUZZ
WHAT CONSULTANTS AT OTHER FIRMS ARE SAYING

- "The Cadillac of consulting firms"
- "Diverse and friendly"
- "Too hands-off"
- "Revenue before client results"

THE SCOOP

Last of the old school

Deloitte's name is a prestigious one in the consulting world, owing largely to its strong brand recognition as an old-school accountancy. In fact, Deloitte is known as the last of the so-called "Big Four" firms, retaining both an accounting and a consulting practice. This wasn't the firm's intention back in 2002. Following the financial scandals that dogged firms associated with troubled giants like Enron and Andersen, Deloitte Touche Tohmatsu decided to separate its consulting and accounting practices to steer clear of charges of conflict of interest—a separation that was pulled off successfully by industry peers Ernst & Young and KPMG. But an expensive plan to spin off the Deloitte consulting arm under the name Braxton was scrapped in 2003. Shortly thereafter, Deloitte CEO Doug McCracken stepped down and was replaced by 20-year Deloitte veteran Paul Robinson, who still leads the practice.

Another rebranding strategy followed, as Deloitte Consulting and Deloitte Touche Tohmatsu were blended into one business, known simply as "Deloitte." The firm is known in various national and global markets as Deloitte Touche Tohmatsu, Deloitte & Touche and Deloitte Consulting, but commonly referred to by the brand Deloitte.

IT all over the place

IT consulting is integrated among Deloitte's many divisions. In 2004, Deloitte's consulting practice employed 21,000 people globally. The Technology Integration arm of the consulting division offers architecture and network services, CIO advisory services, development services, enterprise connection services, enterprise systems management and information dynamics. The firm also boasts a Technology, Media & Telecommunications (TMT) group, made up of more than 5,000 partners, directors and senior managers, along with thousands of support staffers, serving nearly 80 percent of the technology, media and telecom companies in the Fortune 500. Deloitte also offers software implementations and outsourcing, and its Human Capital and Strategy & Operations divisions also offer tech-oriented services.

Consulting cashes in

In June 2005, Deloitte member firm leaders from around the world met in New York to plan the company's growth strategy. The firm was particularly positive about the prospects for its consulting businesses. All consulting revenues for the firm experienced 9 percent growth in fiscal year 2005, a sign that Deloitte's decision to keep consulting services close to home was a good one, execs said. In 2004, revenue from Deloitte's consulting and advisory divisions was $5.9 billion, while aggregate revenue for the firm globally came in at $16.4 billion (up from $15.1 billion in 2003).

Global ambitions

Deloitte continues to derive more than half its revenues from offices outside the U.S., and this global approach shows no signs of slowing down. In November 2005, the firm outlined a $50 million expansion plan for India, including the addition of 2,500 local staffers. Member firms in India expect annual revenue growth of more than 20 percent per year over the next four years. The company has also poured millions into China in recent years. In June 2005, Deloitte China announced a merger with Beijing Pan-China CPA Ltd. This was followed in September 2005 by a Deloitte Touche Tohmatsu China merger with Pan-China Schinda, another top Chinese CPA firm. The firm predicted that Deloitte China's headcount would more than double to roughly 10,000 in the next five years. Deloitte also has expanded through mergers in Korea.

Notable hires

In March 2005, Deloitte stepped up to the PR plate, hiring Keith Lindenburg as its new director of national public relations. A 20-year PR vet, Lindenburg joined Deloitte Services from the public relations firm Waggener Edstrom in New York, and previously served as VP of corporate communications at IBM. And in December 2004, Deloitte named Brian Derksen, a 25-year veteran of the firm, deputy chief executive officer.

Finding a frequency

In January 2005, the firm announced a partnership with HighJump Software, a 3M company, to deliver supply chain execution products that incorporate radio frequency identification (RFID) technology. In fact, Deloitte has jumped on board the RFID bandwagon, hiring experts such as John Greaves, a former leader of the U.S. national standards body for RFID, to boost initiatives in the fast-growing field.

Tracking the top in tech

Deloitte keeps its name in the tech headlines with regular studies and surveys, including the Deloitte Technology Fast 500, tracking the fastest-growing tech companies worldwide. Deloitte's Technology, Media and Telecommunications industry group regularly issues forecasts on global technology, highlighting trends and challenges facing the industry. Deloitte consultants have published influential books such as 2003's *The Innovator's Solution*, by Clayton M. Christensen and Michael E. Raynor. More targeted research includes an October 2004 report on voice over Internet protocol (VoIP) adoption by global businesses.

A personal touch

Though the firm is huge, Deloitte seems to devote resources to making employees feel that they're part of a family. In June 2005, the firm announced the launch of Personal Pursuits, a career management program that aims to encourage employees who have opted out of the workforce to stay connected to Deloitte and continue developing skills and networks needed to facilitate a smooth return. Deloitte estimates that the program, which costs the firm about $2,500 per year for each participant, actually saves money in turnover expenses over time. Thanks to programs like these, the firm also has been named to *Fortune* magazine's list of 100 best companies to work for, for seven years running. For 12 years in a row, Deloitte has been named among *Working Mother* magazine's 100 Best Companies for Working Mothers, with high ratings for its flexibility, work/life balance and advancement programs for women. The firm takes diversity seriously, too, sponsoring affinity groups dedicated to African-American, Hispanic, South Asian and gay, lesbian and bisexual employees.

Deloitte does good

The firm is also visibly dedicated to good corporate citizenship. In May 2005, Deloitte announced that a number of its member firms had begun providing 14,000 hours of pro bono advisory services to the United Nations Development Programme to help mobilize reconstruction funds following the South Asian tsunami. Deloitte staffers also contributed financially following the disaster, donating millions of dollars worldwide. In June 2005, thousands of Deloitte employees worldwide took part in IMPACT Day, a global volunteering event. Projects included helping small business owners with career guidance in South Africa, teaching Hungarian students about business, donating blood in Brazil and helping U.S. job-seekers with their resumes.

GETTING HIRED

A case study

An insider reports that, as an experienced hire, he was subjected to several rounds of interviews. He describes the process after a human resources recruiter contacted and interviewed him over the phone. "He liked me and decided to have a technical consultant call me for a technical interview," a barrage of questions about programming languages and technology issues, to see if the candidate "knew what I was talking about, technically." Finally, the recruiter invited him for face-to-face interviews with a partner and two senior managers, who "drilled me about teamwork and asked a lot of behavioral questions."

Making the grade

Deloitte also actively recruits on campuses around the country to fill full-time positions and summer internships, targeting specific MIS and MBA programs. The company offers internships in specific cities, and seems to require that students apply via the Internet, whether or not they interview with a recruiter. Full-time recruits come from big-ticket business programs like Carnegie Mellon/GSIA, Chicago/GSB, Harvard, NYU/Stern, University of Pennsylvania/Wharton and others, as well as MIS programs. Recruiters also seek candidates at large career fairs and conferences, including the National Black MBA Association Conference and the Exposition National Society of Hispanic MBAs Conference and Career Expo.

OUR SURVEY SAYS

Individual results may vary

Insiders report a company culture that varies from office to office. "Firm culture and style are very heterogeneous and depend on the industry line, the partner and the office that you work with," a consultant reports. Insiders seem to like the people they work with. "Colleagues are generally very easy to get along with," says one source. Deloitte consultants are "results-oriented people that want to succeed" says another, adding that there are "very business-savvy individuals throughout the firm." A consultant notes that in his office, consultants are encouraged to "network during working hours and many times after hours through arranged happy hours and other planned events."

Clocking in

Deloitte follows a 3,4,5 schedule where consultants spend three nights and four days traveling and onsite with clients, and the fifth day working from home. But insiders say the actual hours depend on the project. "3,4,5 is not enforced," one consultant says. "How long you are at the client site depends on the workload and what the client wants." Another insider notes that because none of the clients he worked with are local to his home office, he could expect "a Monday through Friday travel schedule," adding that "while Deloitte frequently touts that you will be back in your home office on Fridays, this is often not the case." Another source puts the average workweek at "50 to 60 hours."

Travel "can be a nightmare because of the global staffing," a Houston-based source reports. "I spent most of my time on projects in the Northeast, a very difficult commute." He recommends that consultants should "try not to get staffed by a staffing manager, but by local partners and [senior managers]: They tend to get more regional projects, but not always." Another source writes that since Deloitte "has a global staffing matrix," a consultant can work for managers and partners from all over: "Some of them are flexible hour- and travel-wise, some of them are not."

Others sources call the travel "harsh" and say it can play a direct part in a consultant's opportunity for advancement in the company. They explain that consultants must "be willing to travel anywhere, anytime" and that "if you are unwilling to travel whenever and wherever they want you to, your career will suffer for it."

Advance!

Deloitte touts opportunities to "enhance your knowledge and skills" through reimbursement and/or time off for training, certification or membership in professional organizations. Consultants, however, report that "opportunities for advancement have to be aggressively sought" and are "available, but you need to shine." One North American insider says the local firm hosts bi-weekly "lunch and learns" and requires that each consultant fulfill a "mandatory learning plan."

Generally, "the firm has a commitment to improving employees and investing in providing employees with learning opportunities." However, one source contends that "a lack of partner interest in individuals" is a real problem, while another suspects that "industry hires [are] not valued as much as recent grads who had all their experience with Deloitte. But this may be different from office to office." In any event, insiders acknowledge that the firm has tools in place to improve upon consultants' skills and education, though one claims that its "ability to manage careers" seems "a little bit limited."

Different faces in different places

Deloitte won kudos in 2005 from *Diversity Inc.*, *Latina Style*, *Fortune* and *Working Mother* magazines for its diversity efforts. These awards recognize Deloitte as a whole, however, so that an industry notably lagging in diversity—such as IT consulting—may not witness first-hand Deloitte's strong reputation for diversity in its offices.

A Pittsburgh-based insider maintains that his home office, occupied by a preponderance of white heterosexuals, does not reflect Deloitte's diversity policies, but rather, the city's particular demographics. "I know other Deloitte offices have a strong support for their affinity groups (African American, gay and lesbian, Hispanic), and in general I think Deloitte does a fair job of trying to promote diversity and collegiality."

And, despite Deloitte's many awards for being a female-friendly firm, not all consultants feel a female presence in their offices. One source says there are "hardly any women" in his home office: two female senior managers, and no female partners or directors. However, he adds that "when you're at a client all the time," it's hard to comment on diversity.

Paying out

While sources seem satisfied with their salaries, insiders say the company "expects a lot: long hours, long travel" for your money. As far as perks go, the offerings are pretty basic. The firm offers standard medical, dental and vision, 401(k), flexible spending plans, a pre-tax transportation plan, flexible work arrangements, parental leave, and disability and long-term care insurance programs, as well as a mortgage assistance program. It also offers reimbursement for child adoption costs, a child care program and an elder care consultation and referral service.

"The firm has a commitment to improving employees and investing in providing employees with learning opportunities."

— *Deloitte source*

3 IBM Global Services

New Orchard Road
Armonk, NY 10504
Phone: (914) 499-1900
Fax: (914) 765-7382
www-1.ibm.com/services/us/index.wss

LOCATIONS

Armonk, NY (HQ)
Over 300 offices in 170 countries

PRACTICE AREAS

Consulting
Application innovation • Business transformation outsourcing • Center for Business Optimization • Financial management • Human capital management • Marketing, sales & services • On-Demand Innovation Services • Strategy & change • Supply chain & procurement

IT Services
Application development & systems integration • Application management services • Applications on demand • Business continuity & recovery • Customized training solutions • Equipment buyback & disposal • Infrastructure & systems management • IT performance • Maintenance • Networking • Outsourcing/Hosting • Packaged application implementation • Security & privacy • Service-oriented architecture • Storage • Technical support • Wireless

THE BUZZ
WHAT CONSULTANTS AT OTHER FIRMS ARE SAYING

- "Everywhere"
- "Strong company; excellent reputation for software engineering"
- "Young inexperienced consultants; the best consultants are gone"
- "Too huge", "no sense of identity"

THE STATS

Employer Type: Division of IBM
Ticker symbol: IBM (NYSE)
Senior Vice Presidents: Ginni Rometty, Mike Daniels, Bob Moffat Jr.
2005 Employees: 190,000
2004 Employees: 180,000
2005 Revenues: $47.4 billion
2004 Revenues: $46.4 billion

UPPERS

- "An incredible network" of colleagues, training and resources
- "Endless opportunities to do new things" with "cutting edge technology"
- "Prestige of working for a firm that's known worldwide"

DOWNERS

- "High-pressure utilization model"
- "Bureaucracy" associated with a public corporate giant
- "Complicated bonus structure"

EMPLOYMENT CONTACT

www-1.ibm.com/employment

THE SCOOP

From hardware to services

They don't call it "Big Blue" for nothing. IBM, the largest IT firm in the world, offers IT consulting through its towering Global Services division. As IBM continues to step away from its role as a purveyor of computer hardware toward a more service-oriented model, Global Services has taken an increasingly powerful role in the firm, contributing $47.4 billion of the company's $91.1 billion in revenues for fiscal year 2005. The division is expected to keep taking a growing slice of the IBM pie—2005 revenues for Global Services were up 2 percent from the previous year.

The Global Services arm of the firm is broken up into consulting and IT services divisions. The consulting division offers application innovation, business transformation outsourcing, strategy and change, and supply chain services, among others. Under the IT services umbrella, IBM offers a host of services such as networking, customized training, security, and outsourcing and hosting. Like many of its tech services peers, IBM has poured resources into its outsourcing division, which makes up the bulk of Global Services' profits.

Taking consulting by storm

Though its name is still largely associated with computers, IBM has made a dedicated effort to redefine itself as a consulting and services player. In 2001, revenues from the company's services division outpaced those from its hardware arm for the first time in the firm's long history. This trend got a big boost in 2002, when IBM acquired PricewaterhouseCoopers Consulting, adding some 30,000 employees in 52 countries. The consulting world had to sit up and take notice—suddenly, IBM was a force to be reckoned with, becoming the largest consulting services organization worldwide. A series of smaller acquisitions solidified this position, including the 2002 purchase of Matra Datavision, a French consultancy specializing in product lifecycle management (PLM) solutions.

The 2002 appointment of Sam Palmisano as IBM's CEO also boded well for the direction of IBM's services division. Palmisano used to head Global Services and wasn't shy about his plans for its growth. In 2005, IBM made a series of steps designed to move the company away from a "commodity" model (focused on selling parts and technologies) and into a "services" model (selling the brainpower of its consultants and other resident experts). One glaring example of this new push was

IBM's decision to unload its PC business, in a deal that closed in the spring of 2005. In May 2005, IBM began a series of shakeups in the Global Services division. For starters, the firm announced planned layoffs of between 10,000 and 13,000 employees, mostly in Europe. The reorganization was seen as a move to push IBM's business consulting strengths ahead of its more traditional "body shop" computer services, analysts said.

Size matters

The streamlining also has been viewed as part of a plan to differentiate IBM's IT services from those of its tech supplier rivals, like Dell, and from its consulting rivals such as HP, EDS and Accenture. With IBM dwarfing even its nearest competitors in size and reach, those smaller rivals have had to resort to a strength-in-numbers approach. In October 2004, for instance, EDS announced the formation of the "EDS Agility Alliance"—a partnership drawing on the resources of Cisco, Dell, EMC, Microsoft, Sun Microsystems and Xerox—an effort to augment its position in the services arena. According to EDS vice president Robb Rasmussen in an interview with InfoWord.com, even partners with overlapping product lines have come together to serve customers. "Our partners have lost business to IBM's service group as well," he added.

Global Services evolves

In July 2005, Big Blue announced a reorganization of the Global Services business. Calling the move not a response to problems in the business, but rather a "natural evolution," company execs said the realigned group would focus more on "high-value" skills in line with those offered by IBM's original Business Consulting Services division established after IBM acquired PwC's consulting practice. The natural choice to lead the group in its new iteration was Ginni Rometty, who had previously run BCS and helped push through the integration of the new consulting business after the PwC acquisition. Rometty's new title became senior VP of enterprise business services. Also appointed to lead the new division in the July shake-up was Mike Daniels, who formerly headed up sales for IBM Americas. The pair of execs replaced John Joyce, who left the firm to join a private technology investment company. Another exec pushed up the ladder was Bob Moffat, tapped as Integrated Supply Chain leader for the firm.

One new component of the retooled Global Services division is business performance transformation services (BPTS), which captures a market outside the traditional IT industry, driven by clients converting more internal spending—such as general administrative and research and development expenses—to external investments in such areas as logistics management, engineering services, HR processes, procurement, marketing, and finance and administration. IBM bolstered its business process capabilities to better serve this market in 2005 through the acquisitions of Equitant (order-to-cash services), Ascential Software (data integration) and Healthlink (health care process consulting). An early example of BPTS was IBM's work with the New York Stock Exchange, which contracted with the firm's engineering division to develop a new order management and messaging system supported by 3,000 custom-designed handheld devices for trading floor brokers to place buy and sell orders via a wireless network.

In March 2005, IBM announced a new strategy for attracting mid-sized businesses to its consulting services. The firm outlined a plan to invest $300 million in a "partner" approach, aimed at forming relationships with regional consultancies catering to smaller clients. Recognizing that the giant firm could better target small and mid-sized clients—a rapidly growing target audience for IT services—with the help of more modestly-sized partners, IBM unveiled a range of collaborative programs. Through its "Express Managed Services," IBM explained, regional partners could work with Big Blue to resell IBM services such as business management consulting and outsourcing.

Filling out the ranks

As a whole, the Global Services division employs about 190,000 people in 170 countries. In August 2004, IBM announced that it planned to hire 18,800 people worldwide that year, 880 more than originally anticipated, with two-thirds of those jobs in Global Services. Employment at IBM has generally trended upwards in recent years, a contrast to 2002, when the company laid off around 15,000 workers (though twice that many became IBMers following the PwC acquisition).

IBM around the world

Of course, the "I" in IBM stands for "International," and the firm has done its best to live up to its name. In December 2004, the firm acquired Danish IT services companies Maersk Data and Dmdata, giving IBM's services division a powerful presence in the region. The firm has landed major clients in Europe, including Portugal's Banco BPI and broadcast network Retevision. In June 2005, IBM inked a seven-year deal with European brewing giant Carlsberg to manage the company's IT infrastructure and services across 12 of its subsidiaries in Europe. In October 2004, IBM signed its largest-ever IT services deal in Austria, with insurance company Wiener Staedtische Group. Latin America has been another success story for Big Blue, including a $6.9 million, seven-year contract to provide IT operation and maintenance services for CorpBanca Venezuela, following an earlier successful $6 million partnership with the bank's Chilean branch. In Mexico, the firm has been working with Mexican retailer Omnilife to support desktop PCs running on Linux in local schools.

The company has made big strides in the Asia-Pacific region, as well. Singapore Airlines signed a deal to outsource its IT operations to the firm in October 2004. That same month, Esquire, Korea's leading fashion marketing company, contracted IBM to manage its IT infrastructure under a seven-year agreement. The firm also signed a $10 million agreement with Singapore-based Equinix in May 2004 to offer enterprise customers a range of e-business services, as well as managed services and IT outsourcing.

High-impact clients

Closer to home, in July 2005, the firm announced that it entered into separate multi-year contracts with Altria Corporate Services and Philip Morris USA to provide data center, hosting and network services. In April 2005, Northeastern supermarket behemoth Pathmark Stores engaged IBM in a seven-year contract for a variety of IT services, including data communications and anti-spam technology. Other mega-deals have included an ongoing $400 million contract with Sprint to provide application development and maintenance support for some Sprint software systems, and a seven-year agreement with Dow Chemical Corporation to manage its worldwide IT infrastructure, as well as to provide electronic mail for over 50,000 Dow employees and contractors, support for 2,800 servers and field services in 63 countries, and to transform Dow's voice communications using Voice over Internet Protocol (VoIP) technology. Dow took the unusual step of canceling an existing contract with IBM rival EDS for the deal, which analysts valued to be worth more than $1.1 billion.

Cashing out

Observers weren't as impressed, however, when JPMorgan Chase withdrew from a $5 billion outsourcing contract with Global Services in September 2004—an arrangement that had been the biggest outsourcing contract in banking. JPMorgan decided to reintegrate its tech infrastructure following its merger with Bank One, taking back the 4,000 IT staff it had transferred to IBM in January 2003. Some analysts saw the withdrawal as a sign that outsourcing in the sector might not live up to its initial hype. But the move, while costly for JPMorgan, had only a minor impact on IBM's operations.

Friendly skies

Meanwhile, IBM has continued to make a name for itself as a go-to resource for airlines, who increasingly want to adopt the firm's "on-demand" approach to IT services. Global Services has worked with JetBlue Airways to design self-serve check-in kiosks, and has provided similar solutions for Air Canada, Alitalia, British Airways, United Airlines, U.S. Airways, Southwest Airlines, KLM Airlines, Japan Air Lines, Gulf Air and Air New Zealand.

Public partners

Though IBM isn't as public sector-oriented as firms such as Booz Allen, the firm does have some government clients. In March 2005, IBM signed a deal with the State of Texas to develop and implement a statewide Web-based voter registration system, designed to help the state meet the requirements of the Help America Vote Act of 2002, including establishing a statewide, centralized database of registered voters. And in September 2004, Global Services was listed as part of a team overseen by Lockheed Martin in a $9 billion contract to provide IT products and services to the U.S. Air Force.

Transforming retail

IBM's IT services also include helping clients implement the increasingly ubiquitous technology of radio frequency identification, or RFID. As Wal-Mart unveiled an ambitious plan to enable its operations with RFID by 2005, IBM came on board to help develop and test solutions. The firm also helped the retailer's partners in China, and in 2004 IBM announced plans to open an RFID Solution Center in Japan.

A view from the top

IBM consistently tops the IT industry's best-of lists for technological innovations, including its Web services and business continuity capabilities. It's also recognized for its workplace practices, earning honors from the Environmental Protection Agency for its unique solutions for commuters (such as rematching and telecommuting). In 2004, IBM became the only company chosen for 17 consecutive years by *Working Mother* magazine for its top 10 list of the 100 Best Companies for working mothers.

A company with class

IBM's community work often involves classrooms nationwide. In fact, IBM has made education a pet project in recent years, investing $75 million worldwide in a school reform program appropriately tagged "Reinventing Education." In September 2005, IBM announced the pilot of a new "Transition to Teaching" program, an effort to help employees become fully accredited math and science teachers when they elect to leave the company. The program, the first of its kind in the U.S., reimburses participants up to $15,000 for tuition and stipends during the student teaching phase. If successful, IBM said, the program would expand significantly and possibly involve other companies, as well.

GETTING HIRED

All aboard Big Blue

IBM's consulting division refers would-be applicants to the main Big Blue careers web site for job openings and other employment information. Candidates can submit applications online and search a database of job fairs and campus recruiting events.

Insiders tell us IBM's hiring practices are quite polished. "For a big firm," a source says, "the process is very streamlined. You go to ibm.com/jobs, find the position you want and submit your resume, all electronically. Somebody gets back to you within 48 to 72 hours." A source who was hired with professional experience reports, "I was interviewed by the practice executive and a project manager. Case questions are included in interviews."

Cream of the campus crop(s)

For campus recruiting, a consultant says, "We do not have a single formula— different labs recruit from certain favorite schools where they know the program." A colleague notes that the firm tends to favor "the cream of the crop from well known schools. A lot of them are MBA grads." The consultant adds, "I don't think they restrict their recruiting to certain schools; they tend to go to a variety of schools. I think they're trying to recruit people who are more local to the projects—that's a recent move—to hire people who tend to be in the large cities. This is an effort to minimize travel, but that wouldn't keep them from hiring someone who was qualified for the position or for a specific project."

College-level candidates, a source says, "are pre-screened on campus, then they come in for a management practice interview, then one to two technical interviews with people who will be their peers. If you pass those stages, feedback from all parties combined will make the decision." At this level, the insider says, there are "no case questions—they have a guide to help us assess characteristics and capabilities of applicants and to probe their experiences. The focus is on understanding how applicants contributed to their prior experience, which would be relevant to their job here, as well as how they worked in a team environment. It's not so much a case study, but more of a formula to seek proof of your capability."

OUR SURVEY SAYS

The global matrix

Simply by virtue of its size, insiders say, IBM boasts a vast and varied culture. As one consultant explains, the firm is "very much a matrixed organization, and allows for a wide range of cultures to exist in different pockets based on the presence of strong leaders." The source adds, "Top-level culture fosters key qualities of personal motivation, personal leadership and accountability at the individual level. And while there are broad themes of innovation and responsibility—core cultural values—it puts a lot of responsibility and trust in individuals to do as they see fit in their personal nooks and crannies of the company."

Another insider, who describes the culture of IBM's consulting division as "positive" overall, says, "When I was first hired by IBM, I had a lot of people who really helped get me up to speed—my manager and the people on my first team. I find that I like the culture of the teams and my network." While "the bureaucracy often gets in the way of getting things done efficiently," the source adds, "I think that's just a consequence of how huge IBM is." At the same time, another source notes, when PwC merged its consulting business into Big Blue, "they brought a lot of their culture with them." These days, the source reports, "the culture is hard working, people keep moving and expanding their careers and learning as much as they can, and people are in that mindset."

IM for answers

Teamwork is big at IBM, which naturally takes advantage of technology to bring out the best from all of its players, sources tell us. "I can instant message with an array of people…and get information from the right thinkers at the right time," a consultant raves. A colleague agrees that IBM is made up of staffers who exhibit "teamwork, professionalism, intelligence, maturity" and a "go-getter attitude," though "not in the negative sense." The source adds, "As a rule, people are willing to help others in a way that I find very positive."

Be your own boss!

At the same time, sources love the "autonomy" the firm grants them. "It's almost like being my own self-employed business," a consultant raves, noting, "I conduct my own schedule, I do my own booking and deliverables—so even though I have managers, I really report to myself." This has its pros and cons, the source explains, noting that a lot of responsibility, from projects to self-promotion, is placed on the shoulders of consultants. But for the most part, insiders appreciate the freedom. "Obviously there are some dependencies within the team, but I have the flexibility of working onsite or remotely (via telephone or online) so I'm not tied to my desk from 9 to 5 Monday through Friday like at typical jobs," a consultant notes.

Utilization vs. balance

Though consultants agree that IBM "pays attention to" work/life balance—the firm made *Consulting Magazine*'s best 10 list for work/life programs in October 2005—achieving it isn't always possible when facing hefty utilization targets, they suggest. As an insider puts it, "The nature of project work is that it is innately flexible; it's not like you have hours—things are not dictated that way. If you have to take a day off to attend to some personal stuff, there's usually no problem...On the other hand, in public sector work, we have very high utilization rates, so while IBM says that they promote work/life balance, having a high utilization rate kind of contradicts that. You have to put the hours in." A co-worker agrees that the company is "very aware of" work/life balance, but that the firm "is only able to do so much about it." Adds the source, "sometimes, with individual circumstances, some may not be able to handle the hours, so management tries to help to the best of their ability. You see some sign of burnout sometimes, but that's inevitable." "It's a double-edged sword," agrees a colleague, noting that "you have a utilization target of 90 percent, and that's over and above the travel. Travel is basically your own time."

There are signs that the company has taken steps to ease the burnout factor associated with travel, insiders say. Though most sources report a steady travel load of four days on the road and one at the office (or, in most cases, telecommuting), "now there's a move back again to find more regional work," one insider says. According to another consultant, "Many people are able to work locally, as opposed to having to travel—this is because of our enormous size." The consultant adds that "at IBM, we're not globetrotters traveling around the world," though "the more niche your skill is, the more likely it is that you'll travel a lot." Still, says a colleague, "IBM has changed in the last four to five years in terms of some of its rules with PwC's influence. They've allowed spouses to travel to the client site on the weekends, instead of the consultant flying home. Also, we used to only stay in hotels when traveling to the client site, but now we can stay in an apartment."

No weekend surprises

Work hours for an IBM consultant tend to "vary by project and time in the project," and are "usually mutually agreed to. You know what you need to get done and you know you need to work heavily during a period of time," says a source. The consultant adds that "the average person probably works 45 hours a week. We're not usually expected to work on the weekends—it doesn't happen very often. There's no expectation that they'll see you Saturday morning, like our friends at Accenture might expect."

Still, IBMers are an ambitious lot, sources suggest—in the words of another consultant, "I work all the time. It's almost like I'm never not working," though the source adds, "The work I do on the weekend is not demanded by the firm." "Personally, I do some work on the weekends," agrees a co-worker, who says that "it's something I enjoy doing, and a lot of times there are commitments that I have to adhere to, like bids and proposals. They say you should work on these for a few hours on Fridays, but a lot of times the work carries into the weekends because there are pretty tight deadlines on this stuff."

Who's the boss?

IBM consultants have a network of mentors, managers and supervisors to report to and help them along in their careers. Consultants "take direction from project managers (involved in your day-to-day activities), administrative managers (don't get involved in day-to-day activity much—more human resource-type stuff), resource managers (help try to get people into the right jobs), and more senior members of various practices provide you with substantial career direction. In this matrix organization, the closest you get to supervisors are administrative supervisors (HR decisions), but it's mostly project managers who direct day-to-day work," explains a source. While all of this management may sound oppressive, our sources report being very satisfied with their supervision. "The thing with IBM is, it's down to you. Even though you have a hierarchy, it's not the same as at other companies. I can reach out to my manager whenever I want to. I'm the one who initiates a monthly call with my career manager to touch base and let him know what I'm thinking and doing," a consultant notes.

One insider notes that IBM's focus on career development sets the firm apart: "They assign you to a mentor/manager, and they really try to realize what your goals are and help you move in that direction by placing you on projects and making sure your education is in tune with your goals. A lot of other firms pigeon-hole you into certain positions—what you sign up for is what you get." The source adds that "mentors are reassigned every year so you're not with the same person." Says a colleague, "These relationships help make IBM a positive place, and bring some cohesiveness into the environment."

Lots to learn

Training at IBM takes place on the job, online and during "several large conferences per year, which are good opportunities to learn about a range of topics," a consultant reports, noting that "IBM has a whole department devoted to education." Under the firm's "Individual Development Plan," a source explains, "you say, this is the direction that I would like to grow in IBM, and you put down specific courses you would like to attend, along with a time frame, and you discuss them with your manager and sign off on them." The firm's "Global Campus" program allows "access to hundreds of online courses, so you can download them to your laptop and do them when traveling or at home," the source adds. Another consultant notes that while "classroom training has not been a priority for the company in the last couple of years," this is not "atypical in the consulting world now." The source notes that the firm offers "a lot of funded training opportunities for people who are going for certification."

Brooding over bonuses

Compensation at IBM is generally described as "better than average." The firm "definitely has the resources to compensate more than fairly," quips one consultant.

Still, a colleague notes that "people are satisfied with their compensation, but they're not satisfied with what it takes to get more of a bonus or to get greater compensation within grade levels. In order to move from one level to the next, you have to take on more responsibility and more business development responsibilities." In fact, bonuses "are a touchy subject" at IBM, one insider says, as they've naturally softened along with the tech market over the past decade. As a colleague explains, "One problem with IBM is that it sets targets way too high for profitability and revenue. They've continually changed the bonus model over time. It used to be tied to the individual's performance and the practice performance. Now it's become based on the division performance and IBM's performance. So if your own group did well, and you as an individual had good utilization, you would get a good bonus. Now, IBM as a whole has to do well to get a bonus."

Consultants describe IBM's benefits and perks as "nothing special." "Most of the benefits are pretty standard," says a consultant. "One thing that's good is that the hotel/car rental/travel rates that IBM negotiates, we can use for personal use as well." Another consultant appreciates the firm's "many decent conference opportunities, software updates, technical exchange weeks and recognition events, in addition to educational events," which staffers genuinely "look forward to." As a plus, the source adds, many conferences and events take place "in places like Las Vegas or Orlando, where there are extracurricular activities." In addition, pipes in one consultant, "we have a concierge service program, but I don't know anyone that uses it."

Work/life for women

For a tech-oriented firm, IBM receives high marks from its consultants for its support of diversity with respect to women. "I see a lot of women in different levels of responsibility and they're not treated any differently than their male counterparts. I think IBM works at solving work/life balance issues for women. They support women in different roles and with different responsibilities," a consultant says. "There is a BCS women's networking group that I have gone to (mostly conference calls), which is a support network for women in the company. I've never felt that because I am an (older) woman that I was discriminated against in any way," a colleague adds. Another source explains that it actually may be easier for women to achieve work/life balance in the senior ranks at IBM, since managerial levels offer more "flexibility," as opposed to "entry levels where you travel more, [and] have to take more direction from others."

Overall, IBM is "a firm committed to diversity," says a source, who notes that "the firm holds a diversity training seminar every year for everyone to attend to talk about

Visit the Vault Consulting Career Channel at **www.vault.com/consulting** —with
insider firm profiles, message boards, the Vault Consulting Job Board and more.
VAULT CAREER LIBRARY   **55**

how IBM is making strides in creating opportunities for people of all minorities (including women and homosexuals, etc.) and how it's encouraged within the firm." The source adds, "I would say it's not just all talk. I see a lot of it put into practice." In addition to "support groups for specific groups," such as black engineers, the firm offers "mandatory diversity training every year," insiders report.

Support groups also are available for gays and lesbians at IBM. As a consultant explains, "The company has taken, in the last five years, a very open stance toward medical benefits and other privileges for same-sex domestic partners, and I think it's accepted." A colleague adds that management is "very positive about fostering diversity and really bringing different groups into the fold—that we're one IBM. Individuals are accepted for what they know, not who they are."

On demand outreach

Just as IBM offers "business on demand," a consultant tells us, the firm has taken strides to foster "community on demand" through various community service and outreach programs. The firm has "people who act as official liaisons in the community to encourage people to participate. We also have a nationwide adopt-a-school program in which we're actually doing hands-on work at schools in the area, painting, etc.," the source adds, and "we have a grant/donation program; we submit grants for equipment and then donate it to the organization that you donate your time to." Other charitable activities include a payroll deduction program that allows employees to contribute to a choice of programs, employee matching contributions and pro bono projects.

"Top-level culture fosters key qualities of personal motivation, personal leadership and accountability at the individual level."

— *IBM Global Services insider*

Cisco Systems, Inc.

170 West Tasman Drive
San Jose, CA 95134
Phone: (408) 526-4000 or
(800) 553-NETS
www.cisco.com

LOCATIONS

San Jose, CA (HQ)
More than 100 offices worldwide

SERVICES

Advanced Services
Partner Support Services
Services for Cisco Technologies &
  Networking Solutions
Technical Support Services

THE STATS

Employer Type: Public Company
Ticker Symbol: CSCO (Nasdaq)
President and CEO: John T. Chambers
2005 Employees: 38,413
2004 Employees: 34,371
2005 Revenues: $24.8 billion
2004 Revenues: $22 billion

UPPERS

• "Very fair and highly motivating
  compensation package"
• Encourages internal advancement
• Young, energetic, fun co-workers

DOWNERS

• You have to "love the technology"
• Some middle managers are "full of
  themselves"
• Late-night conference calls

EMPLOYMENT CONTACT

tools.cisco.com/careers/applicant/
ciscorm/careers/applicant/ index.jsp

THE BUZZ
WHAT CONSULTANTS AT OTHER FIRMS ARE SAYING

• "They run the Internet"
• "A caring employer"
• "Need to evolve with new business
  model"
• "Young, no track record"

THE SCOOP

The parents of networking

Founded in 1984 by a married couple of computer scientists from Stanford, Calif., Cisco is home to the technologies that form the backbone of the Internet as we know it today. The team, Leonard Bosack and Sandra Lerner, began small, running network cables between two Stanford buildings. The firm became known for innovations in routing, attracting $2 million in venture capital funding in 1987. That same year, Cisco (the name is derived from regional neighbor San Francisco) developed the Interior Gateway Routing Protocol (IGRP), which allowed for the construction of large-scale internets. By 1989, on the strength of just over 100 employees and three products on the market, Cisco raked in an impressive $27 million from its revolutionary networking technologies. The firm went public the following year—the same year the term "World Wide Web" was coined.

By the mid-1990s, Cisco was an international enterprise, with offices in its new San Jose headquarters, as well as in Sao Paolo, Tokyo, Amsterdam and many others. The 1990s also saw a series of acquisitions as the firm snatched up developing technologies to corner the networking market. In 1998, Cisco became the first company in history to achieve market capitalization of $100 billion in just 14 years of business.

Righting the Cisco ship

Cisco wasn't spared the effects of the shaky tech economy at the beginning of the 21st century. The firm's announcement in 2001 that it would be laying off as much as 11 percent of its workforce was described by analysts as the "antithesis" of Cisco's corporate culture, and a gloomy omen for the tech industry as a whole. The firm reportedly took a creative approach to its layoffs, offering employees a third of their salary plus benefits and stock-options awards while working for one year at a not-for-profit group associated with the company, in lieu of the traditional severance package. While the firm has been rebuilding since those turbulent times, its headcount still trails the 44,000 Cisco staffers it boasted in 2001. To date, the firm employs more than 38,000 people worldwide.

From switches to services

While the firm continues to derive the lion's share of its revenues from the products it sells (including routers, switches and other advanced technologies), Cisco's services contributed $3.9 billion to its $24.8 billion revenues in 2005 (as a whole, the firm's revenues rose 12.5 percent over the previous year). Cisco's Internet Business Solutions Group, led by VP Gary Bridge, provides many of these services, helping Global 500 clients achieve efficiencies in their businesses by identifying and implementing technological solutions.

Usually, Cisco services are bundled with the sale and implementation of Cisco technologies and, as such, engagements aren't always categorized as either product or service contracts. But Cisco's services span an array of industries, including education, financial services, government, health care, legal, manufacturing, retail and transportation. One education sector client, the University of Arizona, has tapped Cisco to help build a scalable foundation for network security. Government agencies, from local counties to entire countries, have hired the firm to implement IP communications services. And major health care clients, such as a hospital in Beijing, have turned to Cisco to help develop a network for digitally archiving and accessing records such as radiology images.

Reeling them in

The firm has continued to expand through acquisitions in recent years. In 2003, the firm brought networking company Linksys into its fold, which effectively marked Cisco's entry into the multi-billion dollar home networking market. In 2005, the firm's biggest buy was Scientific-Atlanta, Inc. Cisco snapped up the firm, which provides set-top boxes, end-to-end video distribution networks and video system integration, in November for around $6.9 billion. The deal brought around 7,500 former Scientific-Atlanta employees to Cisco. Other 2005 acquisitions included select intellectual property and telephony assets of Toronto-based Digital Fairway Corp. (in November); network memory space firm Nemo Systems (September); intelligent network and service management firm Sheer Networks (July); and semiconductor provider Vihana Inc. (May).

Knowledge is power

Cisco provides a host of white papers, presentations and other content on its web site geared toward "executive thought leadership." The firm helps clients share best practices, while CEO John Chambers provides a quarterly publication aimed at informing executives about Internet trends and innovations. Cisco also publishes a series of thought leadership books—the *Connected Series*—covering current issues in a wide range of industries. Each book, aimed at senior business leaders, is made up of essays (contributed by business leaders and edited by the firm's Internet Business Solutions Group Mobile team) that cover case studies, analysis and predictions for the future of the industry. The most recent addition to the series, *Connected Workforce*, published in June 2005, includes essays on how "mobile technologies will fundamentally change the face of business." Other titles in the series include *Connected Transportation*, *Connected Government*, *Connected Homes*, *Connected Schools*, *Connected Health* and *Connected Cities*.

The essays, contributed by 14 senior business leaders and edited by the firm's Internet Business Solutions Group Mobile team, include case studies and predictions for the connected workforce of the future.

Cisco citizens

Cisco prides itself on its corporate responsibility. The firm has consistently been named one of the 100 Best Companies to Work For by *Working Mother* and *Computer World* magazines, and ranked No. 26 in *Fortune* magazine's 2006 list of the 100 Best Large Companies to Work for in America, topping its No. 27 slot in 2005. More than 40 percent of the firm's employees donated volunteer hours to their communities in 2005, and the firm contributed more than $65 million in cash and in-kind donations toward a range of efforts worldwide, including relief efforts for the Asian tsunami and Hurricane Katrina. In 2005, the firm introduced its first annual Citizenship Report, summarizing Cisco's responsible business practices and social investment programs for the year. The report is partially aimed at catching the eye of sharcholders, as it outlines how the firm's efforts at good corporate citizenship benefit the bottom line. For instance, Cisco touts its responsible energy practices, noting that decreased energy consumption has saved the company more than $6 million per year.

The firm has worked with the World Health Organization to establish the Cisco Health Academy, which operates in 24 schools in Egypt and 21 schools in Jordan to tap the Internet for health and wellness information aimed at inhabitants of remote and underserved areas. In Jordan, the firm's education initiative provides information, equipment and expertise to support the country's goal of creating a knowledge-oriented economy. In November 2005, the firm announced that it was joining forces with the National Center for Women & Information Technology (NCWIT) to increase awareness of education and career opportunities for girls and women in science, technology, math and engineering. Cisco also introduced a comprehensive digital library that offers information and tips for parents, educators and students aimed at encouraging girls' participation in high-tech endeavors.

GETTING HIRED

Targeted searches

Cisco's careers pages online provide information on the firm's culture, benefits and diversity, in addition to those all-important job openings. In fact, the firm maintains not one job search engine but several, geared toward various career stages, regions and areas within the company. For example, the firm's Global Government Solutions Group lists openings separately. The firm also allows Cisco hopefuls to set up a personal profile and a job search engine to have openings e-mailed to them.

Cisco offers internship opportunities, typically ranging from three to six months. The firm also recruits recent grads to participate in its one-year "Associates Program," which provides unique experience in sales and sales engineering at Cisco. Applicants must have graduated within two years prior to the program, be prepared to relocate, and have a cumulative GPA of 3.0. (Of course, they also need to be "dedicated, achievement-oriented, and possess a proven ability to learn," the firm notes.) For MBA grads, the firm maintains a separate job search engine online listing suitable openings.

Interview upon interview

A staffer reports that the firm's "hiring practices vary widely by target group," adding that they've seen "everything from an interview and offer the same day, to two months of multiple interviews with no offer." A recent grad who went through a campus interview with Cisco representatives reports also spending a full day at Cisco's offices for "about seven total" interviews, "one right after the other." According to this source, "They were largely behavior-based interviews because they are willing to train you when you first join on, so you don't necessarily need all the technical experience out of college. However, if you are not right out of college you need serious experience."

Another source, who joined the firm with more experience, reports going through "approximately six rounds of interviews with both engineers and management," adding that "most of the interviews were face-to-face, but there was one that was held over the phone." The format, the insider adds, "varied from panel-like sessions with some engineers to one-on-one sessions with the managers. Since this was a technical position, most of the questions were very technical [and focused on] networking. A couple of the interviews with the managers included behavior-based questions (e.g., what would you do if a customer was upset about a particular situation)." In addition, the source says, "Throughout the interview process, I was treated with great respect, and communications from Cisco HR regarding hiring status was good."

OUR SURVEY SAYS

Cisco casual

Cisco staffers, sources say, enjoy a "positive" corporate culture which "encourages career growth, communication with management and results." Self determination is big at the tech giant—as one insider puts it, "Cisco Systems has a very open culture where it empowers its employees to make decisions and take risks." In the words of another consultant, it's a "very casual work atmosphere" where employees are "treated with respect...and like adults." "Cisco employees are very good at helping each other succeed and we are constantly measured on how well we team and collaborate. Employees are encouraged to voice their opinions and to socialize and initiate changes to improve the team, organization or even the company," raves another source.

For the most part, Cisco offers "flexible work hours," says an insider, though this may vary depending on location and position. One staffer notes that "hours are not defined but the culture reflects late starts in the morning, i.e., 9 or 10 a.m. to late evening hours such as 7 and 8 p.m. or later. Hours vary [based on] the worldwide Cisco location and conference calls with India or Italy, to name a few." Another insider agrees, "IT projects are very outsourced...so you have to like the late night calls to the other side of the world." Still, there is the occasional grumble about work hours: As one consultant puts it, "Cisco considers your work/life balanced as long as there is no life included."

Working together

At Cisco, consultants appreciate both their co-workers and their supervisors—with the occasional quibble. One staffer applauds the firm's "superb top management," and "extremely bright and motivated workers." "The managers are very supportive and your co-workers are all young energetic and fun people," reports a source. But one insider grumbles that, while the top and bottom levels are great, the middle could use some work: "Middle management tends to be tremendously full of themselves (many are successful ex-entrepreneurs), over-confident and not well trained. Unfortunately the skills used to build a successful startup and individual products don't necessarily translate well into building a successful, cohesive large business."

"The culture [encourages us] to help others out while competing at the same time," says an insider in Cisco's management training program. "This might seem impossible but it really happens at Cisco. For some reason, people just seem very driven but relaxed at the same time." The source adds, "There is not much break from it since you live, play and work with these people. But you don't really get sick of them because everyone is so much fun. It is very competitive, though, since everyone was one of the best in whatever they did back in college."

True believers

One staffer urges that only fans of Cisco's approach to high-tech need apply. As the source puts it, "the employees at Cisco are so bright and talented. They really do hire sharp people. And you really have to love what you do; that is, in sales, love the technology. I did not, and you cannot swing a fake-out in the face of these geniuses. For the amount that Cisco expects you to know, you cannot fake it. You must love the technology to survive here."

Rotating around

Insiders tend to agree that Cisco encourages career growth, allowing employees to seize the opportunity to move forward. "Cisco encourages its employees to move around to various positions in order to gain additional experience and skills," says a source. As another consultant explains, "Cisco has a very beneficial rotation program," and "after 18 months, it is encouraged of Cisco employees to rotate to different departments. This procedure allows employees to broaden their scope of experience, because Cisco places internal promotion above external promotion. Thus, the opportunity for advancement is extremely high."

Staffers at Cisco agree that the firm has a "diverse employee population." "Corporate diversity is extensive with all nations represented at Cisco. Diversity is encouraged in every aspect of job functions, from the lowest to the highest positions," a consultant says.

Fair and motivating

Salaries and bonus packages at Cisco vary according to position. Generally, a source reports, "lower-grade employees are paid a lower bonus rate, [while] higher paid salaries earn larger bonuses." In addition, the source notes, "every employee at Cisco is given stock options. The stock option amount is dependent on the position grade. The higher the grade, the more stock options you are granted." According to another insider, "U.S. salaried employees qualify for substantial biannual bonus payments that are indexed on individual achievement, corporate target achievement, group customer satisfaction scores and group target achievement," which makes for "a very fair and highly motivating compensation package." Perks at Cisco include anywhere from two to four weeks of vacation, tuition and certification reimbursement, and "free drinks and popcorn" in the office.

Accenture

1345 Avenue of the Americas
New York, NY 10105
Phone: (917) 452-4400
Fax: (917) 527-5387
www.accenture.com

LOCATIONS
More than 110 offices worldwide

PRACTICE AREAS
Consulting
Change Management • Corporate Strategy • Customer Relationship Management • Enterprise & Performance Management • Finance Management • Human Resources Management • Service Management • Shareholder Value • Supply Chain Management • Workforce Performance

Operating Groups
Communications & High Tech • Financial Services • Government • Products • Resources

Outsourcing
Application Outsourcing • Business Process Outsourcing • Infrastructure Outsourcing

Technology
Business Intelligence • Enterprise Integration • Enterprise Solutions • Information Management • Infrastructure Solutions • IT Strategy & Transformation • Microsoft Solutions • Mobile Technology Solutions • Radio Frequency Identifi-cation • SAP Solutions • Systems Integration

THE BUZZ
WHAT CONSULTANTS AT OTHER FIRMS ARE SAYING

- "Outstanding IT"
- "Smart"
- "Boring"
- "Run down"

THE STATS

Employer Type: Public Company
Ticker Symbol: ACN (NYSE)
CEO: William D. Green
2005 Employees: 123,000
2004 Employees: 103,000
2005 Revenues: $15.6 billion
2004 Revenues: $13.7 billion

UPPERS

- "Highly competent, motivated people"
- "Career diversity"
- "Great place to start a consulting career"

DOWNERS

- "Lack of face-to-face interaction with [your] direct team"
- "Too competitive"
- "Size of the firm...It is far too easy to get lost in the shuffle"

EMPLOYMENT CONTACT

uscareers.accenture.com

THE SCOOP

Andersen no more

With more than 129,000 employees in 48 countries worldwide, Accenture has made a name for itself in IT and strategy consulting in a relatively short period of time. The company has been known as Accenture (a name invented by a Norwegian staffer during a company-wide branding challenge) since 2001, before which it operated as Andersen Consulting. Andersen Consulting, along with sibling company Arthur Andersen, resided under the Andersen Worldwide corporate umbrella until an arbitrator's decision in August 2000 severed the contractual ties between Accenture and Andersen Worldwide and, indirectly, the Andersen firms.

Rebranding pays off

Since this split, Accenture has put some powerful muscle into distancing itself from the Andersen name, mounting global advertising campaigns to showcase the new brand. The strategy seems to have paid off: The company was ranked the 50th most valuable global brand by *BusinessWeek*, and *Fortune* magazine has named Accenture the "most admired" company in its industry in the U.S. for three years running.

The company organizes its services around five operating groups: Communications & High Tech, Financial Services, Government, Products and Resources. Of these groups, Communications & High Tech takes the lion's share of business, posting $4 billion in revenues for fiscal year 2005. The firm's services are divided between business consulting (the more strategy-oriented arm) and technology and outsourcing (more tech services in focus). Globally, the firm divides its business into three geographic regions: the Americas; Europe, the Middle East and Africa (EMEA); and Asia-Pacific. Of these, the EMEA region led revenues in 2005 with $7.8 billion.

As Accenture goes...

Accenture came out swinging in fiscal year 2005, posting revenues of $15.6 billion, up 14 percent from the previous year. Consulting revenues, at $9.56 billion, made up 61 percent of the total, while outsourcing contributed the other 39 percent. Wall Street watchers hailed the firm's fiscal results, noting that Accenture was pulling ahead of the pack in terms of profitability. But the positive results gave the industry as a whole reason to cheer, as well—many analysts saw Accenture's success as a leading indicator for a turnaround in IT services globally.

After some rough debut years, Accenture was ready for a turnaround. The firm started off on a high note in 2001, as then-CEO Joe Forehand presided over an initial public offering in July, raising about $1.7 billion. An additional $93 million came in through another IPO in May 2002. But Accenture soon went the way of many consulting giants, resorting to layoffs in 2001, which added up to about 2 percent of its workforce. The company attempted to lower its payroll costs through a voluntary "FlexLeave" program, which allowed consultants to take sabbaticals of six to 12 months at 20 percent of their current pay and continued benefits, with a guarantee that their job at Accenture would still be there upon their return. September 2002 and March 2003 saw an additional round of cuts, mostly among mid- to high-level managers.

The Accenture employment rolls have continued to swell more recently, with about 20,000 positions added between fiscal years 2004 and 2005. Since September 2004, the company has been headed by 27-year Accenture veteran William Green, who previously served as group chief executive of the Communications & High Tech operating group. Forehand continues to serve as chairman, though he will retire at the end of August 2006, and CEO Green will take on the added role of chairman at that time.

A Bermudan accent

Accenture is unusual among its tech services peers in its choice of location—the firm is incorporated in Bermuda. The firm has said that, prior to its IPO, with more than half of its 2,500 partners being non-U.S. citizens, as a cultural matter it chose the neutral location of Bermuda for its parent company. Accenture also owns an operating company in Luxembourg. But the tax-friendly address has led to some sniping among outsiders, including a few Congress members, who argue that the company shouldn't have access to federal contracts. The firm counters that it indeed pays all appropriate taxes in the countries in which it conducts business, including the U.S. In July 2005, Accenture went to Capitol Hill to try to clarify its tax status. According to an article in *The Wall Street Journal*, Accenture asked Congress to clarify that the firm was exempt from a 2004 international tax law forbidding U.S. companies to move offshore to avoid domestic taxes, on the basis that it was not and never had been a U.S.-based or U.S.-operated organization and had never operated under a U.S. parent corporation or partnership. The firm argued that it was already exempt from the law, but wanted to get confirmation from the Internal Revenue Service, and began a campaign to add language to a bill that would solidify its position. But Democratic lawmakers came out against Accenture's position, and tax writers rejected the firm's appeal.

Too much information

Citing a need to help clients with "information overload," Accenture announced in July 2005 that it would invest $100 million over the next three years to accelerate growth in information management services. Accenture referenced analyst estimates indicating that the info management market could exceed $27 billion by 2007, at a growth rate of more than 9 percent each year. The firm named Royce Bell to head a global practice covering more than 5,000 Accenture consultants worldwide, specializing in services such as business intelligence and content management. According to the firm, these staffers will serve up a "comprehensive array of offerings designed to help clients harness, view, manage, analyze and store data, text and other information to improve decision making, financial and operational management and customer service."

Investing in growth

In June 2005, Accenture swelled its ranks with the acquisition of Capgemini's North American health practice for $175 million. About 600 Capgemini staffers joined Accenture's own Health & Life Sciences Practice, bringing the total in North America to around 4,600 employees. Accenture execs said the purchase helped the firm strengthen its position in the industry, especially as the health care world increasingly moves toward leveraging technology. Accenture's airline-oriented subsidiary, Navitaire, expanded its suite of hosted tech solutions in September 2005, acquiring key assets of Forte Solutions, including all of Forte's airline customer contracts. Forte's operation management software, known as the Geneva system, enables airlines to forecast, organize, plan, predict, measure and report on activity in an integrated, real-time environment. The buy added 14 new airlines to Navitaire's client list, and 25 employees to its staff rolls.

Booming in Bangalore

CEO William Green has made no secret of his aggressive plans for outsourcing, declaring that he'd like to boost outsourcing revenues to 50 percent of Accenture's total. The firm seems to be heading in that direction: In fiscal year 2005, outsourcing made up 39 percent of net revenues, compared to about 30 percent in 2004. Accenture, like its competitors, has poured its outsourcing dollars into India. The firm opened a software development center in Bangalore in October 2002, and the firm's headcount in India has exploded, from 4,300 in 2003 to more than 16,000 at the end of 2005. Accenture also boasts a unique approach to recruitment in the region, emphasizing progressive policies that encourage female employment and work to combat discrimination and sexual harassment. According to *Business Line*, as of March 2005, about 25 percent of Accenture's employees in India were women, and the firm reportedly promotes flexible options like day care centers and home office set-ups.

Accenture's outsourcing clientele includes U.S. leaders like Best Buy, which signed a six-year deal with the firm in July 2004. Other notable outsourcing scores include a $575 million human resources outsourcing contract with telecom giant BT, a 10-year contract to manage key aspects of the financial data management processes for Citadel Investment Group, and an extended IT outsourcing contract with Caixa Catalunya, Spain's third-largest savings bank, valued at more than $290 million. In August 2005, Accenture announced an expansion of a contract to provide Dow Chemical Company with a range of business application development, implementation and support services. The firm has been working closely with Dow in China as the chemical giant establishes a shared services center in Shanghai.

Changing China

China is another growth area for the firm. Accenture has stepped up to help manage the modernization of many Chinese state-owned businesses, contracting with clients such as the Bank of China, China Mobile and China's four telecom carriers. Elsewhere in Asia, in September 2005, Accenture was tapped to help Korea's Dongbu Insurance enhance its accounting and financial management operation by implementing an enterprise resource planning system and providing change management services.

Winning over the feds

Back in the U.S., Accenture has become a player in the government-services sector, snatching up contracts for both federal and state clients. One of the largest such coups came in May 2004, when the firm beat out heavy hitters including Lockheed Martin and Computer Sciences Corporation for a multi-billion contract to work on US-VISIT, a border security program, for the Department of Homeland Security. The project involves working with "Smart Border Alliance" partners Raytheon, the Titan Corporation and SRA International to develop and implement a new entry and exit system governing the more than 400 points of entry to the United States. Once again, the firm's offshore incorporation stirred controversy as some House of Representatives legislators moved to block Accenture's access to federal funds, though the attempt was blocked by the House in 2004.

In February 2006, the U.S. Air Force awarded Accenture a five-year, $79 million contract to design, build and operate a new financial management system known as DEAMS, Defense Enterprise Accounting Management System. In July 2005, Accenture scored a big win with the U.S. Army, which awarded the firm a $431 million contract to design, build, run and maintain a new financial system. The new system, which will help the Army standardize and streamline financial processes, will replace three existing information systems, and is expected to be one of the largest of its kind worldwide. Other federal contracts include an $87 million deal with the U.S. Mint to upgrade its marketing systems, signed in January 2005.

Modernizing social service systems

Accenture has applied its IT acumen to helping state governments modernize their systems for delivering essential human services. In June 2005, the Texas Health and Human Services Commission (HHSC) awarded Accenture a five-year, $840 million contract to transform the way citizens apply for social services. Accenture also leads a group of companies known as the Texas ACCESS Alliance to deliver technology and business operations services in support of the state's modernization plans. HHSC's plan will allow Texans to apply for Medicaid, food stamps, Temporary Assistance for Needy Families (TANF) and other programs in person or via the Internet, phone, fax or mail, providing anytime, anywhere access. Other states are monitoring how the Texas integrated eligibility program develops, as they deliberate their own plans for increasing efficiency and reducing the cost of administering social service programs.

States step up

State engagements often come with political scrutiny. An outsourcing disappointment arose for the company in August 2004, when Florida officials dropped an $87 million contract for computer help desk services at state agencies, after criticism arose around how competitor BearingPoint, which shared part of the contract with Accenture, had won the business. But the firm continues to rack up plenty of work at the state level. In addition to the Texas Health and Human Services Commission contract, Accenture was tapped by the State of Ohio in May 2005 to lead the design and implementation of a new IT system to modernize the state's management of financial, human resource and payroll operations. And in April 2005, the firm inked a $98 million deal with the State of Arizona Department of Administration to help transform its current telecom capabilities to next-generation technologies.

Blockbuster engagements

In the private sector, Accenture's engagements are often large and ambitious. When Blockbuster Video sought a Web-based DVD rental model to compete with popular subscription service Netflix in 2004, it turned to Accenture to help develop the program. And when the world's largest private educational measurement association—Educational Testing Service (ETS)—needed help managing its supply chain, including printing, tracking and shipping tests, it tapped Accenture for a $142 million contract.

Elsewhere in the world, Accenture's engagements keep rolling in. In 2005, the UK's National Health Service awarded Accenture a contract to deploy x-rays and scans to be stored and mailed electronically, rather than printed on film. In March 2005, Accenture announced its successful partnership with London's Royal Shakespeare Company, through which the firm supports the theater group both financially and with consulting services. And in October 2004, Accenture was tapped by the Carinthian Regional Hospital Operating Company to redesign and transform a major Austrian hospital, LKH Klagenfurt, to become the second-largest new hospital in Austria, in a deal worth $4.5 million.

Cuddling up to Microsoft

Many tech services giants enjoy close ties with Bill Gates' empire, but Accenture has a particularly cozy relationship with Microsoft—so close, in fact, that for a time rumor had it that the firm might be acquired by the IT giant. Those rumors haven't come to pass, but Accenture continues to make Microsoft a big part of its solutions. In July 2004, Microsoft honored Accenture with its 2004 Global Enterprise Services and Technology Partner of the Year Special Recognition Award, making the firm the only Microsoft partner to have received the award twice.

Tracking tech trends

Accenture cranks out research at a steady pace, including regular studies and surveys. In April 2005, the firm surveyed business travelers, noting the increasing popularity of booking travel online. Each year, Accenture collaborates with *InformationWeek* magazine on the Global Information Security survey, tracking opinions among IT and security professionals. Another study, "IT Investing for High Performance," released in July 2005, surveyed CIOs from more than 300 Fortune 1000 companies and similar organizations, tracking IT spending trends.

Recent appointments

In May 2005, Accenture announced the appointment of Karl-Heinz Floether to the new position of Group Chief Executive - Technology & Delivery. Floether, who formerly served a successful stint as chief executive of the Financial Services group, assumed responsibility for all of the firm's technology, quality and delivery capabilities. In February 2005, Kevin Campbell, an Accenture vet, was named to the new position of global managing director of business process outsourcing.

Citizen of the world

Accenture emphasizes good corporate citizenship through a variety of initiatives worldwide, beginning with its own workforce. *Working Mother* magazine has recognized Accenture three times as one of the 100 Best Companies for Working Mothers. In March 2005 and again in March 2006, the firm marked International Women's Day with a series of coordinated activities in 20 cities around the world. Activities, focused on the role of women in business, included leadership development sessions, career workshops and a streaming Web cast on women at Accenture broadcast to all offices, with many top Accenture execs participating.

Corporate giving at Accenture takes a variety of forms, managed by the firm's Corporate Citizenship Council. When the company made its IPO in 2001, its partners made a significant endowment of Accenture shares to fund a global giving program. Worldwide, staffers at Accenture have participated in activities such as helping establish an HIV clinic for children in South Africa; the Special Olympics World Summer Games in Ireland; business training for young Nigerian professionals; web site development for teachers in Brazil; and school improvement projects in Philadelphia. In September 2004, the company signed on as a management consulting and IT services advisor to the new Smithsonian National Museum of the American Indian, also offering financial contributions and establishing a scholarship fund for American Indian students.

In November 2004, Accenture granted $200,000 and donated consulting hours to Room to Read, an organization that provides educational opportunities for underprivileged children in developing countries, specifically India, Nepal,

Cambodia and Vietnam. And in June 2004, Accenture made a $2.9 million donation to the African Medical and Research Foundation (AMREF), comprised of $1.7 million in cash and $1.2 million in in-kind consulting and related services. The gift was designed to help implement a new electronic training program to boost the ranks of qualified nurses in Kenya, which faces a shortage of qualified nurses amidst a host of public health challenges.

GETTING HIRED

Student focus

Accenture actively recruits on college campuses for both full-time positions and a limited number of 10-week summer internships for undergraduates. "Campus hires are still the most prevalent" at Accenture, sources say, with Baylor, Columbia University, Indiana University, Marquette, Northwestern, UCLA and the University of Illinois at Urbana-Champaign, among the schools from which the firm frequently selects employees. Another insider suggests that trend could be changing, however, as "more experienced hires with industry knowledge seem to be the focus of recruiting, resulting in a shift from…recruiting new graduates."

Ask away

Campus recruitment "includes multiple campus interviews followed by a day of interviews at the chosen office location." Generally, student candidates begin with a 15-minute screening interview in which "typical questions include, 'Why did you choose consulting?' and 'Why Accenture?'" according to one source. Another insider says, "The first interview is really for [the recruiters] to determine if you look like you would fit into their business model and business culture. Interview questions generally revolve around your resume and your motivations for pursuing a position with the firm. They also emphasize how much you know about the firm and [its] services." The screening interview is followed by a second-round interview comprised of behavioral questions, according to an insider recruited in 2005. This insider explains that recruiters ask the candidates to describe certain experiences and then "they will follow up with a lot of questions based on your stories." The source advises to always "have questions to ask" in return. Finally, recruiters invite candidates for a one-day visit to a particular office for another round of interviews that are "fairly laid back but still emphasize fit, past experience and your interest with the firm."

Experienced hires can expect a similar process, with the addition of a "minimum of two skills interviews," according to one consultant, although this isn't always the case. Another source describes his interview process: "I had two rounds of phone interviews with recruiters from the San Francisco office and two rounds of in-person interviews…at the Los Angeles office. I was prepared for a case interview, but they asked behavioral questions and seemed very concerned about my expectations of the lifestyle."

OUR SURVEY SAYS

The young and the restless

Along with Accenture's traditional emphasis on campus recruiting, sources suggest that the firm maintains a youthful and competitive culture. Consultants note that Accenture is a company made up of "highly competent, motivated people" and "hard-working, type-A personalities." "The people are young and like to have a good time," adds another source. A consultant recruited in 2004 says Accenture "is a very dynamic organization, which really suits me. I am the kind of guy who cannot sit at the same desk, go to the same office, do the same thing for more than six months."

Some Accenture sources note how highly they value the people they work with. "As a recent grad, one of the top reasons for joining Accenture was the fabulous peer group. I made some of my best friends (not to mention husband!) at Accenture." But it isn't always easy to feel part of a community. One insider reports that "as most people work at client sites, it is easy to feel disconnected. The company has tried to improve that 'lack of community' by creating mentoring groups, but they have not stayed active for long." The firm notes that these mentoring groups have been in place since the 1990s and, in the end, as one source notes, efforts such as the mentoring groups make the overall tone of the culture "supportive." But while many consultants laud their co-workers and the culture of their firm, others feel that the firm's atmosphere can be "extremely competitive [because of] forced rankings in peer groups." Another source agrees, calling the culture "very competitive."

All the live-long day

A few sources contend that work hours take away from a sense of work/life balance. Several insiders cite 100-hour weeks and weekends spent at client sites, though these lofty hours seem to be the exception. A source explains that "most projects will work you for as long as it takes to get the job done, which in most cases is at least 50 hours per week, though I tend to work more like 60 hours and I heard of a couple 100-hour weeks for some co-workers."

A balancing act

The company officially offers consultants flex time, part time, job sharing, telecommuting and other work/life balance accommodations, but insiders claim that everything depends on the assignment. Work/life balance is "determined by which project or project stage you are associated with. Currently I have no work/life balance...[I have been] working 14-hour days, seven days a week, but on previous projects it was a straight eight-hour day." This leads some sources to believe that Accenture's efforts to balance workload and personal life "is a lot of lip-service to creating an atmosphere that would allow employees a work/life balance, but there is no real effort to make that real."

Other sources see the firm's efforts to implement a work/life balance for its consultants. An insider notes, "There has been a continued focus in this area [over] the past couple of years, resulting in a continual improvement," but adds that "over the years it has become better, [though] you still have to do whatever it takes to deliver." Accenture is "just starting to integrate flexible work arrangements into line consulting positions" and "with more people becoming family-oriented, the firm does do some work but it needs to pay more attention to certain aspects of work/life balance," suggests a third Accenture employee.

Several consultants chalk this work/life imbalance up to the general nature of the consulting industry. One says that while Accenture's attention to the matter is fairly good, "the nature of consulting is skewed toward work. That's part of the job." Another sees it similarly: While Accenture tries "to promote work/life balance...realistically, you have to push back if you do not want to work a lot, which may or may not bode well with your supervisor."

Go with the flow

Travel is, of course, part of the consultant's world, though Accenture insiders do not seem overly bothered by that requirement. Sources say "travel is expected most of the time" and that "travel can be intense" in a good way: "I had the opportunity for two international projects, which was the best." Travel, predictably, depends on the project but a "typical [schedule] is Monday through Thursday away, and Friday at home," while another insider reports of being "on local engagements for the past 15 months."

Pleased with pay

Consultants generally report satisfaction with their salaries and, in a number of cases, consider pay a real plus of working at Accenture. Benefits include annual bonuses, "recruiting bonus awards" and "a very good health plan, as well as numerous other perks from travel discounts to gym membership discounts." There is also a profit sharing program and performance equity grants for executives.

Insiders also compliment Accenture's many newly-built offices, though most admit that, as line consultants, they're "usually at client sites or working from home," and rarely get to enjoy the new amenities.

Be in-the-know

Advancement at Accenture is generally up-or-out. One source says promotion "for junior positions is fairly selective, for mid-level positions, very selective," and "for senior executive positions, extremely selective." As far as timing is concerned, insiders report that "promotions can occur as frequently as every two to three years" and "it will take anywhere from 14 to 18 years with the company to achieve the partner ranking." One consultant laments this fact, however. "There is no such thing as a fast-track any more; you just need to 'do your time' at [each] level, which is terribly demotivating," he urges. Another source mentions that "consultants with only undergraduate degrees can move into leadership and strategic positions as they develop their expertise."

Some sources suggest, however, that Accenture's promotion policy is more subjective than it may appear at first. Several consultants sense that "there is some bureaucracy, as 'who you know' can be more important than what you know," as one put it. Several insiders referenced such office "politics," saying that the "overall size of the company...tends to limit personal growth. It is hard to overcome a lot of the political aspects in order to advance your career." Other consultants agree, claiming that "promotions are performance based" to a great degree, but still, "someone has to push for you to be promoted." Project placement also impacts promotion. One source explains that "if you are on a project outside of your work unit, your chances of being

Visit the Vault Consulting Career Channel at **www.vault.com/consulting** — with insider firm profiles, message boards, the Vault Consulting Job Board and more.

VAULT CAREER LIBRARY   77

promoted are slim, even if you are a top performer. The luck comes into play when you are assigned to a project. Although the company emphasizes your control over your career, your luck is a better indicator."

Beefing up your skills

Consultants gain "expertise" mainly through on-the-job experience. Consultants say the company is "a good training ground for consulting" and one explains that "in my four years here I have been a coder, business analyst and project manager all across different industries," highlighting the wide variety of exposure he's received in his short time at the firm.

Accenture also provides formal training programs for its employees. Consultants train for two weeks at a site in St. Charles, Ill., before being assigned to a project, and they return for subsequent training sessions intermittently. Generally, a source writes, "for junior resources, the training program is excellent: basic consulting skills, basic communication skills, etc. For mid-level and senior executive positions, the training is limited."

Many insiders praise the training program, but complain that work assignments can impede access to formal training opportunities. As one consultant notes after a year at the company, "I have actually never set foot inside the Accenture office after my initial two-week training program," and adds that "training has been cancelled four times due to project requirements." Accenture also offers continuous training opportunities online with the development of some "engaging interactive classes" through the company's "myLearning" program.

A "Great Place" for all

Accenture has formal programs for women to foster diversity in the work place, which one male consultant calls a "tremendous women's network and initiative—every group in line consulting has a formal women's group…These initiatives have a formal name: 'Great Place to Work for Women.'" He explains that every major engagement has a women's network which provides special meetings and mentoring opportunities for women. This doesn't always translate into great promotion opportunities for women, according to another source, who asserts that "female executives are far less common than their male counterparts."

Accenture also enjoys a reputation of being sensitive to mothers, having made *Working Mother* magazine's list of 100 Best Companies for Working Mothers for three consecutive years. However, one young woman says, "I don't feel any more secure about having children while working for Accenture. In fact, I was recently told that once it's known you are expecting a baby you should be very firm about your plans to return after the birth or you will be given tasks that mean little and don't help advance your career at all."

A source says that "ethnic minorities are well represented" at Accenture. The company arranges mentoring programs for minorities, as it does for women, and also partners with student and professional minority organizations, conducts a campaign for contributions to minority scholarships and makes recruitment efforts on local campuses. But, one insider claims these efforts aren't enough, citing "low numbers and retention of underrepresented minorities." This source continues, saying that while certain minority groups have established themselves in ample numbers at Accenture, other groups such as "African Americans, Latinos and Native Americans" remain underrepresented.

Generosity abounds

Sources say there are "many opportunities that the firm offers for community involvement and charity events," and even "too many to describe." The company sponsors a triathlon, contributes to Habitat for Humanity and Junior Achievement, "plus many local charities." Another source says "charity involvement is encouraged at the local community level" and mentions that "a global outreach program is subsidized for consulting to Third World organizations."

Visit the Vault Consulting Career Channel at **www.vault.com/consulting** — with
insider firm profiles, message boards, the Vault Consulting Job Board and more.

VAULT CAREER LIBRARY   79

6 Lockheed Martin Corporation

6801 Rockledge Drive
Bethesda, MD 20817
Phone: (301) 897-6000
Fax: (301) 897-6000
www.lockheedmartin.com

LOCATIONS

Bethesda, MD (Corporate HQ)
425 offices worldwide

PRACTICE AREAS

Aeronautics
Electronics Systems
Information & Technology Services
Integrated Systems & Solutions
Space Systems

THE STATS

Employer Type: Public Company
Ticker Symbol: LMT (NYSE)
President & CEO: Robert J. Stevens
2005 Employees: 135,000
2004 Employees: 130,000
2005 Revenues: $37.2 billion
2004 Revenues: $35.5 billion

UPPERS

• Distinct, dedicated culture
• Flexible schedules

DOWNERS

• Culture can be conservative
• Salary "on the low side"

EMPLOYMENT CONTACT

E-mail: jobs.lmc@lmco.com

THE BUZZ
WHAT CONSULTANTS AT OTHER FIRMS ARE SAYING

• "Strong competitor with broad reach"
• "First name in systems integration"
• "Too focused on DoD"
• " One hand doesn't know what the other is doing"

THE SCOOP

Uncle Sam's right hand

Formed in 1995, the Bethesda, Md.-based Lockheed Martin Corporation attributes some 80 percent of its business to the U.S. Department of Defense (DoD) and other federal agencies, making it the largest provider of IT services, systems integration and training to the American government. The remainder of the company's gargantuan sales numbers, which reached $37.2 billion in 2005, comes from international governments and commercial sales of Lockheed's products, services and technology platforms. The company, which employs 135,000 worldwide, is separated into five business areas: Aeronautics (which achieved $11.7 billion in 2005 sales); Electronic Systems ($10.6 billion); Space Systems ($6.8 billion); Integrated Systems & Solutions ($4.1 billion); and Information & Technology Services ($4 billion).

When Lockheed met Martin

Glenn Martin started Martin Marietta in 1917, and the company became the first supplier of bombers built in the United States. During the post-World War II decade, the company developed missiles, electronics and nuclear systems, and ultimately merged with American-Marietta Company, a construction materials and chemical products manufacturer, in 1961. Laden with debt after successfully repelling a hostile takeover bid by Bendix in 1982, Martin Marietta sold many of its businesses and joined Lockheed Aircraft in 1995.

Siblings Allan and Malcolm Loughead (pronounced "Lockheed" and spelled phonetically upon incorporation) teamed with Fred Keeler to form Lockheed Aircraft in 1926. The company quickly became a leading aeronautics firm, producing such classics of American aviation as the P-38 Lightning fighter, the U-2 spy plane and the SR-71 Blackbird spy plane, as well as several Cold War-era submarine-launched ballistic weapons, military transports and airliners. Felled by the cancellation of its key aircraft and a cost-overrun scandal, the government bailed out Lockheed from the edge of bankruptcy in 1971, and the company found itself at the center of a corporate bribery scandal in the late 1970s that overturned governments in Japan and Italy and prompted more stringent anti-bribery laws in the U.S. After developing the Hubble space telescope and the F-117A stealth fighter in the 1970s and 1980s, the merger with Martin Marietta came about to form Lockheed Martin.

Ask not what IT can do for you, but what IT can do for your country

Lockheed Martin's Information & Technology Services division might not be as glamorous or shiny as its Aeronautics and Space Systems units, but its services certainly play a larger role in the lives of the average civilian. With responsibilities that range from issuing Social Security benefits to monitoring the country's borders, Lockheed Martin is one of the leading IT development and integration firms in the country and is partnered with the government in numerous federal civil agencies, the Department of Homeland Security, the DoD and other intelligence services. With over 30,000 IT professionals on its roster, Lockheed Martin provides services in 25 countries and operates systems that transmit more bits of data than every U.S. cable provider combined. In May 2005, Lockheed grabbed the No. 1 spot on *Washington Technology*'s top 100 contractors in the federal IT market, for the 11th consecutive year.

Lockheed Martin's IT division specializes in six areas: Business Process Management, E-Government, Enterprise Architecture, Homeland Security, Information Security and Systems Integration. Current clients include the U.S. Air Force, Army, Marine Corps and Navy; Departments of Agriculture, Commerce, Energy, Health and Human Services, Housing & Urban Development, Justice and Transportation; the Social Security Administration and the U.S. Postal Service; and the People's Republic of China and the UK.

Naval gazing

In August 2003, Lockheed Martin acquired the government technology services unit of Affiliated Computer Services (ACS) for around $650 million and, in the same month, revealed plans to create a new segment—Maritime Systems & Sensors—that would consolidate the company's seafaring operations. In December 2004, Lockheed acquired naval electronics manufacturer Sippican, whose businesses include electronic warfare countermeasures, oceanographic and meteorological systems, navigation and communications systems, and autonomous submarine vehicles. And early 2005 saw Lockheed receive a contract from the U.S. Navy to build a new fleet of 23 Presidential Marine One helicopters.

In December 2005, Lockheed announced an agreement to buy Aspen Systems Corporation, a Rockville, Md.-based information management company that posted $165 million in revenues in 2004. Aspen's main clients are civil agencies of the U.S. government, with engagements involving business process and technology solutions, such as program management, constituent relationship management, records management and IT support. The employee-owned Aspen has more than 1,700 staffers, all of whom were offered employment at Lockheed Martin upon completion of the acquisition in January 2006.

Mass security

The New York City Metropolitan Transportation Authority announced in August 2005 that it had selected Lockheed Martin to develop a surveillance and security system to cover the metro region's major tunnels, bridges, and train and subway stations. Lockheed, amassing $200 million from the contract, intends to design an "integrated electronic security system" that includes closed-circuit television, motion detectors, and what the company describes as "intelligent video" software that immediately determines whether a parcel has been abandoned on a train or if unauthorized personnel have accessed a restricted area. Lockheed Martin's Transportation and Security Solutions, established in June 2003 and with a staff of 2,200, will take the lead on the program at its Rockville, Md., headquarters.

Winning the Web war

The U.S. Army announced in July 2005 that Lockheed would be assuming management of its Army Knowledge Online portal (AKO), an online network accessed by 1.8 million users in military service, in early October. The first phase of the $152 million contract includes responsibilities such as help desk management and hosting the Army's home page. Phase two involves the creation of new AKO architecture, managing two data centers, and executing network management and security. The eventual third phase of the contract will ultimately make AKO the single point of entry for other Army systems and programs. The AKO site is an enterprise portal to a series of features and links, including e-mail, distance learning and training exercises, a global people-locator for AKO members, and an exceedingly restricted repository for sensitive and classified documents and information. Prior to this contract, seven separate contractors previously managed various components of AKO during the program's five-year existence, and the Army expressed its satisfaction in anointing a single manager to reduce redundancies and cut costs.

The check's in the mail

Defense and security may be Lockheed's bread and butter, but the firm rakes in plenty of civil service contracts, too. The firm has lent its IT know-how to foreign countries, helping them upgrade their postal systems using advanced address recognition and mail automation technologies. In February 2006, Lockheed scored a shared contract with Bull to help upgrade the French Post Office's mail processing information system, providing automation solutions to boost efficiency and accuracy under a $175 million initiative. And in October 2005, Lockheed was tapped by Sweden's national postal service to upgrade its address recognition technology and mail automation capabilities. The firm has performed similar work for the UK's Royal Mail.

Count 'em up

Back in the U.S., in September 2005 the firm announced a six-year, $500 million contract with the U.S. Bureau of Census to develop and operate an information processing system for the 2010 census. Leading a team of IT experts, including Computer Sciences Corporation, Nortel PEC Solutions and Pearson Government Solutions, the firm will develop and deploy the Decennial Response Integration System for the Bureau, which will allow for the filing of census surveys via the Internet. Lockheed won a similar contract for the last national census in 2000, the largest, most sophisticated and accurate census undertaken thus far. For 2010, the Census Bureau has gotten even more ambitious, integrating data capture and operations capabilities for the first time using Internet technology.

Another big civil coup was also announced in September 2005, when the firm landed an engagement with the National Archives and Records Administration (NARA) to build a permanent archives system to preserve and manage the federal government's electronic records—or "acts and facts," as Lockheed puts it. The contract, worth $308 million, covers six years of work developing the Electronic Records Archives system for NARA, which will capture electronic information regardless of format, save it permanently and ensure its availability in future hardware and software applications. The full system is scheduled for completion by 2011, with a functional subset up and running within two years.

The friendly skies

In December 2005, the firm announced the national rollout of the En Route Communications Gateway (ECG), designed by Lockheed for the Federal Aviation

Administration. The communications system, in use at all Air Route Traffic Control centers in the country, provides critical radar communications data for air traffic controllers. Sue Corcoran, VP of Aviation Solutions for Lockheed, explained that the ECG "provides state-of-the-art commercial technology that supports growth and a seamless transition to future modernization of the air traffic control infrastructure."

Lockheed's contributions to the air traffic industry have certainly not gone unnoticed. In November 2004, Lockheed received the Industrial Award from the Air Traffic Control Association for outstanding achievement and contribution to advancing the safety, quality and efficiency of air traffic control. Lockheed has been honored by the association seven times in the past eight years.

Aiming for excellence

Lockheed continues to work on standardizing its processes, garnering quality certifications that help it earn future contracts. In December 2005, the firm's Information Technology Unit's Application Development and Maintenance group earned the Software Engineering Institute's (SEISM) Capability Maturity Model® Integration (CMMI) Maturity Level 5 rating (the top rating possible) for process excellence in producing and supporting software applications used at dozens of civil government and defense agencies.

Parsing pensions

Lockheed Martin announced plans in October 2005 to cut benefits plans in hopes of saving some $125 to $150 million annually. Employees hired after January 1, 2006, are ineligible for the company's customary pension plan, which assures staffers a percentage of their salaries after retirement, and retiree health care benefits. In exchange, new hires are promised eligibility for a defined contribution plan to replace the traditional benefit pension plan, as well as a 401(k) savings plan and more vacation days. CFO Christopher E. Kubasik explained that health care benefits for retirees had become increasingly unpredictable (and costly), whereas a clearly defined savings plan like a 401(k) allows the company to know with near certainty how much it will have to pay each year. The changes, which Kubasik described as "a win-win situation," give new hires three weeks of vacation upon joining the firm instead of two, and enable employees to immediately sell the Lockheed stock provided by the company as part of the 401(k) savings plan, rather than waiting until they reach 55 years of age.

Visit the Vault Consulting Career Channel at www.vault.com/consulting — with insider firm profiles, message boards, the Vault Consulting Job Board and more.

VAULT CAREER LIBRARY

85

Lending a hand

Lockheed staffers are a community-minded bunch, donating tons of time and cash each year to help out where needed. In Owego, N.Y., in 2005 alone, Lockheed staffers donated more than $750,000 to charities and nonprofits. As if that wasn't enough, employees also volunteered more than 73,000 hours to various community service projects. The firm also stepped up to the plate following Hurricane Katrina in 2005, contributing directly to the American Red Cross and establishing the Lockheed Martin Hurricane Katrina Employee Assistance Fund with an initial contribution of $1 million, followed within a month by a second contribution of $1 million. Employees contributed approximately $3 million in cash and vacation donations. To assist its staffers in the affected region, Lockheed established a hotline for employees to call for help, staffed by its own volunteers.

GETTING HIRED

Unlocking Lockheed

On the careers pages of its web site, Lockheed offers a calendar of recruiting events for college students, as well as a mechanism for submitting resumes online. The firm says it looks for students with GPAs of 2.8 or higher in majors such as engineering, finance and business. Engineering and business majors with good academic credentials can explore intern and co-op opportunities online. Experienced professionals can also look online for various meet-and-greet events, such as open houses, and search for job openings. The firm also offers information for transitioning military members interested in joining up.

Rapid-fire questions

An insider tells us that for interviews, "there is a script, with set questions to select from, where nearly every one starts with 'Tell me about a time [when].'" The source reports being "asked many rapid-fire questions about my field. Questions were designed to seek knowledge of the subject matter [and to] determine whether I would be comfortable working with an all male group (I'm a female)." The source adds that it was "one intense interview, as they really needed someone who could start immediately. I was told where I would be working that day and started the next morning."

"Typically, employees will interview with their department manager and the HR department," another source reports, and will be faced with "typical behavior questions." A colleague, interviewing for a management role, reports meeting with "all customer department heads, additional stake holders and the team that I would be leading. It was definitely the most thorough and exhausting interview I had ever undergone. I believe it lasted about six hours total. I was allowed to ask any questions I wanted and had them answered, as well."

OUR SURVEY SAYS

A distinct culture

Insiders at Lockheed tend to hold strong opinions about their corporate culture, which is seen as rather unique. "Lockheed has a distinct corporate culture and it takes a little while to learn how things work around here," says one source. Another says the firm's ethical culture stands out most: "We have a very aggressive ethics training and development program that everyone in the corporation goes through. Not only is this done when [we're] hired, but employees go through repeated and enhanced training on at least an annual basis. Additionally the company sends out scenarios electronically to employees to keep it in the forefront of our business activity and conduct.

Lest you think Lockheed sounds like a stuffy place, though, one source reports that "the company is very easygoing when it comes to diversity, hours and dress code. Work your hours, don't wear clothes with holes in them and be nice to others are normal practices." According to a colleague, "I work with great people. Everyone in my group is extremely helpful. Even people in other groups are willing to help if they can. My immediate manager and department manager both listen and try to help us do our job as much as possible." And another insider adds, "The work is demanding, sometimes frustrating, but strongly supported by senior management."

The Lockheed way

When it comes to getting ahead at Lockheed, staffers' experiences vary. While one source grumbles that it's "more about who you know and how long you have been there than what you actually do or are capable of," many colleagues disagree. "Once you learn the Lockheed way of doing things, there is definitely room for advancement from within. Also, you can always try out different areas of Lockheed

Martin by applying for job in a different business unit…through the internal web site," a source says.

As another insider puts it, "Advancement is not difficult as long as you play the corporate game (e.g., participate in the charity activities). If someone does not want to play, then it is difficult for them to get better-than-average ratings, raises, etc." And the firm isn't too "up-or-out," a source tells us: "Good people can rise quickly to middle level positions, but senior/executive positions can be hard to come by—a blessing for many of us who choose not to go there, which is a respected choice."

Flex Fridays

As for work hours, a source in human resources explains that "most employees work a 9/80 or a 4/10. A 9/80 means you work nine hours a day Monday through Thursday and get every other Friday off. The Friday that you do work, you only work until 4:15; otherwise office hours are 7:30 a.m. to 5:15 p.m., with a 45-minute lunch. A 4/10 means you work 10 hours a day Monday through Thursday and get every Friday off." Another source reports that "40 hours a week is required with the expectation of 10 percent minimum overtime." With regard to vacation time, an insider notes that "how you take your time off is up to your manager. You will be reminded that taking a vacation is not a right but a privilege, even though it is a company benefit."

Lockheed's other benefits are described by an insider as "excellent and valued at approximately 40 to 55 percent of salary, depending on a number of factors." A colleague notes that the firm "recognizes employees with various awards, most monetary, [though] some are simply certificates and recognition." According to another source, the firm "does provide tuition reimbursement of 100 percent, so I obtained my MBA from a top school at their cost."

Pride and pay

"Salary is competitive, if not on the low side," one insider tells us, with "high performers paid marginally above average and below-average performers." Still, the source adds, "Job satisfaction is high despite being able to obtain a higher salary at a different company, so many stay." A colleague agrees: "The salary package, while very important, is not the primary reason I am here. I suspect that subordinates, peers and superiors alike would say the same thing. I am in this industry because I believe that it is critical to this country. I have worked for others in the industry. I am at this company because I believe that we do it better than anyone in the industry. I make a reasonable wage and am adequately compensated."

Interns at Lockheed also get paid, with an offer package "based on the number of hours you have [completed] in school," a former intern reports. "As a graduate student I was classified as a senior and was paid $15 per hour. Interns do get paid holidays, but no other benefits."

Embracing and understanding diversity

As a high-profile corporation, Lockheed puts a lot of energy into promoting a diverse workforce, insiders suggest. According to an HR insider, the firm "is committed to enhancing its employee diversity, as well as employee understanding of diversity. Every year LMCO hosts a diversity week where employees can visit different booths to gain a better understanding of what diversity means."

VAULT
7
PRESTIGE
RANKING

Oracle Consulting

500 Oracle Parkway
Redwood Shores, CA 94065
Phone: (650) 506-7000
www.oracle.com/consulting/
index.html

LOCATIONS

Redwood Shores, CA (HQ)
More than 75 offices worldwide

PRACTICE AREAS

Applications consulting
Business solutions
Extended services
Technology consulting

THE STATS

Employer Type: Public Company
Ticker Symbol: ORCL (Nasdaq)
CEO: Lawrence J. Ellison
Executive VP, North American Sales and Consulting: Keith G. Block
2005 Employees: 49,000
2004 Employees: 41,000
2005 Revenues (consulting only): $1.8 billion
2004 Revenues (consulting only): $859 million

UPPERS

• Flexible work hours
• Ample opportunities for advancement
• Global positions and travel

DOWNERS

• Offshoring affects corporate culture in the U.S.
• High turnover in some areas
• Poor internal communication

EMPLOYMENT CONTACT

www.oracle.com/corporate/employment/index.html

THE BUZZ
WHAT CONSULTANTS AT OTHER FIRMS ARE SAYING

• "Know the market well"
• "Professional"
• "Barely know some of their own products due to turnover"
• "Expensive, narrow focus"

THE SCOOP

Database dominance

Founded in 1977 as Software Development Laboratories, Oracle is among the granddaddies of the software world, second only to Microsoft in size and scope. Company founder Larry Ellison is credited as the first techie to recognize the commercial possibilities of relational database technology—an innovation that has made him one of the world's richest people. Known for its database dominance, Oracle is organized into two areas: software and services. The services division, making up roughly 20 percent of the company's revenues, is broken down further into consulting, advanced product services and education.

A small slice of a big pie

Consulting is the largest arm of the services division, bringing in 15 percent of total company revenues in 2005, down from 16 percent and 19 percent in 2004 and 2003, respectively. Though these numbers don't make up a huge slice of the firm's pie, keep in mind that the $11.8 billion Oracle is a pretty hefty pie—consulting revenues alone in 2005 were $1.8 billion. In 2005, the firm derived 53 percent of consulting revenues from North American engagements. The rest came from Europe and the Middle East (39 percent) and Asia Pacific (8 percent).

Oracle all over

The firm's consulting customers include big names in the corporate world (7-Eleven, Sun Microsystems, Sony Corp.), as well as public sector organizations (the U.S. Army and Navy, Chicago Police Department, the city of Arvada, Colo.) and international entities (Lloyds TSB, Poste Italiane, New Zealand Exchange). Industries served by the firm include aerospace and defense; automotive; chemicals; communications; consumer products; education and research; energy; engineering and construction; financial services; health care; high technology; homeland security; industrial manufacturing; life sciences; professional services; public sector; retail; travel and transportation; and utilities.

Consulting customers usually turn to Oracle for an all-encompassing solution, spanning services from software to implementation. Unlike tech services rivals such as IBM and HP, which have at least nominally tried to separate their services from the products the companies themselves produce, Oracle isn't shy about promoting and installing its own solutions as part of the consulting package.

Slow growth

Since Oracle often sells its services alongside its software and applications packages, implementing these services after software licenses are purchased, the firm's consulting revenues tend to trail software revenues by several quarters, Oracle explains in its annual report. And with a shift of resources to lower-cost countries, consulting revenues have slowed down in recent quarters, the firm admits. The firm also says consulting revenues have declined because of attrition rates in the U.S. due to increased demand for tech talent, and "as a result of our decision to work more closely with partners who are performing an increasing number of the implementations of our software." In fact, Oracle's combination of software dominance and its services business means it often works with firms with which it also vies for contracts. For instance, the firm enjoys strong collaborative relationships with companies like Accenture, EDS, IBM and Unisys, firms that Oracle readily admits to being both partners and competitors.

Selling services

Oracle focuses on a global solutions delivery approach in which it assembles global teams dedicated to each customer, blending resources from both onsite and remote delivery channels to match client needs. In 1992, Oracle split the its 10,000 salespeople into two teams, one focusing on selling database software and the other on applications. Cutting out two layers of management, then president Ray Lane took the helm of sales operations at the firm, with Ellison manning the applications side of the business. By the late 1990s, when Oracle revenues were ebbing, revenues from services maintained a positive flow. From 1996 to 2000, with Lane serving as president and chief operating officer of the firm, revenues tripled. In 2000, Lane resigned and in 2002, Oracle named Keith Block its executive VP of sales and consulting in North America. Block served as a senior consultant at Booz Allen Hamilton before joining the firm to climb the consulting ladder back in 1986.

Strategic acquisitions

In recent years, Oracle has made a number of strategic moves aimed at dispelling any doubts about the firm's future profitability. In fact, CEO Ellison has declared a goal of 20 percent year-over-year revenue growth in the next few years. After winning an antitrust lawsuit against the Department of Justice, in December 2004 Oracle finally announced its long-anticipated acquisition of rival PeopleSoft for approximately $10.3 billion. PeopleSoft brought more than 11,000 employees to the Oracle family, but the firm cut around 5,000 positions in the following months, including staffers from both the parent company and its new acquisition. In its 2005 annual report, the firm predicts that the PeopleSoft purchase will boost consulting revenues over time.

Another big buy came in September 2005, when the firm announced plans to purchase Siebel Systems for around $5.85 billion. The deal, which closed in early 2006, makes Oracle the biggest customer relationship management (CRM) applications company in the world. Other 2005 acquisitions include retail applications firm Retek, data management software firm Times Ten, and identity management solutions provider Oblix, to name just a few.

Sharing the wealth

Oracle's ambitious community efforts include both corporate giving initiatives and plenty of hands-on volunteer time by employees. In 2004, the firm made $8.5 million in cash donations, as well as $151 million in in-kind software donations, to organizations worldwide. Oracle's pet causes include education, the environment and medical research, and more than 28 percent of the 8,000 employees at Oracle headquarters participate in volunteer efforts.

GETTING HIRED

Onboard with Oracle

On the company web site, Oracle hopefuls can search for job postings through the firm's "iRecruitment" search engine. The firm also provides information on its internship opportunities, for which it typically selects 35 to 40 outstanding candidates each year. Currently, Oracle says, the firm only reviews internship applications from candidates with computer science or equivalent majors attending college in North America. Interns receive compensation, along with fully funded housing and transportation, plus fun extras like helicopter rides around the Golden Gate Bridge and other San Francisco area sightseeing trips.

Visit the Vault Consulting Career Channel at **www.vault.com/consulting** — with insider firm profiles, message boards, the Vault Consulting Job Board and more.

VAULT CAREER LIBRARY　　93

Patience, please

Over and over again, Oracle insiders warn that the firm's "unstructured" hiring process requires some patience. "You need to find an internal white knight to continually kick the process to move your application for employment forward," says a source, who adds, "I personally recruited and hired four people, but it took a lot of work by me to push the applications through the process to get them hired." "It was a 'hurry up and wait' approach," agrees a colleague. "After they told me they would hire me it took three months before I got an offer letter." "Never give notice until you get the offer letter from Oracle," advises another source, adding, "This process can take weeks or months. It is supposed to be getting better for new candidates."

As for the interview process itself, you can expect to meet with a number of staffers, with a mix of behavioral and technical questions. One source reports, "Each interviewer conducted a 30-minute interview that consisted of situational questions. The key to successfully passing the final interview questions/scenarios is to be able to think outside the box." Another insider notes, "It is good to have an understanding of industry best practices in addition to Oracle technology."

OUR SURVEY SAYS

India encroaches

Oracle Consulting, insiders report, offers the "ability to travel," a "flexible work schedule" and "great opportunities for advancement." But the firm's global expansion has rubbed some staffers the wrong way. "Our internal processes are very broken and cumbersome. The addition of directing menial steps through India has caused delays, rework and irritation. It has become a common joke in Oracle," one source says. A co-worker agrees: "The dream scenario for senior management would be a handful of managers in the U.S. and everything except sales done in India. Sadly, successful offshoring requires good management and communication, neither of which exists in Oracle."

One staffer notes that "at a high level, the direction of the company is strong and I support the mergers/acquisition plans." But another consultant suggests the picture is difficult on the ground. "Due to the established large management structures," he says, "there is micro-management and strong rivalry amongst departments at the cost of the individual contributors. Unless you are in a management position with the option to delegate down, you are a resource with often contradicting orders...Employee turnover is high and morale extremely low. The results are frequent internal re-orgs. Working in the same position, I have [a] third manager in three years." As another insider puts it, "There is too much ego running the company and not enough heart or sense."

Earning it

Salaries for Oracle consultants are described as "lower than BearingPoint and similar firms." As one source explains, "This is a product company and consulting salaries for lower level employees [are] sometimes very low. Bonuses vary widely from one manager to another. At the very high levels it can be six figures. Salaries within the same job role can vary very widely. Make sure you negotiate the salary; you may have the same base salary for a decade." Another insider says that while salaries are "not as competitive as key companies like SAP," they're "generally good." The firm reportedly offers "great stock options." But a consultant advises, "Get as many certifications as possible. There may not be time or funding for this after you join the company."

Capgemini

750 Seventh Avenue
Suite 1800
New York, NY 10019
Phone: (212) 314-8000
Fax: (212) 314-8001
www.us.capgemini.com

LOCATIONS

New York, NY (U.S. HQ)
Paris (HQ)
Offices in 30 countries

PRACTICE AREAS

Consulting Services
Outsourcing Services
Technology Services
 Agent Technology • Application
 Development & Integration •
 Business Intelligence (BI) •
 Infrastructure & Security • IT
 Transformation-Strategy &
 Architecture • Mobility • Open
 Source • Oracle • Portals • Radio
 Frequency Identification (RFID) •
 SAP • Siebel

THE STATS

Employer Type: Public Company
Ticker Symbol: CAP.PA (Paris Bourse)
CEO: Paul Hermelin
Chairman: Serge Kampf
2005 Employees: 61,000
2004 Employees: 60,000
2005 Revenues: €6,954 billion
2004 Revenues: €6,235 billion

UPPERS

• "Very friendly"
• "Excellent environment to develop
  professional and personal
  relationships"
• Travel is "manageable"

DOWNERS

• Still experiencing transitional
  effects of the 2004 rebranding
• "Mostly a sink or swim mentality"
• Limited training opportunities

EMPLOYMENT CONTACT

www.us.capgemini.com/career

THE BUZZ
WHAT CONSULTANTS AT OTHER FIRMS ARE SAYING

• "Cream of the crop in commercial
  consulting"
• "Brainy"
• "Still trying to get it together"
• "Strong in Europe, but not in the
  U.S."

THE SCOOP

C'est Capgemini

Based in Paris, Capgemini is a truly international company, with more than 61,000 employees around the globe. The firm is organized around three disciplines, namely consulting, technology and outsourcing. Capgemini consultants cover 11 industry sectors: Automotive; Consumer Products; Distribution; Energy, Utilities and Chemicals; Financial Services; Health; Life Sciences; Manufacturing; Public Sector; Retail; and Telecom, Media & Entertainment. The firm's consulting arm offers transformation consulting, customer relationship management, supply chain, and finance and employee transformation services.

The firm hasn't been Capgemini for long—just since April 2004, in fact, when it changed its name from Cap Gemini Ernst & Young in a $72 million rebranding campaign. CGE&Y was born from a 2000 merger between France's Cap Gemini and the consulting arm of Ernst & Young, and the challenges of culture clash and a struggling economy combined to create a rocky start for the firm. Plenty of red ink and layoffs marked the firm's first couple of years in business, as the Paris-based management team learned to run a new U.S. division from overseas while the North American wing struggled to meet the expectations of its new corporate parent.

Belt-tightening

By fiscal year 2004, the outlook still wasn't totally rosy for the firm. Revenues for 2004 were €6,235 billion, up from €5,75 billion in 2003. But in September of that year, the firm lowered its expectations for the year and launched a plan to cut costs by approximately €120 million by the end of the year. The belt-tightening included the planned slashing of 1,000 jobs, on top of the 400 already cut in the first half of the year. London's *Financial Times* reported in September 2004 that Paul Hermelin, CEO of the firm globally, was resisting pressure to step down following an unexpected operating loss in the first half of the year and the exit of its CFO, William Bitan (he was replaced by Nicolas Dufourcq, a managing director). Analysts began buzzing about a lack of confidence in management at the firm.

North American buzz

Back in North America, rumors began to swirl about a possible sale of the division. HP and France's Atos Origin were both seen as likely bidders. But as one analyst asked *BusinessWeek* Online in October 2004, "Who would want to take over Capgemini? When you acquire something, you acquire the problems, not just the benefits." In any case, the firm denied these reports in November 2004, claiming that its focus was on improving turnover and margins in North America. And by the end of the month, the firm had positive news to report, with stronger-than-expected third-quarter sales, up more than 20 percent.

The company unveiled an ambitious plan to right its North American operations in early 2005. In an interview with AFX International Focus in March 2005, Capgemini CEO Paul Hermelin said "restructuring was not enough" for the firm's U.S. consulting operations. "This division is suffering because its pricing policy is significantly higher than those of the market, and the objective we have given ourselves is to cut our production costs by close to 20 percent," he added.

Refocus, resize, resell

In May 2005, the firm announced that its Project & Consulting, or P&C, line of business in the region was being "refocused and resized," following the sale of its health care consulting practice in April 2005 to Accenture for $175 million. Capgemini execs predicted an annual savings of more than $100 million through the reduction of support function costs, including a 30 percent reduction in IT spending and greater use of offshore resources for back-office functions. The firm announced a plan to "change the management culture" in the region, insisting on affordability (with no more than 3 percent of revenues allowed to go toward overhead), accountability, and efficiency.

Meanwhile, management both in France and the U.S. has changed hands. In April 2004, Chell Smith, a 14-year consulting and tech services vet, was appointed chief executive officer of Capgemini's North American division, taking over for John McCain (no relation to the politician), who has presided over CGE&Y's early, rocky era of downsizing. Smith, one of the few female execs in the tech services world, is known for supporting the progress of women at the firm, promoting work/life balance and taking advantage of telecommuting herself, when possible.

Adieu, Danon

In October 2005, the company made headlines when its Paris-based chief operating officer, Pierre Danon, was sacked after his name turned up on a short list to be the new chief executive at French hotel group Accor. Danon, who had been with the firm since March 2005, was credited with helping to turn around Capgemini's U.S. IT operations. A source told the *Financial Times* that the company had no choice but to let Danon go, noting that, "In the U.S. our biggest problem is staff attrition. It is very difficult to convince people to stay when you personally want to leave."

Dividing territories

In June 2005, the firm began a transition to a geographically-oriented profit and loss model in North America, naming four consultants to be area directors of its regions in the U.S. Tim Crichfield, formerly CFO of Capgemini's North American strategic business unit, was tapped to head consulting and technology services in the Midwest area; Lanny Cohen, formerly market segment and sales leader for Telecom Media & Entertainment, was named head of the Eastern region; Bill Campbell, formerly North American geographic sales leader, was appointed director of the Southern region; and Kevin Poole, formerly supply chain leader for North American consulting services, was named head of Western operations.

Capgemini began trumpeting its North American turnaround in September 2005, noting that its outsourcing business was on track to make a profit during the second half of the year. The firm noted several North American engagements in recent quarters. In September 2005, Capgemini was engaged by Bombardier, the world's third-largest civil aircraft manufacturer, for a seven-year business process outsourcing contract. Capgemini also cited an outsourcing partnership in collaboration with HP; a contract with Limited Brands to overhaul the company's IT systems at stores such as Victoria's Secret and Express; and an $8.9 million contract to design, implement and maintain a new Oracle-based financial management system at Washington's National Gallery of Art. In the Telecom Media & Entertainment practice, the firm noted, contracts were signed to design and develop a film distribution system for Sony Pictures, and to create customer service representative tools for Time Warner Cable.

Outsourcing, the right way

Outsourcing has proved to be a strength of Capgemini's, making up 33 percent of the group's overall revenues in 2005. Capgemini calls its approach to global delivery "Rightshoring," a term intended to convey the blend of onshore, near-shore and far-shore locations into a single integrated, seamless service. In 2005, the firm was given the National Outsourcing Association's Outsourcing Service Provider of the Year award, in recognition of its investment—and big wins—in outsourcing.

High-energy deals

One such win came in October 2005, when Capgemini beat out EDS for a seven-year outsourcing deal with London's Metropolitan Police Service (MPS) worth around $612 million. The firm was part of a consortium selected to take over the IT operations for the police service, along with BT and Unisys. In March 2005, the firm was awarded a five-year, $35 million contract with British Energy, the largest producer of energy in the UK. Another high-energy deal was inked in May 2004, when Capgemini contracted with TXU Corp., a Dallas-based energy company, to form Capgemini Energy Limited Partnership, a new company initially devoted to providing business process and IT services to TXU (which owns a less than 3 percent stake in the venture). The 10-year agreement was valued at more than $3.5 billion, and involved the transfer of 2,700 employees from TXU to Capgemini. One analyst, quoted in *BusinessWeek* Online, said the agreement was the first "megadeal" of its kind for a North American branch of a foreign company in many years, calling it "one of the sexiest deals in IT services." Yet another energy industry deal came in November 2004, when Capgemini announced a 10-year, $1.9 billion outsourcing contract with Schneider Electric, transferring about 800 of the industry giant's employees to Capgemini sites globally.

One of Capgemini's most buzzed-about outsourcing contracts was signed in June 2004, as Capgemini took over responsibility for the IT systems of UK's Inland Revenue agency. The engagement, known as "Aspire", is worth more than $3 billion, and is said to be one of the largest outsourcing contracts in history. The project began with a six-month transition process as former employees of EDS—which lost the contract to its rival—joined the Capgemini ranks. Capgemini is partnering with Fujitsu Services to deliver the contract.

Boosting the ranks in India

In September 2005, the firm announced plans to set up an additional tech services facility in India to meet growing demand for outsourcing from the U.S. and Europe. The company's Indian subsidiary employs around 2,200 people (up from 400 in early 2003), with offices in Mumbai and Bangalore, and another planned in an additional Indian location. Reports indicated that Capgemini planned to increase its Indian headcount to 4,000 by the end of 2005.

Partnering pays off

In April 2005, the firm announced a partnership with HP and Intel—CP-Connect—designed to apply technologies to help consumer products companies boost their business performance and revenues. Together, the companies offer a range of new (and newly-packaged) services such as product lifecycle management, radio frequency identification and enterprise resource planning. The firm also enjoys friendly relations with industry heavies like Microsoft. In 2003, the firm was named co-winner, along with HP, of Microsoft's Global Services Partner of the Year, in recognition of the partner "that has demonstrated leadership and has been the most valuable global services partner in delivering Microsoft solutions to mutual customers in the past year." The firm expanded its global alliance with Microsoft in July 2004, as the companies agreed to invest more than $50 million in accelerating the development of joint solutions for the health care, energy, automotive and other markets.

Helping out down South

Capgemini isn't a firm that toots its own horn when it comes to community service, but the company did report on its efforts following Hurricane Katrina. The firm said that it had made "substantial contributions" to both the Red Cross and the Salvation Army, and was working with governments and businesses in the South to help repair IT systems. Additionally, Capgemini employees in the U.S. donated time to recovery efforts.

GETTING HIRED

Natural selection

Selectivity seems to be the name of the game at Capgemini. Inside sources note the company's rigorous hiring process for students coming out of graduate and undergraduate programs. "The hiring process is pretty straightforward," one consultant reports, but students must pass through several screening layers before the firm will offer them a job. Candidates begin with "career fair presentations, then comes pre-selection, a first round of interviews on campus, followed by a second round of office interviews for selected students with office tours, and then the final decision." The result is a "very selective" process where Capgemini extends offers to select candidates within "a week from the day of the office visit," though insiders warn about some lag time. The firm also hires experienced candidates through referral or through hiring firms.

Capgemini has had a reputation for gleaning competitive graduates from large and prestigious universities—including Louisiana State University, Texas A&M, the University of Texas at Austin and Rice University—though one insider reports that specific technical skills on a resume also may get your foot in the door, independent of academic degree or school pedigree. "SAP is hot," the insider reports. "People who have put this on their resume are being hired with little proven ability." Insiders report that case questions are typically not asked, but that the interviews generally rely more on behavioral-type questions. A typical question may include, "Describe a situation where you had to resolve a conflict," and the candidate will then be expected to "explain, defend and review" his/her answer.

OUR SURVEY SAYS

U-N-I-T-Y

Survey respondents seem impressed by the atmosphere of camaraderie in Capgemini's North American offices where they see "diversity with unity," as one source puts it, admiring the "great work environment [and] wonderful colleagues." A number of consultants consider working with their colleagues to be a major plus. "The opportunity to solve real hard problems and help our clients achieve results," one consultant states, "is only possible when you have a great team of people working with you. I have experienced the tremendous drive, intelligence and persistence in doing what is right for our clients from all the team members that I have worked with. That is what makes me still work for Capgemini." One source, however, misses the days when Capgemini was still married to Ernst & Young, and wishes the rebranded company would do something to "encourage the sense of community we once had."

Trickle down theory

Corporate reorganization following Capgemini's 2004, $72 million rebranding may have impacted how consultants feel about the company and how it affects their work locally. Many respondents cited attrition and changes at the management level as both a blessing and a curse. "Due to the recent rounds of cuts…there is a lot of room for rapid advancement and responsibility," one consultant notes. On the other hand, another insider reports, "There have been a lot of changes in leadership and that affects the overall perception of the great work we do. That has been the worst thing so far," he says. Another source avers that "if we can just stop changing the leadership every six months, we can do better than most of the other companies out there."

Self-improvement

Some Capgemini consultants would like to see the company work on retention and cultivation of its employees. Sources say that Capgemini offers 401(k), profit sharing, continued education and certification, and sometimes discounts with company clients. But some insiders note that compensation is less than satisfactory, and others have problems with how the company promotes and helps its employees develop their careers. One consultant feels that Capgemini could make more of an "investment" in employees through "proper training courses" and "appropriate compensation." While one consultant says that from his experience "one can advance as fast as one wants to advance," another thinks that Capgemini "could do better" to make it clear to employees which career paths are available to them. Echoing this sentiment, another suggests that Capgemini shepherd its first-year employees so that "newcomers don't have to struggle to find projects."

Gender gap

Capgemini insiders commend the diversity of their workplace. One source, though, notes that the industry in general should improve on how companies assess performance for women when they leave work to have a child, while another suggests that Capgemini give its female employees more flexibility to balance work and family, specifically by providing them with "traveling requirement relaxations so they can spend more time with their families."

Community action

Capgemini employees are actively involved in community service, participating in various charitable walks, blood and food drives, and Habitat for Humanity. These activities, though, seem to be done of consultants' own accord, since the firm doesn't offer many formal firmwide community service opportunities. One consultant says that the firm sponsors community efforts only "a little bit, but this is based on the old E&Y vice president's connections to previous charities." Another insider adds, however, that even though there are few formal efforts, the firm "strongly encourages individual employee participation in community events."

HP Services

VAULT PRESTIGE RANKING: 9

3000 Hanover Street
Palo Alto, CA 94304-1185
Phone: (650) 857-1501
Fax: (650) 857-5518
www.hp.com/hps

LOCATIONS

Palo Alto, CA (HQ)
Offices in 160 countries worldwide

PRACTICE AREAS

Business Applications
Business Continuity & Availability
Consulting & Integration Sevices
Education & Training
Industry Services
Infrastructure Services
Leasing & Financing
Managed Services
Outsourcing Services
Packaged Services
Support Services
Technology Services

THE STATS

Employer Type: Public Company
Ticker Symbol: HPQ (NYSE)
CEO: Mark Hurd
Executive Vice President, HP Technology Solutions Group (includes Services): Ann Livermore
2005 Employees: 69,000
2004 Employees: 65,000
2005 Revenues: $15.5 billion
2004 Revenues: $3.7 billion

UPPERS

• Has a strong reputation in the consulting industry
• Flexible approach to work hours

DOWNERS

• Still rebuilding from restructuring initiatives
• Size can be overwhelming

EMPLOYMENT CONTACT

www.jobs.hp.com

THE BUZZ
WHAT CONSULTANTS AT OTHER FIRMS ARE SAYING

• "Hi-tech gurus"
• "Employees have a good reputation"
• "Layoff city"
• "Hardware vendors shouldn't necessarily consider themselves solution developers"

THE SCOOP

From the garage to consulting

Hewlett-Packard entered the tech consulting world in stages, as it took steps to help its clients integrate and implement the firm's broad range of IT products. Though HP's first PC was introduced to consumers in 1980, the firm can trace its roots back to 1938, when founders Bill Hewlett and Dave Packard started the company in a now historically landmarked garage in Palo Alto, California.

Like many of its peers with roots in the tech hardware world, HP has devoted a separate division—HP Services—to solutions including Business Applications; Business Continuity & Availability Services; Industry Services; Infrastructure Services; Managed Services; Packaged Services; Support Services; Consulting & Integration Services; Technology Services; Leasing & Financing; and Education & Training. The division has been known as HP Services since 2001—before that, it operated as the Professional Services Organization, and later, as HP Consulting. More than 69,000 of HP's approximately 151,000 employees worldwide work under the Services umbrella.

A major deal

As HP Services worked to establish an identity in the burgeoning tech consulting realm, facing powerful players like IBM, the parent company was undertaking the largest deal in the history of IT. In 2001, HP announced that it would join forces with Compaq to form an $87 billion company. The merger, which became official in May 2002, created a mega-corporation serving more than 1 billion customers in 162 countries with products, technologies and services.

The merger also left then-CEO Carly Fiorina with the formidable challenge of redefining HP in a competitive marketplace. Upon taking over the top position in 1999, Fiorina had dubbed the firm "the new HP." Following the Compaq deal, she was faced with the challenge of defining the "new new HP."

Adapting to a new era

HP's new era was a boon to the Services division, which was called the "favorite son" of Fiorina, despite its relatively smaller contribution to the corporation as a whole. The parent company continued to invest in the group, touting a new "Adaptive Enterprise" strategy in May 2003. The strategy, as the company defined it, was aimed

Visit the Vault Consulting Career Channel at **www.vault.com/consulting** — with insider firm profiles, message boards, the Vault Consulting Job Board and more.

V/\ULT CAREER LIBRARY   **105**

at helping businesses "manage change and get more from their IT investments." Of course, this was essentially what the consulting group had been doing all along, but the "Adaptive Enterprise" concept proved to be a savvy branding device for the firm.

In 2004, the division had to do some adapting of its own, when HP's services, servers, software and storage units were combined under the Technology Solutions Group umbrella, headed by executive VP Ann Livermore. The new VP told the publication *eWeek* in August 2004 that the group would draw on a "synergy between the software and consulting business." The firm's approach to championing and installing its own software and solutions separates it from other tech services competitors, who have taken pains to prove themselves "agnostic," ferreting out solutions from across the tech marketplace. Asked whether or not the HP Services group could remain "technology-agnostic," Livermore said, "Every customer would know we have a bias toward HP technology because we're most familiar with it. Every systems integrator is biased toward the technology they're most used to based on their expertise. And customers want that. The discussion about bias is a red herring in the services industry."

Slow and steady...

HP's results for fiscal year 2004 showed some solid gains, though perhaps not enough to wow Wall Street. For the year, HP reported revenues of $79.9 billion, up 9 percent from the previous year. Of that amount, $3.7 billion came from HP Services, a 13 percent increase over 2003. By the close of 2005, total company revenue was up 8 percent compared to 2004, at $86.7 billion for the year. HP Services continued to grow at a 12 percent rate, bringing in $15.5 billion of the company's revenues.

Farewell, Fiorina

Fiorina, one of the most prominent female CEOs in the U.S., saw her tenure cut short in February 2005, when she was forced out by the board of directors. Fiorina's bold approach to the Compaq merger had put her leadership in the spotlight, and when the firm failed to make impressive financial gains, investors grew restless. But Fiorina walked with a severance package estimated at $21 million. Robert Wayman was named acting CEO as the firm commenced its search for a new leader.

Hurd in the news

The speculation ended abruptly in April 2005 when HP announced the appointment of former NCR CEO Mark Hurd to the top slot, sending share prices skyrocketing. A 25-year veteran of automated teller machine giant NCR, Hurd was hailed as a strong choice for the position. "Mark Hurd has the potential to fix HP's problems. It will be a tough job but he could be the person that could do it. He digs into details and is a hands-on manager that examines every alternative," an observer told CNN at the time.

A leaner HP

In July 2005, Hurd demonstrated this hands-on approach by introducing a tough, ambitious restructuring plan, including the axing of 14,500 jobs worldwide—or 10 percent of its workforce—scheduled for the next year. Though HP execs weren't specific about which positions would be slashed, Hurd characterized them as "redundant positions," such as support and HR jobs. The firm hoped for $1.9 billion in savings from the plan, though its initial layout in restructuring costs was expected to top $1 billion. Other strategic changes included the folding of the firm's Customer Solutions group into the Technology Solutions Group, and cuts to the firm's retirement benefits plan (including no more pension for new U.S. employees). In a message broadcast to employees, Hurd noted, "When a company is structurally inefficient like we are, short-term fixes don't work," adding, "I know this is not the best news you can get, but it's what's required for HP to become the great company it can be, once again."

Defining the division

HP Services finds itself in an awkward position with respect to competitors like IBM. Despite early speculation that the company would make a mega-purchase to firm up its consulting presence, HP lost out on opportunities to do so, such as the sale of PricewaterhouseCoopers' consulting division, which went to Big Blue. And analyst speculation that HP might look to break itself up into smaller chunks for sale on the market hasn't materialized, either; observers note that Hurd is more likely to forge ahead with his new, leaner version of the firm intact.

But the company hasn't shied away from smaller acquisitions through the years. HP expanded its strategic services presence south of the equator in September 2005, when it signed an agreement to acquire substantially all of the assets of New Zealand consulting firm CGNZ Ltd and two related entities. The acquisition was expected to add a strong enterprise resource planning practice to the company, as well as a presence in a number of New Zealand industry sectors. In May 2004, HP Services added Dallas-based ManageOne and the U.K.'s CEC Europe Service Management consulting companies to its customer support unit. In February 2004, the firm agreed to acquire Triaton GmbH (with subsidiaries in Singapore, China and Brazil), Triaton France SAS and U.S.-based Triaton N.A, Inc. (USA), wholly owned subsidiaries of the ThyssenKrupp Group. The acquisition of the Triaton subsidiaries gave HP a stronger foothold in Europe, particularly in Germany.

Continuity clients

Business continuity and avalability and recovery were hot HP topics in 2005. The firm invested $100 million in these services, designed to help companies proactively maintain, recover or resume their critical business processes following virus attacks, natural disasters or other unforeseen events. The firm's recent business continuity and availability clients include business communications company Avaya, financial services software developer Summit Information Systems, nutritional supplement provider Herbalife, and dairy giant Land O'Lakes. Domestically, HP provides business recovery services at centers in Georgia and California; the firm also has set up a number of these centers overseas, from Madrid to Singapore. In March 2005, HP Ireland acquired Schlumberger Business Continuity Services (Ireland), the country's leading provider of business recovery and "hot seat" services, in a multi-million Euro deal. And in April 2004, HP announced plans for a new survey to give execs insight into their peers' best practices and current challenges.

A rosy outlook for outsourcing

Any tech services company these days has to have a competitive presence in outsourcing, and HP is working to carve out a name for itself in this area alongside bigger rivals. The Outsourcing Center honored HP and its outsourcing client, Bank of India, with its 2005 Outsourcing Excellence Award in the Best First Steps category, recognizing the firms' initial steps toward achieving business goals—in this case, the implementation of a standardized banking system, one of the largest such engagements in India.

Early outsourcing wins included a 10-year, $3 billion managed services deal with Procter & Gamble, signed in 2003; a $50 million outsourcing contract with the U.S. Postal Service; and a five-year IT outsourcing agreement with Nokia, valued at around $100 million. HP's outsourcing ambitions were given another boost in March

2005 when the car manufacturer Renault signed a $150 million deal with the firm to manage and update its global desktop computing environment over the next five years—a project covering 87,000 Renault staffers worldwide. Operating from a base in France, HP also planned to develop an "Expertise Center" for Renault to advise and support the company on IT matters. Other big outsourcing deals for the Services group have included a five-year, $112 million agreement with MCI; a five-year, $53 million contract with Standard Register Corp.; and an automated banking upgrade arrangement with TD Bank Financial Group valued at $320 million over seven years. In 2004, HP signed a $1 billion deal with Ericsson (a contract effectively split with IBM in which HP manages infrastructure and IBM takes on applications) and a $500 million infrastructure management deal with Nokia.

The firm grew its business process outsourcing capabilities in April 2005, when it announced a plan to invest $50 million over the next five years to build a new BPO center in Wroclaw, Poland. The center was expected to employ around 1,000 staffers, providing outsourced financial and accounting services.

Deals the world over

All the world's a stage for HP, which landed a number of international contracts in 2005. HP landed a powerful engagement in April when it signed a $48.5 million contract with the European Commission to develop two significant central information systems covering border control, police and visa information. One of India's largest banks, Bank of Baroda, engaged HP that same month as its strategic IT partner to create a uniform, portal-based IT infrastructure covering the bank's domestic and international operations. In March, Canada's Carleton University selected HP to design, implement and manage a $10 million campus-wide upgrade of its network infrastructure. Other international gigs include a contract to help DHL develop a new data center in Prague; an IT support contract with German company Carl Zeiss, AG; and an engagement to help the Central Bank of Montenegro develop a new, automated inter-banking payment system.

In October 2004, the firm announced a seven-year, $100 million contract with Starwood Hotels & Resorts Worldwide to build a new global reservations system to be managed by HP. The firm predicted that the new system would save Starwood $15 to $20 million annually in operating costs. HP also signed on to provide other services to the hotel giant, such as building the infrastructure for and hosting Starwood's branded web sites.

Engagements roll in

In August 2005, HP announced a three-year, multi-million dollar contract with Lucasfilm Ltd., to help the visual effects and sound engineering company with technology and services. HP Services was contracted to deploy a storage environment to securely store and archive critical business information for the company. In June 2005, Toronto's Mount Sinai Hospital selected HP Canada as its partner in a six-year initiative to enhance its IT infrastructure for better patient service, care and safety. Another health care heavy, California's Scripps Health, inked an agreement with the firm to jointly develop a new clinical intelligence system, designed to help Scripps improve patient care and safety. And in December 2004, HP announced a slew of new engagements. For Jim Beam Brands Co., the firm helped upgrade its information-sharing abilities by establishing an improved e-business infrastructure. The firm also worked with Sanyo Electric Company to consolidate and reform its entire IT infrastructure. Meanwhile, the Oklahoma Department of Human Services tapped HP to help upgrade its systems, while the city of St. Cloud, in Florida, signed on with HP to set up a wireless network for use in a new mixed use business and residential district.

HP often combines its hardware and services strengths into a single engagement. A good example of this one-two punch can be found in the firm's print management services deals, where HP contracts with clients to provide both consulting services to streamline the print workflow, and technology and device applications to put its plans into effect. In September 2004, the firm inked the largest U.S. health care print management services contract in its history with Ohio's University Hospitals Health Systems. The firm was tapped to streamline the hospital system's existing print infrastructure across more than 150 facilities.

The source for SOA

In 2005, the tech services industry was buzzing about service-oriented architecture (SOA), which describes an approach to integrating heterogeneous IT systems. In June, HP revved up its SOA presence, announcing a new suite of consulting services and the opening of four competency centers worldwide. By offering both management software and consulting services, HP argued, the firm was in the ideal position to present clients with an effective SOA solution. The firm has worked with tech partners like Microsoft, BEA, Oracle and SAP to push the adoption of SOAs worldwide.

The Microsoft nod

HP got a confidence boost from Microsoft in 2005, when it beat out rivals, including Dell and Accenture, for the annual Microsoft Global Enterprise Services and Technology Partner of the Year award. The win was the third for HP, which has worked closely with Microsoft for 20 years, a veritable lifetime in the tech world. HP also enjoys a close business relationship with America Online, going back more than 10 years. In March 2005, the Internet giant tapped the company to be its provider of integrated support services for its server and storage technology.

A progressive pioneer

HP is seen as a pioneer when it comes to progressive workplace practices. In 1973, the firm became the first in the U.S. to institute the concept of flex-time, or flexible work hours, among its staffers. HP was also one of the first employers to encourage its employees to take advantage of telecommuting capabilities to work from home or from remote offices, resulting in reduced office space needs for the company and improved employee retention, according to the firm.

(Good) citizen of the world

The firm also strives to be a good corporate citizen, publishing an annual Global Citizenship Report detailing its activities ranging from social investment to the environmental impact of its products. The firm touts "e-inclusion," or making sure as many people as possible have access to technology, as a major corporate initiative, donating time and equipment to classrooms and other institutions worldwide. As a whole, the firm gave about $62 million in cash and equipment in 2004. Following the devastating effects of Hurricane Katrina in the Gulf region, HP employees, along with the HP Company Foundation, committed more than $3.5 million to help out with recovery efforts, on top of other contributions such as technology services and PC access for evacuees. HP staff in Houston pitched in with volunteer efforts and collection drives.

GETTING HIRED

Hop online

On HP's web site, HP hopefuls can search for jobs company-wide and create a candidate profile to be stored in the firm's database (the Technology Solutions group doesn't maintain a separate careers site). Job seekers may also opt to have openings that match their profile e-mailed to them.

On its Career pages, the firm provides a list of "tips and hints" for applying successfully—these range from knowing as much as you can about the company to differentiating yourself from other candidates. Successful candidates, HP advises, come equipped with a "dynamic attitude," flexibility, teamwork abilities, analytical, communication and interpersonal skills, and commitment. "Most of all, be natural, be honest and be yourself!" the firm adds.

Hands-on HP

HP offers hands-on internships and co-op assignments for college students. Students must have completed at least their freshman year, and have declared or earned majors in electrical engineering, computer science, computer engineering, mechanical engineering, industrial engineering, information technology, finance or business administration. Interns receive some benefits, including health coverage. To locate internships, use the main job search function on HP's web page. Students also can look up campus recruiting events online; these take place at a host of universities nationwide.

More than 69,000 of HP's approximately 151,000 employees worldwide work under the Services umbrella.

Visit the Vault Consulting Career Channel at **www.vault.com/consulting** —with
insider firm profiles, message boards, the Vault Consulting Job Board and more.

VAULT CAREER LIBRARY   113

BearingPoint

1676 International Drive
McLean, VA 22102
Phone: (703) 747-3000
Fax: (703) 747-8500
www.bearingpoint.com

LOCATIONS

McLean, VA (HQ)
130 offices worldwide

PRACTICE AREAS

Customer Relationship Management
Enterprise Solutions
Managed Services
Strategy, Process & Transformation
Supply Chain Management
Technology Infrastructure &
  Integration

THE STATS

Employer Type: Public Company
Ticker Symbol: BE (NYSE)
CEO: Harry You
2005 Employees: 17,000
2004 Employees: 16,000
2004 Revenues: $3.4 billion (est.)

UPPERS

• "Freedom to specialize in areas of
  interest"
• "Independence and autonomy"
• "Increased focus on people"
• "Challenging, cutting-edge work
  with a talented team"

DOWNERS

• "Slow increases in salary"
• "Still trying to figure out how to be
  a public firm"
• "Emphasis on finance and
  shareholders rather than employees"
• "Poor maternity program"

EMPLOYMENT CONTACT

bearingpoint.recruitmax.com/eng/can
  didates/default.cfm

THE BUZZ
WHAT CONSULTANTS AT OTHER FIRMS ARE SAYING

• "Better than most"
• "Dependable"
• "Profit-driven; less concern for
  results and long-term client
  relationships"
• "Good, but overly tough
  management"

THE SCOOP

Born from the Big Five

BearingPoint can trace its roots to the original "Big Five" group of accounting firms, having spun off from global giant KPMG in January 2000. In fact, it was known as KPMG Consulting until 2002, when it selected its new name, designed to reflect the concept of "setting direction to an end point." But the firm's IT roots are solid, too. When KPMG's consulting arm was established as a separate company in August 1999, Cisco Systems poured $1 billion into the company, and now owns a 10 percent stake in BearingPoint. The firm employs around 17,000 staffers, serving BearingPoint's broad client list of Global 2000 companies, mid-sized businesses and government organizations. Practice areas include business and technology strategy, systems design, architecture, applications implementation, network, systems integration and managed services.

BearingPoint divides its lines of business into three divisions: commercial services, serving consumer, industrial, technology and communications clients; financial services, serving banks, insurance companies and other large financial institutions; and public services, covering federal, state and local government clients. This latter division, which contributed about $1.3 billion to the company's $3.4 billion in revenues in fiscal 2004, has continued to lead the firm through the second quarter of 2005, when it brought in an estimated $333 million in bookings.

A financial flurry

Thanks to strong ties to both the high-tech and government worlds—and a strategically advantageous location in McLean, Va.—the public company started off strong. But the shaky economy made the firm lose its bearings for a bit, and 2002 saw a series of layoffs and restructuring in Europe and then in North America. Shareholders grew antsy, too, as BearingPoint was forced to restate its earnings for the first three quarters of fiscal 2003, cutting profits by $10.8 million. The glitch was attributed to complications arising from the firm's many acquisitions (most notably its May 2002 acquisition of most of Andersen's global consulting operations, a deal worth up to $284 million).

Financial complications have continued to dog the company. In November 2004, BearingPoint announced that it had miscategorized $92.9 million in assets, attributable to a "clerical" error. Soon thereafter, the firm disclosed yet more problems, along with a restructuring charge of as much as $67 million. In addition, the firm revealed that it was evaluating whether to reduce or sell some overseas operations, and that it would issue new debt that could reduce the value of shareholders' interest in the company.

By March 2005, the picture hadn't gotten any rosier—the firm announced that it would delay filing its annual report for 2004, citing a need to ensure compliance with accounting practices as it implemented a new financial accounting system. The firm said it was undertaking a "thorough review" of its statements, and had found that its "internal controls over financial reporting as of December 31, 2004, were not effective." In addition, BearingPoint said it had identified "certain items" that would probably require it to restate earnings for at least the first three quarters of fiscal year 2004.

Still waiting ...

In July 2005, the firm issued a statement saying the completion of its 2004 financial statements was a "top priority," and that it expected to finish the work up by some time in September. Meanwhile, the firm reported, bookings for the second quarter of 2005 totaled around $960 million, the largest for any quarter in the company's history, and the firm was able to secure additional capital with a $150 million line of credit. But in an update in September 2005, the firm noted that, "due to the volume of work and review involved," the filings might take until the end of October. Even so, BearingPoint added, "additional issues" could arise that would stretch the time frame even further. It also warned that its filing for the third quarter of 2005 was unlikely to appear on time. In addition, the firm revealed that the Securities and Exchange Commission had turned an informal investigation of the company's finances into a formal one. On the heels of this announcement came shareholder lawsuits in September 2005, asserting that the company was in default on certain debentures because it hadn't made its SEC filings in a timely fashion. The firm argued that the claims were without merit.

The firm's recent troubles haven't prevented it from bringing home accolades as an industry leader. BearingPoint took home top honors in a customer service survey conducted by Forrester Research in July 2005. In the third annual "IT Service Provider Scorecard," Forrester asked execs who had engaged IT service providers recently about their levels of satisfaction with these businesses. Of the 11 providers on the list, BearingPoint's scores came in highest. For the third year in a row, BearingPoint was named one of America's Most Admired Companies by *Fortune* magazine in 2005, placing fifth in the computer and data services category.

Rumblings at the top

All of this fiscal drama has gone hand-in-hand with plenty of revolving-door management activity, starting at the very top. In November 2004, the firm's chairman and CEO, Randolph Blazer, who had led the firm since before it went public in 2001, bailed unexpectedly and without giving reason—though he did leave with a cool $2.5 million severance package. The firm had barely recovered from the surprise when, a week later, its CFO, Robert S. Falcone, retired. The firm got a new CFO in January 2005: Joseph Corbett, who had been an executive with KPMG, BearingPoint's former parent.

It's up to You

In March 2005, the firm hired another exec with connections—Harry L. You, former CFO at Oracle. Before his eight-month stint at the IT giant, You served as CFO for BearingPoint rival Accenture. Calling the firm's financial woes "embarrassing and inexcusable," he announced that the firm's "first order of business" would be to "reestablish financial credibility and consistency with an unswerving commitment to transparency in disclosure and rigorous financial processes." But things didn't remain stable for long: In May 2005, Corbett resigned as CFO, through a "mutual agreement," according to the company. He agreed to stay on as a consultant until a successor was found. "Harry and I together decided that the challenges facing BearingPoint require that Harry have a CFO of his own choosing," Corbett said.

In July 2005, the firm appointed Judy Ethell as executive VP of finance and chief accounting officer. Ethell, a CPA for 23 years, was charged with completing the firm's internal audit and helping it get its financial transformation efforts in order. The announcement followed the June appointment of Connie Weaver, an industry veteran, as executive vice president and chief marketing officer. And in September 2005, the firm announced a few management changes designed to help the firm better focus on larger, more complex client engagements. These included the appointment of former PricewaterhouseCoopers managing partner Robert Glatz as executive VP for corporate development and global capture—new positions for the firm; former A.T. Kearney VP Andrea Bierce to the newly created position of executive VP for global capture; BearingPoint and Andersen vet Michael Lyman as executive VP and chief strategy officer; and former PricewaterhouseCoopers partner Michael Reuschel as senior VP of the communications and media practice.

Engagements roll in

The firm's fiscal intrigue hasn't prevented big wins among clients, however. The firm received a big vote of confidence from the Federal Deposit Insurance Corporation (FDIC) in August 2005, in the form of a $23 million contract to help consolidate technology security self-assessment and monitoring activities. The firm has been helping the FDIC with similar projects since 2003. Also in August 2005, the firm won an engagement valued at up to $15 million from the Centers for Disease Control and Prevention, its largest contract ever from the CDC. The firm was tapped to help the department's Coordinating Office for Terrorism Preparedness and Emergency Response with a range of services, including strategic planning, business process improvement, and Web development. Since November 2001, the firm has been working with the U.S. Department of Health and Human Services to implement a new centralized financial management system, known as the Unified Financial Management System project, which may become the single largest civilian financial system in the world. Additionally, on a phased-in basis, BearingPoint is replacing redundant and outdated financial systems at agencies such as the Food and Drug Administration and the Centers for Medicare and Medicaid Services.

Helping the homeland

As homeland security and defense spending has been skyrocketing, BearingPoint has been well-positioned to step in with its services. In the public sphere, perhaps the biggest recent win is the firm's September 2004 deal to serve as the prime contractor for the Department of Homeland Security's eMerge2 Program (which stands for "electronically managing enterprise resources for government effectiveness and efficiency"). Under a blanket purchase agreement valued at up to $229 million, the firm is working to implement a DHS-wide solution to deliver accurate, relevant and timely information for the department's decision-makers. In August 2005, the Port Authority of New York and New Jersey awarded BearingPoint a $5.2 million contract to continue work on the Operation Safe Commerce project, a program designed to improve security procedures for cargo containers entering the country. The project involves implementing a range of "best of breed" technologies to monitor containers along the supply chain.

A Naval fave

BearingPoint continues to rack up contracts with its other neighbors down the road in Washington, DC. In October 2005, the firm scored an engagement worth up to $58 million from the U.S. Navy. The contract calls for BearingPoint to provide IT strategy, program development and program management in support of the Navy's creation of an Enterprise IT Program Management Office, one of the Navy's highest priority initiatives as it seeks to strengthen its IT operations. In August 2005, the firm was tapped by the United States Naval Air Systems Command for a contract worth up to $4 million, to provide a range of technical and advisory services related to process improvement. In July 2005, the firm was awarded a $36 million contract to provide program management support to the Defense Manpower Data Center, which maintains the largest and most comprehensive archive of personnel, manpower, training and financial data for the Department of Defense. Another Navy contract was signed in June 2005, when the firm agreed to provide a range of technical and advisory services to the United States Naval Surface Warfare Center, Dahlgren Division, under an agreement worth up to $27 million. The firm got another big award from the Navy in May 2005, when it was awarded a contract to assist with the execution of the Navy's strategic sourcing program, an agreement worth up to $55 million.

From telecom to online shopping

The firm's engagements aren't limited to the military and government. In August 2005, BearingPoint was awarded a managed services contract from Hawaiian Telecom Communications, covering a broad enterprise system implementation. In May 2005, the firm signed a three-year, $18.9 million contract with Purdue University to serve as the prime system integrator for OnePurdue, the school's initiative to modernize the systems that support student services, human resources, research administration and finance. In March 2005, BP got a major contract from Fireman's Fund Insurance Company to implement a new management system for insurance agents. And in February 2005, the firm was tapped by Minnesotan online grocer SimonDelivers to help it with its long-term online delivery plans though a blend of both strategy and IT consulting.

A niche in development

BearingPoint also has seen a flurry of contracts pour in for development work overseas, particularly in troubled (or, as the firm puts it, "post-conflict") areas such as Afghanistan. The firm was awarded a $6.85 million contract in September 2005 to help the republic of Afghanistan's Ministry of Finance strengthen its cash management capabilities and to develop strategies for treasury processes and human resources management. The contract expands upon work begun by the firm in 2002, when it was tapped to provide a benchmark for a fully-functioning financial management system for the country. BearingPoint has taken on these types of projects in Iraq, Kosovo and Southern Sudan, using local workers where possible.

The firm also helps out in more established areas—in October, the U.S. Agency for International Development (USAID) awarded BearingPoint a four-year, $124.7 million contract to implement a broad program of economic, financial and private-sector reform in Egypt. But these contracts often draw intense scrutiny: In 2004, a $9 million contract with the feds to provide services in Iraq drew controversy when some government officials questioned the competitive bidding process that landed the firm the deal.

Florida follies

The firm also has come under pressure in the U.S., largely through its work in Florida, which has caused some critics to carp about BearingPoint's close ties to Governor Jeb Bush. In late September 2004, BearingPoint was cut from a $126 million contract to run the data center for the state, following an investigation that turned up alleged improprieties with the bidding process (rival Accenture also was taken off the project). In December 2004, after more than a year of escalating grumblings over the firm's work in Florida, the Justice Department and Veterans Affairs Department launched criminal and civil investigations into one of the firm's previous engagements—a computer system at Florida's Bay Pines VA Medical Center. The system had failed its pilot phase, prompting federal inquiries and congressional hearings. A report issued by the Department of Veterans Affairs inspector general's office said the contract, reportedly given to BearingPoint without competitive bidding, was "tantamount to issuing BearingPoint a blank check." The firm disagrees with this assertion, claiming that it fulfilled its contractual obligations and continues to stand by its work on the system, which met 88 percent of the requirements established by the VA, exceeding the VA's established target of 80 percent.

Readying RFID

Like many of its tech-savvy peers, BearingPoint has gravitated toward radio frequency identification (RFID), working from its RFID Center of Excellence to help clients such as the Department of Defense understand and implement the expanding technology. In August 2005, the U.S. Army awarded the firm a blanket purchase order to provide various RFID technical services, as the Department of Defense ramps up RFID use for activities such as tracking weaponry across supply chains.

Relaying research

BearingPoint has hopped on board with another new technology: podcasting. In an article in *CMO Magazine* in October 2005, global financial services marketing director Paul Dunay called the audio technology an "unblockable tube to our customers and prospects around a thematic topic that we've identified." The firm launched five podcasts in mid-2005, covering topics such as operational risk and business process management. The five- to seven-minute presentations were described by Dunay as *Reader's Digest* versions of existing BearingPoint white papers, designed both to inform existing customers and attract new ones. In fact, research is a big selling point for BearingPoint. Recent studies have covered topics ranging from the need for Hollywood to adapt their business models to respond to digital opportunities, to key areas of improvement needed for China's banks.

In October 2004, the firm announced the launch of its first-ever custom magazine, *Business Empowered*, a quarterly publication designed to cover the emerging business and technology trends and issues facing chief executives. The publication, part of a larger marketing partnership with Forbes, Inc., had an initial circulation of 50,000. In April 2005, the firm launched the BearingPoint Institute for Executive Insight, a professional knowledge and research organization geared toward C-level executives on critical business challenges.

Setting up shop in India

As the company boarded the outsourcing bandwagon, BearingPoint laid out ambitious expansion plans in India and China in 2003 and 2004. In February 2004, the firm opened a software development and management center in Chennai and planned another in Bangalore, reporting that it wanted to boost its headcount to 2,000 in India. Analysts hailed the move, noting that the firm's lack of presence on the subcontinent was weakening its position in the competitive consulting market. Meanwhile, in China, BearingPoint has an Asian hub in Shanghai, along with offices in Beijing and Guangzhou.

The firm also has invested in less costly areas back home. In March 2005, BearingPoint announced that it was opening a software development center in Hattiesburg, Miss., near the University of Southern Mississippi. The initial aim of the center is to provide government clients with access to highly skilled, cost-effective resources for applications development and testing, technical support and managed services; after it has established itself, the center will serve commercial clients, as

Visit the Vault Consulting Career Channel at **www.vault.com/consulting** — with insider firm profiles, message boards, the Vault Consulting Job Board and more.

VAULT CAREER LIBRARY

121

well. To sweeten the deal, Mississippi offered an aggressive incentive package, including tax credits and workforce development grants.

A centered approach

In recent years, the firm has dedicated resources to a series of centers, such as its new "Testing Center of Excellence," launched in June 2004. The center is designed to enhance the testing capabilities of telecommunications, media, entertainment and utility companies and reduce their overall testing time and costs. And in October 2004, the firm announced its sponsorship of a "business incubator," the Chesapeake Innovation Center, aimed at creating market strategies for new homeland security technologies. The firm launched a new practice, Customer Identity Management, in February 2005, designed to help clients "know your customer" through a blend of customer relationship management, identity management and risk management.

Donating hours and dollars

When it comes to corporate charity, BearingPoint shines. The firm committed an estimated $1 million in in-kind contributions to clients dealing with the effects of Hurricane Katrina, in addition to thousands contributed to the Red Cross by the firm and employees. BearingPoint staffers also gave up thousands of hours of paid leave to help fellow employees affected by the disaster. The firm also showed its generous side following the tsunami in Southeast Asia in late 2004, matching employee contributions for a total donation of around $600,000. BearingPoint has also been active with pro-golfer Phil Mickelson's work with the Special Operations Warrior Foundation, an organization dedicated to funding college educations for the children of Special Operations personnel killed in operational or training missions.

Corporate diversity is also a BearingPoint mission, and the firm has participated in Upwardly Global, a nonprofit program promoting an ethically diverse workforce. The firm was honored by the program in 2004 for hiring two of the program's candidates and participating in its mentoring program to help highly qualified legal immigrant professionals seek employment.

GETTING HIRED

Talent wanted

Aside from maintaining a recruiting system to seek out potential employees, BearingPoint also "recruits from select schools and relies greatly on referrals from employees," says a source. Schools from which the firm plucks talent include University of Minnesota, University of Illinois at Urbana-Champaign, Northwestern University, University of Chicago, Penn State, Carnegie Mellon, University of North Carolina, Indiana University at Bloomington, Duke University, MIT, New York University, Columbia and UCLA. "We hire based on experience and also straight from business schools. We are moving more towards hiring from undergraduate classes as well," one consultant reports. Some insiders grumble, however, that the regionalized search radius needs to expand if the firm is to attract the country's top graduates. A South Carolina-based source explains that the company recruits at "very few selected colleges" and "needs to increase schools and target the top schools in the country and not just those in two or three selected geographies."

No standard procedure

Sources observe that the "highly structured hiring process"—a process that "seems efficient and well managed"—is culled from a "large database" of potential employees. However, the hiring process is hardly uniform and may vary according to group, says one employee, who notes that there is "no standardized approach aside from [an] offer letter." As one insider puts it, "It's up to each manager to define requirements. The central recruitment function provides support." In general, "recruiting is organized centrally," says a source, "but hiring decisions and interviewing is left to solution teams."

Applicants are usually pre-screened by the human resources department, insiders say. "The firm typically then conducts an initial first-round interview comprised of basic skill set and experience questions. The first round can be in person or over the phone. The firm then conducts final-round interviews facilitated by nonmanagers, managers and partners (managing directors), consisting of case studies, personality questions and general background/experience questions," a consultant explains. More tech-heavy positions may also require more quizzing based on experience and know-how in the field, insiders add.

OUR SURVEY SAYS

Working out the spots

Plenty of BearingPointers have positive things to say about their firm. "The culture is very informal and relaxed, yet everyone works really hard," one consultant avers. According to another insider, BearingPointers are "very smart, nice people with few exceptions. I feel like it's a collaborative culture." However, five years after its launch, BearingPoint seems to still be finding its bearings. One consultant sums the culture up as "spotty—it is not consistently delivered across the board." Some of this inconsistency has to do with the firm's transformation from KPMG, along with its recent leadership changes, insiders suggest. "Since our separation from KPMG LLP we have been in a change process of many of the elements of our work culture," says a source. A colleague grumbles that staff are "continuously paying for the mismanagement, poor decisions, [and] lack of true leadership of the former CEO and his direct reports," but adds that the "new CEO seems to have recognized this situation and is trying to make necessary improvements."

This general feeling of cautious optimism regarding the future of the firm's culture resonates with many of the firm's employees. "Culture is hard to identify," a source says. "We are trying to figure out who we are. Our culture is possibly struggling but improving." A colleague agrees: "I've been watching our firm evolve over the past year into a company that treats culture and people with top priority. We still have some work to do, but the results are obvious." Employees point to changes in upper management as the critical reason for optimism. "The change from the partnership model and subsequent shakeup at the senior management levels are fundamentally changing the culture at BearingPoint—a good and necessary thing to remain competitive," a consultant observes. "Cultural change, however, takes a long time but the management team is working in the right direction." BP consultants are thus far very impressed with the stewardship of new CEO Harry You, "who seems to have recognized the situation and is trying to make necessary improvements."

Supervisory distance

BearingPoint's business is centered on a dichotomy between management and personal autonomy for consultants who are typically working offsite with client teams. Though many applaud the firm's "individualistic culture—each person is essentially empowered to take ownership over his/her career"—leadership remains a major concern for some consultants, as MDs and supervisors vary greatly in their management duties. Experiences vary depending on leadership. "My direct supervisor only works two days a week, so that person is a little disconnected," reports one source, "but she is accessible and very supportive." Regarding her supervisors, one consultant offers that "one is excellent and one is very good, but one I have never met in person (during my two years), and the other I see once a year at most. The challenges come in supervising from 800 miles away, or being supervised from 800 miles away." One source adds, "As the nature of the consulting business is to be 'on the road,' it is extremely important to be in a group that has a strong support system."

Walking the work/life walk

Work/life balance also gets mixed reviews at BearingPoint. Some see the concept as a "lot of lip service," with one insider complaining, "They talk the talk, but rarely walk the walk." "There is a constant reminder that evenings and weekends are for getting your work done," gripes another consultant. Agrees a colleague, "I don't feel they consider your life outside of work as important to you as an individual." According to one source, "It is entirely up to the consultant in our company to decide if they want to have a life, and then they have to fight the culture to have one."

Flexibility appreciated

But some insiders seem to have won the battle. "The firm is very considerate of the work/life balance. As a manager, I am also encouraged to ensure my direct reports are managing their personal life as their work," a source reports. One consultant offers, "I'm able to work a flexible schedule that gives me time to tend to my personal life, and volunteer at my local high school." Another source says, "In addition to beach time, I worked from home on proposals for seven consecutive weeks." However, the amount of balance and scheduling flexibility, says one insider, is "based on each individual supervisor" and is "not company wide."

The same might be said for work hours at BearingPoint, which run the gamut from the traditional 9 to 5 to much more. "It just runs at a constant 60-plus hours a week," comments one insider. Another consultant reports working "50-plus" hour weeks, though "it has gotten a lot better." In any case, BearingPoint consultants rarely see down-time: "During my five-plus year tenure with BearingPoint, I have never been on the beach," a consultant notes. According to a colleague, "My workload is sporadic and sometimes requires night and weekend work, but I have the flexibility to balance this and keep total hours worked relatively consistent."

Visit the Vault Consulting Career Channel at **www.vault.com/consulting** — with insider firm profiles, message boards, the Vault Consulting Job Board and more.

VAULT CAREER LIBRARY   **125**

Travel on your own time

As a firm that conducts business worldwide, travel is pretty much a given for BearingPoint consultants, though experienced in different ways. "While on the road assisting our clients we need to comply with other BE responsibilities, usually done on overtime. Also, travel time (about seven to 12 hours a week) is taken from our personal time," a source says. "Our travel requirements are extensive," one source acknowledges. "However, if on long projects, the firm allows for spouse travel, pending allowance from financial budgets on the project." Employees in the DC area are the exception, reports one insider, grateful that "I rarely travel now because I'm in the federal practice." Another DC source reports that "I am intentionally in a non-travel role. I appreciate that my company was able to accommodate my desire to move from a travel to a non-travel position when my personal situation required this."

Rewards and growth

Consultants at BearingPoint reflect a deep dissatisfaction with the firm's financial woes in years past. As a consultant bluntly puts it, "BearingPoint, given its recent financial woes, is not at the forefront of compensation." One insider describes a common perception that "upcoming changes in compensation, from MD on down, will cause great, unplanned and potentially fatal attrition in many practice areas." Another insider has similar concerns about losing top consultants: "I believe that we can be much better at consistently providing competitive compensation. We are now in the process of benchmarking ourselves with the best in the industry and ensuring that we compensate our people that way, too."

Employees are particularly critical about the bonus structure in recent years. "Although I am not generally unhappy with my compensation I have not had a bonus in three years and this is discouraging," reports one senior manager. Most bonuses come in the form of stock options, "but our stock value is quite low so it's not too enticing," scoffs an insider. Bonuses are handed out from time to time, but tend to come from clients rather than the firm, awarded "for creative and exceptional client service/solutions."

A concierge at your service

The firm does contribute to a 401(k), and offers an Education Savings Plan, as well as profit-sharing "at the managing director level." Sources rave about the firm's "generous" vacation allotment, about five weeks per year. Other perks include medical, dental and vision insurance plans, "discounts on health and fitness programs," "a range of various discounts with several of our partners or customers such as Apple," and "concierge service to take care of personal needs to achieve better work/life balance, etc." In addition, says a source, "The firm places a strong emphasis on internal employee social programs and external community service. The firm offers a number of trips to sports events, skiing/snowboarding events, theater, and dinners." But one consultant says of BearingPoint's benefits, "I believe that we have room for improvement here. I have seen some clients whose employee benefits are much better." As for offices, one consultant reports, "[They] depend on location. Mountain View and McLean are great. Denver is out of space, and we are on card table chairs and fold up tables now."

Movin' on up

Promotion remains a sure-fire route to a pay raise, though there's no clear line on the firm's promotion schedule. Most BearingPoint consultants appreciate that performance, not paper credentials, are the basis for most promotions. One self-assured insider says that "I believe our firm follows an up-or-out policy. If it is determined that a person has 'it,' they move up quickly. For example, I have moved up four levels in five years and expect to be a manager within the next six months. In short, if someone has exceptional consulting soft skills, technical skills and a practical business sense, they can expect to move up quickly." Another source agrees: "Promotions are based on semi-annual performance reviews, and guideline objectives set by the firm for each position. The rate that you move up is dependent upon you." This is especially evident in the lack of distinction between employees with and without graduate degrees. One consultant states, "There is close to no distinction between an MBA grad and an undergrad. As long as the undergrad can develop a good relationship with his MD or senior manager, then in the eyes of the MD and senior manager, his lack of qualifications are not even a consideration."

Others see the promotion policy in a different light. BearingPoint consultants who are eager to move up in the ranks report that progress can sometimes be frustrating. "We don't do a very good job of getting rid of the folks that are not performing," an insider complains. Promotions are described by one source as "somewhat performance-based and somewhat the good ol' boy network." As another consultant puts it, "Our firm's promotion policy is merit-based, but the criteria for promotion are not judged across the firm in a standard manner. There are no restrictions as to how long a person can stay at a certain level (not up-or-out). Because it is merit-based, a person can control the pace at which he/she advances. However, the measurements against which a person is measured are not completely objective—there are still a lot of subjective elements to promotion."

Train and gain

BearingPoint is committed to training, and it shows, insiders say. The prevailing complaint about BearingPoint's training opportunities is not that they are inadequate or archaic, but simply that there are not enough of them. The company recently redesigned its training program, offering a new series of instructor-headed training courses called Introduction to BearingPoint (introducing the company, products/solutions, etc.) and Consulting 101 (case study-based training in techniques to sell and deliver to clients). Employees enjoy the new approach. Training "is getting better," one consultant offers. "We moved too much towards e-learning (we're quite a pioneer in that!), but are now including more in-class training programs." One source raves that she "just went to a manager's training in San Francisco and it was great. I would love to have more instructor-led training as it is extremely helpful." Others explain that while they, too, would enjoy more training, the daily demands of the job leave little time for personal development. "The problem lies in getting approval for the money (for external classes)," writes an insider, "or time off for any form of training." Some consultants are able to take time off for training as long as their MDs approve. "I have never been denied a chance to go to training, as long as it makes business sense," an insider says.

Dishing on diversity

Most survey respondents are content with the firm's diversity, though they note that it varies depending on employment level. One consultant says that "at consultant levels [there is] no difference" between gender expectations, while "at upper levels, women must conform to the management style of the men." There's "not a lot of support for working moms," grumbles a source, who notes that new mothers "have to take disability leave for maternity leave. Some directors are supportive while others are not, leading to low percentages of women in leadership positions." Another employee observes that "facilities to support work/life balance for new mothers must absolutely be improved," adding that "improvements with regard to maternity leave, areas set aside in the office for lactation, working mother support groups, onsite day care, etc.," would improve the retention rate of female employees.

The firm's treatment of minorities also gets mostly favorable reviews. One insider suggests that "the company has a good minorities hiring policy," but recommends additional training for foreign workers, since "for many people English is a second language and we should offer presentation and language assistance training. Though most respondents feel the firm looks only at employee performance and capability in hiring and promotion, others see room for improvement in diversity. An insider laments the "old-boy networks" and suggests the firm consider "recruiting from historically minority universities." According to a consultant, gays and lesbians at BearingPoint will find a "don't ask, don't tell culture, which I think is too bad. I would like it to be more open." A colleague sums it up, saying that "personal lives are not used as a basis for anything here."

Giving back

The transitions at the executive level are bringing change to nonprofit areas of the firm, as well. One consultant notes that community service activities "are increasing and seem to be at a high level after a period of perceived low community involvement." The firm "strongly encourages community involvement and leads many efforts, as well as matches 100 percent of employee donations to charities of their choosing," says a source. "We have an annual community event planned by each office. In addition, our office plans at least one community event each quarter," a consultant notes. Reports an insider, "we are giving away $1 million of in-kind consulting services to our clients affected by Hurricane Katrina. We also have volunteer opportunities, clothing drives and food drives. We are very good about community involvement." "During Hurricane Katrina, we sent out an internal notice for donations and an Employee Shared Leave Program so employees could contribute their hours to affected employees. From that, we received an overwhelmingly positive response, both in donations and hours. Our employees are very community-minded and are always willing to help each other," another source says. An insider notes, though, that while there are "quite a few efforts in the local offices" and that "these offices always invite 'traveling consultants' to participate, it is hard to feel a part of the 'local office community' when you spend 100 percent of your time on the road."

Computer Sciences Corporation

2100 East Grand Avenue
El Segundo, CA 90245
Phone: (310) 615-0311
www.csc.com

LOCATIONS

El Segundo, CA (HQ)
1,200 offices worldwide

PRACTICE AREAS

Application Outsourcing
Business Process Outsourcing
Credit Services
Customer Relationship Management
Enterprise Application Integration
Enterprise Solutions
Hosting Services
IT Infrastructure Outsourcing
Knowledge Management
Legal Solutions
Management Consulting
Outsourcing
Risk Management & Claims
Security
Supply Chain Management

THE STATS

Employer Type: Public Company
Ticker Symbol: CSC (NYSE)
CEO: Van B. Honeycutt
2005 Employees: 80,000
2004 Employees: 78,000
2005 Revenues: $14.1 billion
2004 Revenues: $13.4 billion

UPPERS

• Good exposure to various areas of the company
• Reasonable work hours
• Opportunity for advancement

DOWNERS

• Cutthroat environment as you advance
• Minimal perks
• Some morale problems within acquired companies

EMPLOYMENT CONTACT

careers.csc.com

THE BUZZ
WHAT CONSULTANTS AT OTHER FIRMS ARE SAYING

• "Demanding but fair to employees"
• "Superior integrators"
• "Middle of the pack"
• "Bureacracy to the max"

THE SCOOP

A skyrocketing investment

Computer Sciences Corporation has many claims to fame, including being the first software company to go public, way back in 1963. The firm also represents a substantial return on a modest investment: The multi-billion dollar company was founded in 1959 by two young aerospace analysts, Fletcher Jones and Roy Nutt, with just $100. The firm started out as a provider of IT support to government agencies such as the Defense Communications Agency and NASA, branching out into the commercial sector in the 1980s. These days, CSC divides its massive business into three divisions: outsourcing, systems integration and consulting. In 2005, the employee headcount was around 78,000—lower than the 90,000 reported the previous year, largely due to the sale of some of CSC's non-core businesses.

During fiscal year 2005, CSC earned approximately 67 percent of its $14.1 billion in revenues from commercial engagements worldwide. The firm's 2005 annual revenues represented a 4.5 percent increase over 2004. The firm reported record revenues in Europe of $1.28 billion, while worldwide, CSC raked in 24 contracts valued at $100 million or more, with five of them exceeding $1 billion. Many of those big engagements came from the federal sector, with contracts for the Department of Defense (DoD) making up 21 percent of CSC's revenues during 2005.

Takeover buzz

As of November 2005, CSC has been seen as a company "in play." Rumors that either a big defense company, such as Lockheed Martin, or even a tech services rival, like EDS, may be angling to buy the firm appeared in *The Wall Street Journal* in October. The paper, citing sources close to CSC, suggested that the firm was in "early negotiations" with one or more bidders, valuing a potential purchase at up to $65 a share—a figure that would add up to a transaction of more than $11 billion. Such a deal would likely take the firm private, observers noted, which would allow CSC to avoid the intense scrutiny that comes with government contracts awarded to public companies. The buzz sent investors scrambling, driving share prices skyward. At the same time, CSC president and CEO Michael Laphen made a cool $1 million by selling some of his shares under a plan that allows execs to exercise stock options once a certain "trigger" price has been met, according to The Street.com. The company steadfastly refused to comment on the buyout rumors.

A lock on defense contracts

It's no secret that CSC is an attractive target for a defense-oriented company like Lockheed Martin. The firm has ramped up its defense presence steadily in the years following the September 11 terrorist attacks. Stepping up to meet government demands for intelligence and security services, in 2002 the firm created a new enforcement, security and intelligence (ESI) division to serve a range of agencies while aligning itself closely with the newly created Department of Homeland Security. In 2003, the firm acquired DynCorp, a technology services firm specializing in communications, security and aircraft. By 2003, revenues from government sources had reached 40 percent of CSC's total, up from 24 percent in 2002.

Homing in on IT

In December 2004, CSC raked in $850 million from the sale of some of its DynCorp business units and contracts to Veritas Capital. The units, which employ 14,000 people worldwide, primarily provided the DoD with aviation maintenance, physical and personal security, drug eradication, and shipboard logistics, training and staffing services. According to CSC, the sale allowed the firm to focus its efforts on providing IT services to the government sector. In March 2005, CSC formed a new division within its Federal Sector business unit, the Applied Technology Division, which provides managed engineering services, including infrastructure, mission and range support to government agencies worldwide. The new division—which supports roughly 8,300 employees—essentially folded DynCorp's Technical Services division, which was not part of the larger DynCorp sale, into CSC's Federal Sector unit. CSC also owns DynPort Vaccine Company (DVC), a pharmaceutical subsidiary focusing on biodefense products.

CSC provides Web hosting support for a variety of DoD sites. Most recently, in September 2005 the firm was awarded a $42 million contract to provide these services to the Defense Technical Information Center (DTIC). In addition, the firm supports the Naval Surface Warfare Center's Dahlgren Division, in Virginia, with software and systems engineering support, in a $123 million agreement signed in September 2005. The firm signed a conditional $307 million deal in August 2005 to support the U.S. Air Force Air Education Training Command with maintenance and operation services for the 81st Training Wing at Keesler Air Force Base in Mississippi. The firm also supports the Navy's education division, providing IT network, Web and operations support services in an engagement valued at $100 million.

Rallying the troops

CSC's defense contracts piled up throughout 2005. For the DoD, CSC agreed in August to develop, implement and support the Biometric Identification System for Access, a system designed to evaluate fingerprints and other biometric data from non-U.S. citizens before granting them access to U.S. military facilities, such as those in Iraq. The task order was valued at around $22 million. In July, the firm scored a total of $62.4 million in contracts with the U.S. Air Force's Office of Special Investigations. The contracts, which extend CSC's long relationship with the Air Force's investigative arm, cover project support, IT operations and maintenance services, software design and development, document imaging and data warehousing services. The Naval Sea Systems Command also tapped CSC in July to provide program management and total ship systems engineering support, in a contract worth up to $71 million. In June, the DoD's Missile Defense Agency targeted CSC to provide support services to its senior leadership in a deal valued at up to $62.5 million. Services covered under the contract include engineering analysis of missile defense capabilities, program and acquisition planning and analysis, and related defense program support.

The firm helps support homeland security through non-defense agencies, too. In August 2005, CSC was awarded an $86 million contract to provide comprehensive mission support services to the new Water Security Division within the U.S. Environmental Protection Agency's Office of Water, a division established in the wake September 11 to oversee water security and infrastructure. And in January 2004, CSC won a $96 million contract to support the largest environmental cleanup in the U.S. Under the deal, the firm's subsidiary, AdvanceMed Corporation, would provide occupational medicine services to the 11,000 employees of the Department of Energy working at the Hanford site near Richland, Washington.

Prescription for IT

The firm's public sector contracts extend beyond those involving issues of national security. In September 2005, CSC was tapped as part of a team selected by the Centers for Medicare and Medicaid Services to establish one of 10 national prescription drug benefit plans created under the new Medicare reform legislation. The $384 million contract calls for CSC to provide the drug benefit program with support services, including call center operation, enrollment processing and financial management, as well as compliance management services. The Department of Education signed with CSC in May 2005 to provide infrastructure management services, including network, project and security support, to offices throughout the

U.S., in a deal valued at around $176 million. That same month, the FBI awarded CSC a $58 million task order to provide certification, accreditation and information security services to the Bureau's Information Security division. Also in May, the firm won a contract of up to $230 million to provide support services to the new NASA Shared Services Center at the Stennis Space Center in Mississippi. The broad contract covers a range of services including administrative, financial, human resources and procurement support.

CSC tackles federal contracts far and wide, often supporting the U.S. government overseas. In June 2005, the firm was awarded a $75 million task order to support IT operations for the Navy in Japan and elsewhere in the Far East.

Hands around the world

The firm's commercial outsourcing contracts also are spread all over the globe. In September 2005, the firm inked a $135 million outsourcing deal with British Nuclear Group, which provides nuclear site management, decommissioning and cleanup services. CSC supports British Nuclear Group's IT operations in the UK, including help desk and desktop services; software applications support; networks; midrange computing; telecommunications; and managed security. In August 2005, the firm joined forces with Telkom South Africa in a $275 million outsoucing contract with Old Mutual, the largest financial services group in South Africa, and Nedbank, one of the four largest banking groups in South Africa. The deal follows an earlier outsourcing engagement CSC signed with Old Mutual in 1999. The firm landed a billion-dollar deal in July 2005, when it signed an interim agreement to extend an ongoing IT outsourcing contract with DuPont. The contract, valued at up to $1.9 billion, involves providing desktop support in Latin America, including countries such as Brazil, Colombia, Mexico and Venezuela. And in June 2005, the firm made a splash in Asia when it was tapped by ING Life Insurance Company of Japan to provide applications outsourcing, a deal valued at $11.8 million. In January 2005, the firm signed a seven-year IT outsourcing contract with TDC, Denmark's largest provider of communication solutions, valued at around $70 million.

Billions in outsourcing

Closer to home, an IT outsourcing contract extension inked with General Dynamics in April 2005 pushed the value of the engagement to around $1.6 billion. That deal was sweetened even further in September 2005, when a series of extensions worth around $260 million was added to the contract. In June 2005, CSC scored a five-year,

$48 million IT outsourcing contract with Raytheon Technical Services Company, to provide help desk, data center, electronic messaging, desktops, servers, data and voice networks, and staff augmentation services. In October 2004, the firm won a $1.35 billion outsourcing deal for IT services with Ascension Health, the largest nonprofit health system in the U.S.

The firm's commercial engagements aren't limited to outsourcing, however. The firm also provides specialized software solutions tailored to specific industries, such as insurance. In China, the firm was picked for an $18 million software and services contract with China Pacific Life Insurance Company, the country's third-largest life insurance firm, in July 2005.

Expanding worldwide

In January 2005, the firm announced the opening of the CSC Asturias Information Technologies Service Center in Asturias, Spain, part of its Global Transformation Solutions (GTS) World Sourcing network. The site is set up to serve as an offshoring facility for U.S. customers, as well as a nearshoring center for Europe.

On the leading edge

CSC supports innovation through its Leading Edge Forum, which offers two sets of programs: the LEF Executive Program and the LEF Technology Programs. The executive suite is essentially a repository of research, plus specialized conferences and programs, offered to senior executives for an annual retainer. The Technology Programs, geared toward technical execs and other IT specialists, also offer programs, advice and research. CSC also offers 19 Centers of Excellence, dedicated facilities that help CSC experts stay on the cutting edge of technological progress so they can offer the latest developments to clients. The centers are also used for beta testing new technologies.

Tech-based training

For its own staffers, CSC offers an extensive professional development program with more than 2,800 online computer-based training courses offered through Learn@CSC. The courses include both technical and interpersonal skills training. Other programs include leadership development, coaching skills, Catalyst education and the "Pioneer Curriculum" for global business change. In October 2005, the firm was honored with a 2005 BEST Award from the American Society for Training & Development (ASTD) for its global learning and employee development programs.

One such program is the Senior Leader Development Program, aimed at helping senior executives, succession plan candidates and others prepare for leadership opportunities. Eleven CSC employees were honored with All Star awards at the 2005 National Women of Color Technology Awards for their accomplishments in advancing technology and science.

Paying overtime

CSC was the subject of employment law headlines in 2003, when computer maintenance and service workers filed a class-action lawsuit against the firm, alleging that they were entitled to overtime under the Fair Labor Standards Act. According to the FLSA, only tech employees in the creative and managerial fields with a minimum salary of $57,500 could be considered "exempt" from mandatory overtime. The work performed by the computer maintenance and service workers was mechanical, according to their attorney, and not creative; therefore, the workers were entitled to overtime. The subject of overtime exemption is a tricky one in employment law, and the case was watched closely by others in the industry. In April 2005, the firm settled the lawsuit for $24 million, entitling approximately 30,000 current and former employees to make claims.

GETTING HIRED

The source for careers

On CSC's web site, prospective employees can access CareerSource, the firm's "virtual recruiting site," which lists up-to-the-minute job openings in real time. Applicants can search for jobs by location or position; set up personalized job searches with automatic e-mail notification; and register to submit resumes electronically. The site also lists career events by date, event name and location. Though the site features a "University Initiatives" link, it takes visitors to a basic job search engine, with no further information on campus recruiting.

No curveball questions

A CSC consultant in the health care group reports going through two rounds of interviews. During the first round, there was one "typical behavioral interview," followed by a case interview. During the next and final round, there were two "general" interviews followed by another case. "The first interview was very casual (with a senior consultant). The second interview was also pretty easygoing except [I spoke] with the operations manager for the entire global health division. The last interview was a case study that was not even health care-related," the source says, adding, "it was a very standard business case interview."

Another insider reports that "the questions were very basic," listing queries such as "Why do you want to work at CSC?" and "When would you be able to start?" "There were absolutely no trick questions, or even moderately tough questions," the source says, adding, "Any half-wit could wow this particular interviewer."

OUR SURVEY SAYS

Big company, many cultures

It can be hard to pin down the corporate culture at Computer Sciences Corp., since the firm is "made up of many acquisitions of smaller companies," a source says. One insider whose firm was acquired by CSC notes a drop in morale since the transfer, with decreased pay raises, declining opportunities for advancement, and "too many chiefs and not enough Indians." Another source reports that "the people are generally smart and interesting, but it differs from project to project. Some project managers are not very good and others are very bright and sharp. It really depends on which group you are in within CSC."

Taking its toll

A CSC consultant reports that the "hours are very easy for consulting," reporting, "Usually we work from Monday through Thursday and work from home on Fridays (and sometimes there isn't that much work to do on Fridays)." Still, "the corporate culture is cutthroat at the manager level," a more senior source warns, and "opportunities for advancement exist but with advancement comes more work and longer hours." The source adds, "As you move up, you never leave your previous assignment, they just add another one on top. This works for a few years and provides exposure to a lot of different positions, but over time it takes its toll."

In any case, a source says, the work is "interesting." "Projects vary depending on what group you are in, but entry-level consultants are usually generalists within the health care group. There are opportunities for advancement that are defined, but it seems like it's difficult for everyone to advance," the insider notes.

Short on glamour

Compensation packages at CSC are described as "OK," though "not glamorous." While one insider grumbles that "most perks have been removed from senior management and below," there is reportedly a bonus structure in place "based on utilization and review." In addition, a source reports receiving the "usual consultant perks (i.e., miles, hotel points, per diem when on travel projects)," relocation funding, and a "not so great" 401(k) plan with 1.5 percent matching after one year.

"The hours are very easy for consulting. Usually we work from Monday through Thursday and work from home on Fridays (and sometimes there isn't that much work to do on Fridays)."

— *CSC employee*

Visit the Vault Consulting Career Channel at **www.vault.com/consulting** — with
insider firm profiles, message boards, the Vault Consulting Job Board and more.

V/\ULT CAREER LIBRARY   139

5400 Legacy Drive
Plano, TX 75024
Phone: (972) 605-6000 or
(800) 566-9337
E-mail: info@eds.com
www.eds.com

LOCATIONS

Plano, TX (HQ)
Offices throughout the U.S., Puerto
Rico, and 60 countries in Europe,
the Middle East, Africa and Asia
Pacific

PRACTICE AREAS

Applications Services
Business Process Outsourcing
  Services
Infrastructure Services

THE STATS

Employer Type: Public Company
Ticker Symbol: EDS (NYSE)
Chairman and CEO: Michael H. Jordan
2005 Employees: 120,000 (approx.)
2004 Employees: 117,000 (approx.)
2005 Revenues: $19.75 billion
2004 Revenues: $19.86 billion

UPPERS

• Great benefits and salaries
• "Technology is improving"
• "Opportunities to change hours"

DOWNERS

• "Company culture is stifling"
• "Due to layoffs, morale has slipped"
• "Does not encourage dedication"

EMPLOYMENT CONTACT

www.eds.com/about/careers

THE BUZZ
WHAT CONSULTANTS AT OTHER FIRMS ARE SAYING

• "Strong in government market"
• "Strong technical skills but
  expensive"
• "Too eager to claim expertise it
  lacks"
• "Button-holed"

THE SCOOP

Everything's big in Texas

America's famous Texan Ross Perot founded EDS with a $1,000 investment 43 years ago. Six years later, in 1968, the company went public. The company's official name is Electronic Data Systems, but the company's been EDS for so long, anyone would be forgiven for not remembering it. What people do remember, however, is that EDS is one of the largest IT services firms in the world, trailing only IBM's IT services division worldwide.

The Plano, Texas-based giant is currently ranked No. 95 on the Fortune 500 list of companies, with a slight dip from No. 87 a year ago. With roughly 120,000 employees scattered worldwide in over 60 countries, the company raked in $19.75 billion in revenues in 2005.

The company will do anything you want in IT—take over your back office; handle business processes like your HR department; do a sophisticated consulting project— you name it. Its portfolio includes information technology and business process outsourcing services to clients in the manufacturing, financial services, health care, communications, energy, transportation, and consumer and retail industries, as well as to governments around the world.

The pioneering spirit

EDS considers itself an innovator in its field. A pioneer in ATM technology, it also had a hand in the text-analysis tool that allows documents to be searched electronically. Its facilities-management contract with Frito-Lay in 1963 was the first of its kind. The company also developed the first system to process Medicaid claims for the State of Texas in 1966, and continues to support various Medicaid activities to this day. Additionally, EDS offers "Agile Workplace Solutions," a virtual desktop management approach.

A headlining history

Record-breaking IT deals with the federal government in the 1980s spurred the company's growth, until a $2.5 billion deal transformed it into a wholly-owned subsidiary of General Motors in 1984. Perot left the company in 1986 after two years of friction with the auto giant's senior management. GM spun the firm off as an independent company in 1996, though it remained a loyal customer through a 10-

year master services agreement with GM, contributing more than 10 percent to EDS's sales.

EDS remained independent, acquiring A.T. Kearney in 1995 for over $600 million to boost its management consulting presence. And A.T. Kearney helped polish EDS's management consulting image with case studies, big-name clients and record-breaking projects. In 2005, *Consulting Magazine* named Paul A. Laudicina, A.T. Kearney's VP and managing director of the firm's Global Business Policy Council, to its annual list of the Top 25 Most Influential Consultants. However, some analysts have viewed A.T. Kearney as being a drag on EDS's performance: A.T. Kearney posted an operating loss of $10 million on revenues of $806 million in 2005, compared to a $7 million loss on revenues of $846 million the previous year. In January 2006, EDS completed the sale of A.T. Kearney to the subsidiary's management for an undisclosed sum.

Working for The Man

The firm is comfortably ensconced in Washington, DC, signing federal government contracts, even after former board member Dick Cheney took off for the White House in 2000. In 2004, the firm landed a $34 million subcontract by Systel Corp. to work on immigration and customs enforcement programs for the U.S. Department of Homeland Security. The company also has several contracts with the Department of Housing and Urban Development.

One recent government deal hasn't gone as smoothly as planned. In 2000, EDS won the largest U.S. Government IT contract in history to develop and manage the Navy Marine Corps Intranet (NMCI). The deal, however, has already cost the company more than $1.1 billion due to delays in implementing the Navy's IT network. In August 2005, EDS made an announcement defending itself against misleading statements in *Stars and Stripes,* claiming that Zotob virus worms compromised the networks. "EDS was proactive in protecting the NMCI computer network from the Zotob computer virus and has effectively and successfully protected the NMCI network from virus attacks in the past," the company said.

Signal fires

The last few years have not been easy for the IT giant. At the end of fiscal year 2003, the firm was forced to take a $559 million charge for costs related to the NMCI deal. In addition to an $8.4 million structuring charge, the firm's numbers were down $1.07 billion for the year. In response, the firm adjusted its management, hiring former CBS and Westinghouse executive Michael Jordan as chairman and CEO to outline a more coherent strategy, to rein in costs and to spur growth for the floundering company.

Cleaning up shop

Jordan, known in the industry as a "turnaround artist", promised to cut $3 billion in annual costs over two years and to reduce headcount by 20,000. While the 20,000 mark has not yet been reached, in October 2004 Jordan offered 9,200 employees an early retirement package and launched job retraining programs for 20,000 programmers. The company's debt load has decreased, with approximately $250 million in cost-savings from the personnel reduction and from the $2 billion sale of its subsidiary, UGS PLM Solutions, in May 2004.

Despite ever-persistent rumors of an imminent sale to IBM or HP, Jordan tinkered with the company's senior management positions, shuffling key executives and creating new roles to streamline business in an effort to highlight Jordan's commitment to turning the firm around and to recapture its glory years.

Not quite the expected results

The firm is trying so hard to regain its luster as the premier IT services company, that clients experiencing problems while using EDS systems is the last thing the company wants to deal with. In a recent scuffle, Her Majesty's Revenue & Customs in United Kingdom complained that the IT system developed by EDS in 2003 to launch, support and operate a new Tax Credits program was too difficult to use and was not in line with what the company had promised to deliver. HMRC demanded compensation for issues experienced.

The two sides agreed to settle in November 2005, instead of going to court. The settlement amount of £71.25 million—or $126 million—includes an up-front payment and additional future payments. In November, Doug Hoover, EDS Managing Director for the UK, Ireland and Africa stated that "HM government remains a very important client for EDS," and that not settling the dispute would have resulted in a "lengthy and complex legal case."

Medicaid as cash cow

Ever since its initial Medicaid deal in 1966, EDS has grown its Medicaid-related business in the health care sector. EDS processes more than 1 billion health claims annually and administers over $100 billion in benefits each year. In 2005 alone, the firm signed four new engagements and extended two existing Medicaid deals. Oregon, Massachusetts, Kentucky and Wisconsin all signed contracts with EDS to design, develop, implement and maintain a Medicaid Management Information System (MMIS), while Oklahoma and Rhode Island extended their partnership with the firm to continue processing health care provider claims and to provide a variety of other Medicaid financial services.

In April, the Centers for Medicare and Medicaid Services chose the company to operate the Florida Benefit Integrity Support Center and the Florida Medicare and Medicaid Data Analysis Center in a $46.5 million contract. The contract put EDS in charge of investigating fraud in Florida, Puerto Rico and the Virgin Islands. The Centers followed up with a $99 million four-year contract in August to provide systems maintenance and management services for the system that processes Medicare Part B claims.

Asia takes center stage

EDS began spreading its wings overseas in the 1970s with offices in Saudia Arabia, Singapore, Iran, Pakistan, the UK and the Netherlands. An office opened in Mexico City in 1980, followed by facilities in Australia, Brazil, Canada, France, Germany and New Zealand in the mid-1980s. Recently, the company has shifted its focus to India and China. The company announced efforts to expand its Indian headcount to 5,000 professionals by January 2006. In February 2005, when the effort was announced, the company counted 2,400 personnel housed at its centers in Chennai, Mumbai, Pune and Gurgaon. To accommodate new staff, EDS unveiled new centers in Chennai and Pune in September.

EDS established operations in China in 1987 and has served multinational clients there—including GM and Delphi—since the early 1990s. EDS also has a significant presence in Taiwan, where it is a leader in the financial services sector, and Hong Kong, where it has had a strong position in government IT services for more than 15 years. "China is the world's fastest growing IT services market and holds great interest for multinationals based in the U.S. and Europe," said COO Ron Rittenmeyer in September 2005. In an effort to capitalize on this burgeoning area, the company named John Dowd VP and general manager of EDS Greater China in September 2005. The role was created to reflect China's increasing importance to EDS's Asian strategy by consolidating the company's operations in China, Hong Kong, Taiwan and Korea into one unit.

Trading spaces

In June 2005, the firm decided to reduce costs and outsource its global real estate functions to Trammell Crow Company. Trammell took over most of the global real estate services, including portfolio management, facilities management, project management and lease administration for a portfolio of approximately 800 company-owned or leased facilities totaling 27 million square feet of real estate. Approximately 170 employees moved from EDS to Trammell as part of the deal.

In keeping with this move, EDS planned to sell approximately 20 company-owned properties and to lease back a portion of them at a lower cost, generating approximately $200 million in cash in 2005. The cost savings would exceed $200 million over three years, the company explained during the first quarter earnings call.

Deep pockets, bigger hearts

EDS prides itself on its community service involvement, starting with its charity golf tournament, the EDS Byron Nelson Championship. World-class golfers such as Vijay Singh and Tiger Woods competed in 2005, which raised over $6 million in net proceeds, prompting the PGA tour to recognize it for raising more money than any other tournament on the tour for the sixth consecutive year.

But the giving doesn't stop there. The firm also runs the EDS Foundation and encourages its employees to participate in a Global Volunteer Day, a program that's been ongoing for 13 years. Many of its programs are geared towards the arts, culture and health. The company contributes computers and technical assistance to the underprivileged in Dallas, Texas, and Lake Charles, Louisiana. And in the aftermath of the South Asian tsunami and Hurricane Katrina, the firm stepped up its efforts, donating millions of dollars in employee donations and company-matching programs to relief efforts, the Red Cross, UNICEF, CARE and Habitat for Humanity. After both catastrophes, many EDS employees volunteered at call centers to collect donations.

GETTING HIRED

Get a head start

EDS recruits undergraduates for summer internships and co-op programs, but appears to conduct a less aggressive campaign to bring MBAs and other graduate students into its fold. Otherwise, the company fills positions with experienced hires.

EDS offers two types of positions for students: Internships and Cooperative Education. According to the firm, the internship program "integrates classroom study with planned, supervised work." As an EDS intern, students gain valuable job skills in a professional business environment, and have the opportunity to earn academic credit, as well as a salary. Generally, internships are offered during the summer to candidates who have completed their sophomore year of college. In its candidates, the firm looks for strong academics, an interest in pursuing an IT career, and strong communication and teamwork skills, not to mention leadership ability and professionalism.

The Cooperative Education program, open to college juniors and seniors enrolled in their university's co-op program, is an arrangement among students, schools and employers. Co-op students are compensated financially and academically, and are expected to meet the same qualifications as interns.

Qualifiers

Experienced hires take different paths to EDS. Some respond to job postings on the company's web site, while others are recruited by head-hunters and, depending on the kind of work, the candidate's experience getting hired can differ significantly. An insider who joined EDS in the early 1990s remembers the process including "two HR interviews, one team interview [and] one manager interview." The hiring process has been streamlined since then, according to other, more recent accounts. The process now typically begins with a brief phone interview, followed by an in-person "behavioral interview with a diverse team of peers and management." Interviewers seem to place greater importance on a candidate's resume than on technical questions or aptitude tests. An insider supports this, stating that during his interviews with HR personnel and "the leader I would be reporting to in my new role," he noticed that "most of the questions were behavioral, although a few technical questions were asked…I found that something that EDS believes in is that they can train anyone to have the technical skills required to do a job, but the attitudes and behaviors cannot be modified easily, so it was better to interview for those behaviors up front."

Another source details a similar experience: He was "contacted by a head hunter," had a phone interview followed by an in-office interview, and was "hired 90 days later." The source called the face-to-face session "an easy interview" that "lacked task-specific technical questions; demeanor and resume strength were emphasized." The interviewer only asked "some basic questions related to the job." But the process became more involved. As EDS maintains a large number of contracts with government agencies that may require added precautions, it's not surprising that "a drug test was required" and "an intense background-check was completed" before "I was brought on board."

OUR SURVEY SAYS

Climate change

Economics is the dark science that's casting a shadow on EDS insiders. Real and rumored cuts to the workforce beginning in 2004, and persistent speculation over the possible sale of the company to another large corporation like IBM, have created doubt among consultants in the U.S. "Morale is down because of the never-ending rumors of job cuts," an insider reports, while another expresses his sense of insecurity and wonders, "Will I still have a job this time next year?"

Praise for peers

Job insecurity, however, hasn't dampened consultants' opinion of their peers and project managers, particularly when they are working in the field. Sources say "I like my co-workers and the type of work I do," and "when I was working out on an account, working for EDS was great. I had the opportunity to work with really great managers and team members." Overall, insiders say, EDS is a "company of good people dedicated to helping each other and helping our clients."

Generally speaking, insiders say EDS is an "enjoyable workplace, but some things will frustrate you to tears." Sources variously blame this on "top-heavy" management, a lack of "accurate mechanisms to track or recognize employee performance" or changes in "corporate direction" beginning in the mid-1990s. Veteran consultants who retired in 2005 contend that EDS wasn't always frustrating. "I loved the EDS I worked at 17 years ago," says one source who started there in the late 1980s, a time when the company was still experiencing growth spurred by big government IT contracts, though he concludes, "I hated the EDS I retired from." Another employee who left the company in 2005 agrees, claiming, "EDS changed radically over the 16 years I worked there."

A favorable balance

Work/life balance seems to offset frustration and anxiety among EDS insiders. One source says "the company is outstanding [regarding] flex time, telecommuting" and other ways to ease hours. An insider reports that "I've been with EDS for over two years. The company has been good to me and provided a flexible work environment for me and my family, especially during the birth of our child." This consultant lauds EDS's two-week paid paternity leave "that was invaluable for us to spend quality time during the hardest first two weeks."

"It just depends"

EDS employees don't seem overburdened by travel demands. One source says that "travel is hit-or-miss: Some people never travel and others are always gone. It just depends on the job requirements." Work hours, also, seem to vary in intensity based on one's position in the firm. Technicians "in the field work a typical 40 to 45 hours a week," a consultant says, though, unsurprisingly, managers and others work "much longer hours." A more senior source clocks in "50 to 55" hours a week, and adds that his hours have piled up because there are "not enough people to do all the work" due to layoffs, and "those that remain are stressed from overwork because the workload has not decreased. Senior management needs to turn away clients or increase staff, but not to keep selling while reducing headcount."

No "clear path"

EDS says it has "developed processes and tools that empower you to develop your potential and accelerate your career," including a "self-directed career planning process, mentoring program and Global Learning and Development." But insiders say that this training is spotty and that the firm doesn't support certain of its own training initiatives. "EDS requires a lot of annual training," an insider says, "but they don't relieve work responsibilities to complete training. They also don't usually pay for the more expensive classes and conferences that would be most helpful."

Sources are generally down on the promotion policy at EDS. They report that the policy for advancement at EDS is not defined or consistently executed and that promotion seems to rely too often on politics. In short, one source reports, "there does not seem to be a clear path upward." One asserts that opportunities for advancement at EDS "do exist but they are not plentiful. It can be very difficult to advance without rubbing shoulders with the right people," and adds that the company "does not give raises for promotions, regardless of the responsibility increase; everything is considered a lateral move." As another puts it, the firm "does not have accurate mechanisms to track or recognize employee performance...it does not match cost to value. It only tracks cost." Another source says that "management is very redundant;

some positions will have as many as four direct managers. The manager that does your evaluations may or may not reside in the same county as you." To sum it up, one long-time employee describes EDS as a company that "went from a place of great advancement to a place of people running scared wondering if they would have jobs tomorrow; salaries were frozen, bonuses (even for management) became non-existent."

Better benefits

Despite its problems, insiders note, EDS is not a bad company to work for, "if you negotiate properly coming in." Another says that "despite its flaws, it treated me reasonably well, and I believe was no worse nor better than any other company of its size." In the last few years, though bonuses and raises have been "intermittent…and small" and sources describe benefits as standard until you get into senior management positions.

Committed to diversity

Sources readily acknowledge EDS's commitment to diversity. The "workforce is extremely diverse along race and gender lines," says one insider and another source calls EDS a "very diverse employer." EDS reports that it supports dozens of groups dedicated to diversity, both in and outside of the company. These include national and international professional associations for minorities and women, as well as groups formed by EDS employees, such as Women @ EDS and the Hispanic Employee Resource Organization.

But some insiders believe that the way the company promotes its workers means that advancement for some groups is limited. "An immense talent pool resides at EDS," a source reports, "but white males beget more white males. The leadership must promote outside their comfort zone or nothing will change."

Getting involved

Employees seem proud that EDS gets involved in many community activities and charitable causes. "EDS is very involved in highly visible events like the EDS Byron Nelson golf tournament," one source says, and another recalls the "online pledging system" that EDS developed in response to Hurricane Katrina and adds that the firm "began the program by donating $100,000 to the Red Cross." However, one source worries that the company is "starting to cut back on community events that are important but not as visible."

Corporate Headquarters
Unisys Way
Blue Bell, PA 19424
Phone: (215) 986-4011
www.unisys.com

LOCATIONS

Blue Bell, PA (HQ)
Offices in more than 50 countries

PRACTICE AREAS

Consulting
Infrastructure
Outsourcing
Server technology
Systems integration

THE STATS

Employer Type: Public Company
Ticker Symbol: UIS (NYSE)
Chairman: Henry C. Duques
President and CEO: Joseph W. McGrath
2005 Employees: 36,000
2004 Employees: 36,400
2005 Revenues: $5.76 billion
2004 Revenues: $5.82 billion

UPPERS

- "You'll learn a lot"
- "Hands-off" managers
- "Reasonable" travel

DOWNERS

- Slow hiring process
- Skimpy raises
- "Disjointed" culture

EMPLOYMENT CONTACT

www.unisys.com/about_unisys/
careers/index.htm

THE BUZZ
WHAT CONSULTANTS AT OTHER FIRMS ARE SAYING

- "Good integrators and consultants"
- "Good commodity support outfit"
- "Notorious *Washington Post* headliner"
- "Revenue before client value"

THE SCOOP

From typewriters to high tech

Unisys was officially founded in 1986—but its tech roots go back much farther than that. The Blue Bell, Pa.-based firm can trace its family tree back to the 1870s, when Remington Rand produced the first commercially viable typewriter. The company introduced the first commercial business computer, UNIVAC 1, in 1951, and went through a merger in 1955 to become Sperry Rand Corp. Sperry was acquired by mainframe computer giant Burroughs in 1986, forming the Unisys we know today.

The firm carried on its legacy of groundbreaking computer inventions. In 1988, Unisys acquired Convergent Technologies and its proprietary Convergent Technologies Operating System (CTOS). In 1989 Unisys developed Micro-A, the first single-chip desktop mainframe, and in 1993 the 2200/500 mainframe, the first mainframe based on CMOS (complementary metal oxide semiconductor) technology. From there it began to specialize in services and solutions, developing complex technologies like ClearPath Heterogeneous Multi-Processing (allowing applications and databases to run with UnixWare and Windows NT applications and databases on a single platform) and Cellular Multi-Processing, which can handle up to 32 processors at once. To date, the firm owns more than 2,600 technology patents.

A "disappointing" stretch

From a financial perspective, the formation of Unisys didn't exactly go smoothly. Many observers labeled the merger that formed the firm disastrous, blaming a "botched integration process" which caused customers to flee—many to IBM— according to a March 2004 *Financial Times* article. Larry Weinbach, former chief of Andersen Consulting, was brought on board to calm the waters in 1997. He initiated a restructuring plan that directed the company's focus toward consulting and outsourcing, which represented about 80 percent of the company's resources by 2004. The plan helped stanch the bleeding somewhat: 2003 revenues rose by 5 percent to $5.9 billion. But for fiscal year 2004, Unisys reported net income of $38.6 million, a dizzying decline from its 2003 income of $258.7 million, and revenues came in nearly flat at $5.82 billion, and continued on that plane with $5.76 billion in 2005. Admitting that the firm had a "disappointing year," execs pointed to weaker-than-expected demand in the technology business and an asset write-off charge associated with a weakened outsourcing business.

In January 2005, Unisys got a new CEO, Joseph W. McGrath, who formerly served as president and chief operating officer at the company. McGrath, retaining his president's title, joined the firm in 1999 from Xerox. The new CEO faced ever-greater challenges toward the middle of 2005. By the third quarter, Unisys had posted a $54.3 million loss, and announced plans to lay off 10 percent of its staff, roughly 3,500 people. In October 2005, the firm fell out of favor with Wall Street when it was revealed that government auditors were investigating possible overbilling on a contract with the Transportation Safety Administration. But Unisys and analysts covering the company said such scrutiny by the feds wasn't unusual and was certainly no indication of wrongdoing on the company's part. In any case, the firm found its stock at a 14-year low.

Focus, people!

Shortly thereafter, the firm announced plans aimed at refreshing both its image and finances. Acknowledging a lack of focus in the business, Unisys execs declared a new strategy—"visibility." Part of this strategy centers around the firm's concept of a "3D Visible Enterprise," a way of depicting clients' businesses, as well as their business decisions, "to give clients true visibility into their business and IT operations, so they can see the critical linkages and results of business decisions even before they make them."

The firm also reiterated plans to focus on five key areas: enterprise security, open source software, outsourcing, infrastructure and Microsoft enterprise software. In addition, the firm said, it would focus on its top 500 accounts worldwide, making up around 85 percent of Unisys' sales. To cut costs, the firm planned to further develop its use of global sourcing, turning to operations in India, China and Eastern Europe to deliver services where possible. Unisys has also pursued an aggressive approach to boost its hiring of experienced sales and marketing people, hiring top sellers from fellow IT companies.

Cozy with Microsoft

The strategy also involves firming up alliances with tech partners including Microsoft, IBM, Oracle and Intel. Microsoft remains a key player in the Unisys business plan, and this relationship was strengthened in November 2005 with the announcement of the formation of a new business unit focused exclusively on implementing Microsoft products. The firm said it planned to staff the unit with around 2,500 consultants. In July 2005, the firm won Microsoft's Winning Customer

Award for outstanding competitive efforts in the High Performance Computing category. The award recognized a database, based on the Microsoft platform, which helps leading Dutch banks manage their payments products for greater efficiencies.

With IBM, the firm has worked to identify verification technologies and IT solutions for insurers and the U.S. Department of Health and Human Services. Unisys has also teamed up with Oracle on tech solutions for financial services and government agencies, and with Intel on automating government services. Additionally, Unisys announced a partnership with NEC Corporation in October 2005, in which the firms will collaborate on technology research and development, manufacturing and solutions delivery.

Open to open source

Unusually for a top tech services firm, Unisys remains an ardent champion of open source technology. Peter Blackmore, a former HP bigwig who now heads global sales for Unisys, said in November 2005 that open source is a "mature technology," with Linux "really in demand" by powerful clients. These clients, Blackmore explained, include a "major European travel business" considering the adoption of open source in a large server environment. Of course, the firm's dedication to open source, along with its loyalties to powerful tech buddy Microsoft, requires some diplomacy. As Blackmore told ZDNet News at the time, "The combination of Microsoft Windows on the desktop and open-source software on the server can be the most successful strategy for the company."

Services provided by Unisys include enterprise transformation, infrastructure, outsourcing and security, as well as business services such as enterprise transformation, global commerce, customer relationship management, supply chain management, imaging and workflow, systems integration and software translation. The firm organizes its services around six industry sectors: public sector, financial services, communications, transportation, commercial and media.

Citizen services

Unisys provides services to more than 1,500 public sector clients worldwide, including the U.S. federal government and 45 of 50 U.S. state governments. Overseas government engagements have included developing smart cards for the citizens of Malaysia and establishing a command and control communications system for the London Metropolitan Police. Closer to home, Unisys federal clients include the

Department of Agriculture, the Medicaid program and the Transportation Security Administration.

The Department of Health and Human Services gave Unisys a healthy boost in November 2005, awarding the firm a contract worth at least $65 million to standardize computer operations at each of the department's eight locations. Under another contract awarded in September 2005 and worth up to $96 million, Unisys is deploying and operating a next-generation federal inmate telephone system for the U.S. Federal Bureau of Prisons. Unisys was granted a contract in June 2005 to help provide the U.S. Navy's Military Sealift Command with support for certain applications, including a payroll system and service history program. And in February 2005, the firm was tapped to help I.D. Systems, Inc., implement a new wireless tracking system for U.S. Postal Service vehicles using RFID technology.

On the local level, the firm was picked in June 2005 to provide a comprehensive case management solution for the State of California's Department of Industrial Relations, including both application software and professional services. Under a contract inked with the State of Virginia in February 2005, Unisys is implementing a new election and registration information system in a contract worth up to $6.1 million. And in the same month, NYC Transit, which operates the Big Apple's subway and bus services, chose the firm to provide desktop support services for the agency in a deal worth up to $143 million.

Cashing in

In the financial sector, Unisys clients include 22 of the world's top 25 banks, eight of 10 top global life and pension insurers, and five out of 10 property and casualty insurers. In fact, a major source of Unisys outsourcing revenue is check processing; around 50 percent of all the checks written worldwide are processed on Unisys systems. For the Bank of China in Hong Kong, Unisys was awarded a contract in June 2005 to build a new voucher imaging system to help the bank manage its document processing. The firm also signed a multi-year deal in April 2005 to provide IT outsourcing services to Capital One Financial Corporation. In February 2005, the Blue Cross Blue Shield Association signed a three-year national contract with Unisys to offer outsourcing services for claims administration.

Taking flight

Unisys also is well-traveled in the transportation industry—21 of the top 25 airlines and more than 600 airports worldwide use Unisys solutions. The company has jumped on board the e-travel bandwagon, teaming with Lufthansa Systems to offer the Airline Availability Manager solution, which manages and displays open seats available for sale on any flight at a reduced transaction cost to the airline. A major travel client, China's Guangzhou Baiyun International Airport, was named a Laureate for the 21st Century Achievement Award as part of IDG's Computerworld Honors program in 2005. The award recognizes the airport's successful implementation of operation and management systems, which handle 25 million passengers per year.

Another big travel coup came in July 2005, when the firm was awarded a contract to develop and integrate the core operational systems for Beijing's new international terminal, being built in preparation for the 2008 Olympic Games. The new terminal, part of the most advanced international airport hub in China, will double the airport's capacity to 60 million passengers, making way for the hordes expected to arrive for the 2008 summer games. In April 2005, TAM, Brazil's largest global airline, tapped Unisys to provide IT infrastructure outsourcing services. And in August 2005, the firm was selected by Air Berlin, Europe's third-largest low-cost airline, to implement its Unisys Customer Loyalty Solution to retain and attract customers.

Outsourcing heats up

In April 2004, Unisys said it planned to invest around $180 million in India, including a new, state-of-the-art facility in Bangalore. And in March 2005, the firm announced that it planned to employ around 2,000 staffers in India by the end of the year, with its Indian headcount expected to double again in the following two to three years to meet demand. Such expansion and expenditures seem justified, as outsourcing contracts keep rolling in for the firm. In November 2005, Rabobank, the largest Dutch financial services provider, extended its business process outsourcing contract with Unisys subsidiary Unisys Payment Services and Solutions (UPSS) for an additional two years. The firm scored an outsourcing contract in September 2005 to manage the IT infrastructure for ECOPETROL, Colombia's state-owned oil company.

On the radio

Unisys also has made its presence known in the radio frequency identification (RFID) arena. The firm has provided the Department of Defense with RFID support and services for more than a decade, using the technology to track military assets such as equipment and repair parts. Unisys has partnered with RFID firm ODIN Technologies on an RFID contract awarded in July 2005 by the Department of

Defense. The contract calls for Unisys and its partners to connect the Defense Logistics Agency and its suppliers using RFID. In June 2005, Unisys and ODIN were picked to maintain the RFID network and infrastructure for Thomasville Furniture Industries' Creative Interiors Division. Unisys will serve as the main point of contact for all RFID service requests for the furniture giant.

The sporting life

Unisys enjoys a firm presence in the sports world, serving as the official scorer for the USGA's U.S. Open Golf Championship, as well as the Royal and Ancient's Open Golf Championship. In fact, Unisys lays claim to being the first to offer real-time golf scores online. In 2005, the firm provided results information services to more than 100 individual sporting events worldwide, including golf and motor sports.

GETTING HIRED

Lengthy discourse

During the interview process, a consultant says, "I was asked to discuss my experience, understanding of technology in [the] project, and leadership style." Another insider describes the process of landing a Unisys job: "I was interviewed by a 360 degree set of folks. My immediate boss, his bosses, two peers, two partners from other groups and a couple of senior folks who could have ended up reporting to me. It took forever. Making yourself available early in the morning and late in the day (e.g., 7 p.m.) will really expedite the process."

Patience is a virtue

In fact, taking "forever" is a pretty common phenomenon when it comes to the Unisys hiring process, insiders suggest. "It's a shame it took five months to get approval to be hired," one source gripes, adding that "HR over-analyzes and under-hires." Another source advises that "no one should give up just because they think Unisys is not interested. A lot just falls through the cracks." "The hiring process was surprisingly well-done, with the exception of the ridiculous amount of time it took for the decisions to be made," another source chimes in. Finally, a source's words of wisdom: "Go for the best package you can in the negotiations. Don't expect much in the way of raises until you get a promotion."

Real world Unisys

For students, the company offers "real world" experiences through its intern and co-op programs. These paid opportunities, offered to "undergraduate and graduate students with outstanding academic records, excellent communication skills and leadership capabilities," are available part-time and year-round. Student employees get a Career Portfolio from Unisys University containing personal development and training information. Users can access their courses and performance objectives through the system. These objectives, developed with the student's manager, help outline roles and responsibilities; when the employment period is up, students get a chance to go over them with their supervisor. In some locations, students can access subsidized housing through the firm, as well as networking events.

OUR SURVEY SAYS

Searching for culture

Unisys' corporate culture, a source reports, is "excellent in general," though there are "some challenges from time to time and during recent restructuring." Another insider reports that "In the newer services units, we are still searching for a 'culture.'" There are some naysayers out there, though. The firm's culture, grumbles one source, is "extremely disjointed. A few players are involved in key projects. The rest become lackeys." "Unisys is going through yet another evolution in trying to find itself. While there are a lot of good, smart people that work at Unisys, there are not enough of us. Management wants to grow the company, but refuses to pay for that growth," a source complains.

But one insider likes the way things get done at Unisys, noting that, thanks to the firm's dedication to documentation, "you'll learn a lot." The source adds, "I know it may not sound like much, but I have worked at companies that do a terrible job of documentation. In those places, the lack of documentation allows a few selfish people to keep knowledge away from everyone else by hiding the documentation CDs or installing the documentation in some off-the-beaten-path location only they can access."

No red eyes

Travel at Unisys is described by one source as "reasonable for [the] work involved." One insider appreciates that "I can travel on work time, if necessary. I don't need to catch red eye flights." Back at home base, however, a colleague gripes that it's a "miserable warehouse cubicle environment" with "no windows anywhere." Luckily, another insider reports, "Flexible hours and working from home is not an issue, as long as the work is done." The firm notes that it employs a growing virtual workforce and expects that practice to increase.

Take charge

At least one consultant at Unisys describes supervisors as having a "hands-off style." This approach may be a bit too removed sometimes, insiders suggest, as training is seen as "very casual" and "disorganized." But another source says the firm works best for those who are willing to take charge of their own careers: "Unisys has a culture of allowing people to progress and has a good practice of employing from within when it meets business requirements. Individuals have to take charge of their development planning...Unisys provides a separate part of HR called Unisys University which supports managers and personnel training, personal development and skills maintenance. Unisys has a culture of backing the innovator, so people are allowed the opportunity to justify a business opportunity and get help to succeed or fail. Failing is considered a learning process but accepted as the norm."

Though Unisys gets decent marks for its treatment of women in the workplace, an insider comments that there's "almost no promotion from within," noting that "women execs are brought in from the outside. I'd like to see at least one internal success story. Women have to leave to get promoted." The firm contends with this assertion, however, claiming that several positions on the senior team at Unisys are currently filled by female executives who have been promoted from within.

Slow growth

Some Unisys insiders grumble about the firm's compensation, with annual raises of about "2 to 4 percent" since the late 1990s. As a source puts it, "if your aim is exciting and exponential growth, don't work for Unisys. Even when the company was making money in 2000 to 2003, the management gave no bonuses or raises. Now that the company is losing money, the prospect of getting a raise is nil." Benefits are described as "average for corporate America, poor for an IT consulting shop."

"Unisys has a culture of allowing people to progress and has a good practice of employing from within when it meets business requirements."

— *Unisys consultant*

Visit the Vault Consulting Career Channel at **www.vault.com/consulting** — with
insider firm profiles, message boards, the Vault Consulting Job Board and more.

VAULT CAREER LIBRARY   **159**

Sapient

25 First Street
Cambridge, MA 02141
Phone: (617) 621-0200
Fax: (617) 621-1300
www.sapient.com

LOCATIONS

Cambridge, MA (HQ)
16 offices throughout North
America, Europe and Asia

PRACTICE AREAS

Application Outsourcing
Application design & development •
Application management •
Outsourcing services • Sourcing
strategy • QA & testing

Business Applications
Custom applications • Customer
relationship solutions • Enterprise
resource planning • Package
solutions • Supply chain • Web
solutions

Business Intelligence
Data warehousing • SAP Business
Intelligence solutions • Research &
analytics

Business & IT Strategy
Business applications & enterprise
architecture planning • Business-
process consulting • E-business &
Web strategy • IT governance &
advisory services • Marketing
strategy • Multichannel strategy

Marketing Services
Experience marketing • Interactive
agency of record • Web solutions

THE BUZZ
WHAT CONSULTANTS AT OTHER FIRMS ARE SAYING

- "Smart, agile, hot"
- "Impressive turnaround"
- "Work better as a team"
- "They work their people to death"

THE STATS

Employer Type: Public Company
Ticker Symbol: SAPE (Nasdaq)
CEOs: J. Stuart Moore and Jerry A.
Greenberg
2005 Employees: 3,017
2004 Employees: 2,300
2005 Revenues: $319.5 million
2004 Revenues: $253.9 million

UPPERS

- Open, feedback-friendly culture
- Rapid advancement
- Strong adherence to "core values"

DOWNERS

- Work hours have a tendency to
  spike
- Hard to find time to train
- Heavy travel is a given

EMPLOYMENT CONTACT

www.sapient.com/careers/career.htm

THE SCOOP

Tech know-how

Sapient's name suggests wisdom, so it's appropriate that the company is headquartered in the intellectual haven of Cambridge, Mass. The brainy firm's location is no accident—co-founder Jerry Greenberg is a Harvard grad with an economics degree, while his co-CEO, J. Stuart Moore, boasts a computer science degree from Berkeley. The firm has offices throughout the United States as well as in Canada, Germany, India and the UK.

Founded in 1990, Sapient has seen its fortunes rise and fall—and rise again—reflecting the overall trends in the tech market. The firm had to cut staff in 2001 to keep up with lagging revenues, and posted operating losses in 2003. But by 2004, Sapient was back on track, with a headcount of 2,600, up from 1,500 the previous year. Revenues for fiscal year 2004 were $253.9 million, up a whopping 37 percent from 2003, and the company managed to recover from its earlier operating losses. The news got even better in 2005, as revenues jumped 26 percent to $319.5 million. The firm continued to build and maintain strong relationships with clients worldwide, including Avis Europe, BP, Cinergy, Cingular, Enbridge Gas Distribution, Essent Energie, Royal Bank of Scotland, Royal Mail, Scotiabank and Vodafone.

An impressive comeback

How did the tech firm manage such an aggressive comeback? In a May 2005 article, Forrester analyst Stephanie Moore applauded Sapient's ability to reinvent itself, most notably as a player in the offshoring and outsourcing game. Commenting on Sapient's quiet entry into the outsourcing arena, Moore noted that the company discreetly marketed these services to existing clients at a time when outsourcing was "still not considered hip or particularly hot." These days, the firm employs more than 1,350 staffers in India and, according to Moore, maintains a consistent culture across the ocean, with Sapient India serving as "truly an extension of Sapient Cambridge."

Indian innovation

In fact, the Indian press has hailed the firm's presence in the area. According to an article in *The Times of India* in August 2004, the firm endears itself to employees by offering unconventional incentives to boost productivity and reward hard work. In a "silent auction," for instance, senior staffers offer their services for auction, with the more "wacky" services standing the best chance of being accepted. For example, said a Sapient India insider, "a VP offers to be a slave for a whole day to a particular team that wins the bid. Or a director promises to cook omelets for the team that bids the highest. All the proceeds go to a nonprofit organization."

Sapient further differentiates itself from outsourcing competitors in the types of jobs it takes on overseas. The firm shies away from the rock-bottom deals like mainframe maintenance and staff augmentation that boost other tech firms' offshore portfolios. Instead, as Forrester's Moore noted, Sapient sticks to its core competencies both in India and elsewhere, offering high-end application development services that lead to longer-term relationships with clients. These long-term engagements are key to Sapient's revenue rebound.

Widespread clients

The firm serves a broad range of clients in the U.S. and overseas in automotive and industrial, education, energy services, financial services, government, health care, retail and consumer products, technology and communications, and travel and hospitality. Sapient organizes its service offerings around three categories: planning, creating, and management and outsourcing. Within those categories, the firm offers a host of services including business and IT planning, business intelligence and application management.

Getting in on intelligent design

In June 2005, Sapient announced its acquisition of Business Information Solutions, LLC, a provider of SAP-related professional services specializing in business intelligence solutions. Making an effort to capitalize on the growing market for SAP solutions, Sapient is hoping that the BIS acquisition will build on its existing business intelligence capabilities and extend its outsourcing services to include the management of SAP applications. Commenting on the acquisition, Sapient executive vice president Alan Herrick stated, "The opportunity in the SAP services market is growing rapidly as many large organizations seek to improve competitive advantage by leveraging their SAP investments." Currently, Sapient provides business intelligence solutions to a range of clients, including Edssent Energy—a leading European gas and power utility company—Opodo and the U.S. Marine Corps.

Getting creative

In late 2005, Sapient announced its intention to lend its IT savvy to the rapidly growing Internet advertising arena. In January 2006, the firm grew the marketing component of its business with its purchase of Miami, Fla.-based Planning Group International (PGI), a well-regarded marketing agency specializing in online, offline and multi-channel marketing strategies and programs. PGI's client list includes heavy hitters like Burger King, Citigroup and Celebrity Cruise Lines. With the acquisition, Sapient formed a new business unit, Experience Marketing, offering advertising, brand development, direct marketing, data mining, paid search, and media planning and buying. The unit is led by former PGI chief Gaston Legorburu, who has been appointed a senior VP with Sapient. The acquisition isn't the first time Sapient has made a splash in the marketing world: In late 2005, the firm announced that it helped Goodby, Silverstein & Partners, the ad agency for auto company Saturn, to deliver a "rich consumer experience" for Saturn's web site visitors.

Results-oriented

Sapient specializes in hands-on engagements designed to get results. In late 2005, Sapient was awarded a six-and-a-half-year contract to manage the offshore software development capabilities of Vertex Financial Services, a leading UK outsourcing provider. The contract extended the firm's three-year relationship with Vertex, during which Sapient has completed projects such as developing a new billing solution supporting more than 3.5 million customers. Sapient said it planned to open an office near Vertex headquarters in Cheltenham, UK.

In June 2005, shipping company DHL tapped Sapient to design a new and improved web site to help customers simplify the shipping process. According to an article in *BtoB* magazine, page views doubled in the first few weeks after the site was relaunched, and DHL reported a 30 to 35 percent increase in online scheduling. The firm was tapped in December 2004 by energy giant BP to develop a global Internet platform designed to help the client integrate standards and technologies among its more than 200 web sites. Sapient helped to deliver an updated Web interface, navigational structure and technology architecture standards serving all of BP's business lines worldwide. And in September of that year, the firm helped the Department of the Navy eBusiness Operations Office develop the Joint Expeditionary Warfare Logistics System, an integrated logistics decision support and execution system that allows the Marines, Naval Construction Forces and other expeditionary naval units to access shared information across geographies. The system was honored with the Intergovernmental Solutions Award, recognizing innovative technology solutions that provide intergovernmental collaboration and show measurable results.

Redesigning health care

Sapient also has carved a niche for itself in the health care market. In May 2004, the firm won a deal valued at up to $1.8 billion to help plan, design and implement a 10-year project to build an electronic patient records system for the city of London, connecting more than 30,000 doctors and 270 acute, community and mental health NHS Trusts in a single national, secure system. Described as the world's largest civilian contract of its kind in the world, the project makes up a hefty chunk of Sapient's revenues in the UK. High-profile health care projects closer to home include engagements with the University of Chicago Hospitals and the State of California's Office of the Patient Advocate.

At home in higher ed

Sapient maintains strong ties to the education sector, helping to integrate cutting-edge IT with academics. The firm was honored in 2004, along with the Massachusetts Institute of Technology, with the *Computerworld* 21st Century Achievement Award in Education and Academia for its work on MIT's OpenCourseWare application. The firm also has completed engagements for Harvard, such as the development of MyCourses, a multi-channel course management system for students and faculty at Harvard Medical School.

New money man

In December 2004, Sapient got a new chief financial officer, Scott Krenz, who formerly served as corporate vice president and treasurer at EDS. Susan D. Cooke, who previously served as Sapient's CFO, remained at the company as senior vice president. In September 2004, design and software pioneer Clement Mok was promoted to the position of global director of design planning for the firm, leading Sapient's digital marketing and Web design services.

Consulting kudos

In both 2004 and 2005, the firm was ranked among the 10 Best Firms to Work For in *Consulting Magazine*'s annual survey. The firm got further kudos in 2005 when it was named Career Champion by the publication, which noted Sapient's commitment to career development, employee feedback and openness. German magazine *Capital* ranked the firm No. 9 among its list of Germany's best employers for 2005, and *Consulting Magazine* honored Sapient co-CEO Jerry Greenberg as one of the Top 25 Most Influential Consultants in 2005. And in 2004, Sony Electronics honored the firm as Partner of the Year for its work on the electronics giant's e-business initiatives, including online sales and merchandising.

GETTING HIRED

Getting savvy with Sapient

Sapient's online hiring information is limited, though the firm does offer a comprehensive search engine for locating and applying to jobs. Sapient's hiring process, in the words of one source, is "quite intensive." As the source describes it, "We have five rounds of brainstorming. The first round begins with two questions that are business problems and need to be coded. After that a review happens, which is a technical review. Subsequently, we have rounds which are more personality tests and are meant to show if the candidate is good enough to fit into the company's culture."

Another insider supports this explanation, noting that there are "three interviews: one for core values/culture fit; one case study, based on domain and position; [and] one 'strategic context' interview that checks alignment with Sapient's purpose." The source adds that "three interviewers have yes/no decision rights."

Sapient Saturday

Sapient reportedly recruits from "top engineering" schools such as MIT, as well as "top regional" universities. A consultant who was recruited from a campus event describes the experience: "[The] second and final round was at an office for a Super Saturday event. Twenty-two people were in the Santa Monica event, representing four schools. Check-in to the hotel started at 9 a.m. where we met some Sapient people. After that, we went to the office where there were presentations by workers and CEO Jerry Greenberg. This was followed by an interview, which was all behavioral, and a group exercise where we made a presentation in front of a few Sapient people."

Likeability is key

A colleague adds that "there were no difficult questions, no case interviews and [it] was mostly a day of socializing and interacting with employees...it seems like they judge you mostly on your likeability rather than your actual potential abilities as a consultant." But other insiders suggest that there are case questions in some instances, though these are "protected and no examples should be published"—so you're on your own.

OUR SURVEY SAYS

Dedicated to the culture

Sapient's culture is described as "very strong"—in fact, it's "the most important thing here," says a source. Numerous insiders concur: According to one, Sapient's "very strong culture [is] what has kept me here for my 10-plus years. The dedication of the firm to the culture is palpable and evidenced from the CEOs down to new hires."

At the same time, another consultant says, "The culture can be intense—fixed time [and] fixed price requires that. People work hard and have fun doing it, though." It's a "very fast-paced, collaborative culture. People are great to work with and share similar beliefs to the core values," agrees an insider. As for work/life balance, a consultant says, the concept of a "'Well Balanced Life'" is something that the company has tried to pay some homage to, but hasn't done an extremely good job at. WBL comes from the individuals and the teams. Individual account leads and directors pay more attention than others. It's hit or miss."

Spiky hours

Hours tend to range from 45 to 55 per week, sources suggest, but those in the upper echelons can put in some heavy weeks. One director says, "For me, [workload] doesn't really spike, given that 80 to 90 hours a week is normal. For an average employee, they should expect a spike (from 50 hours to 60 or 70 hours) once every three months or so." As for travel, an insider reports, "The 'expected' travel is three nights and four days away, with the fifth day in the office. The reality is that one does what's right for the client, which is often five (or seven) days on the road at a time."

Open lines

An insider praises the fact that Sapient's culture is "very open," with "no sense that you work 'for' any particular manager," and "CEOs are very easy to talk to [and] encourage open, honest feedback." In fact, the insider reports, "Feedback is huge at the company—people are always asking for it and employees give it very freely." As another source puts it, "We have a great open culture where you can voice your opinions and grow in a direction that suits your growth plans; [it's] not a set up-or-out consulting mentality."

This openness is a boon to those who want to get ahead at Sapient, a consultant says. "Opportunities for advancement totally depend on how you perform in your team...There is a feedback process and you can ask for feedback at any point in time, so you can correct your approach immediately." "People tend to advance rapidly; success is definitely recognized—and frequently," another insider says, noting that there's "no real 'glass ceiling' where people's careers tend to stagnate." Agrees a source, "Do well and you will be advanced automatically, as managers are responsible for people's growth." "Sapient has quarterly reviews for promotions for associates and semi-annually for senior associates, which gives you a chance to prove yourself and get promoted in a quarter," a consultant chimes in.

Sapient consultants enjoy a "potential 15 percent annual bonus," plus "semi-annual stock option grants." Staffers also get "two weeks vacation plus holidays; company subsidized coffee and an onsite gym," a source tells us. In addition, says an insider, "there are some discount policies on food courts and cafe joints." But a source grumbles that "compared with other consulting firms in the space, Sapient underpays." Training is described as "good," but a consultant frets that it's hard to "get time out of the schedule to pursue [training] due to stringent deadlines of project work."

DiamondCluster
International Inc.

John Hancock Center
875 North Michigan Avenue
Suite 3000
Chicago, IL 60611
Phone: (312) 255-5000
Fax: (312) 255-6000
www.diamondcluster.com

LOCATIONS

Chicago, IL (HQ)
11 offices worldwide

PRACTICE AREAS

Growth
Market Penetration • New
Business Development • New
Growth
Operations Improvement
Execution Excellence • Operations
Strategy • Profit Improvement •
Turnaround Management
Technology
Architecture Assessment and
Strategy • IT Assessment and
Strategy • IT Portfolio Assessment
and Strategy • Outsourcing
Advisory • Security Assessment
and Strategy • Technology
Program Management

THE STATS

Employer Type: Public Company
Ticker Symbol: DTPI (Nasdaq)
Chairman: Mel E. Bergstein
CEO: Adam J. Gutstein
FY 2005 Employees: 751
FY 2004 Employees: 652
FY 2005 Revenues: $193.2 million
FY 2004 Revenues: $154.8 million

UPPERS

• "Small and close-knit firm"
• "Flat team structure"
• "Academic atmosphere"

DOWNERS

• "Competition within the firm is
fierce to get ahead"
• "Consultants are asked to do a lot
more than at some larger firms"
• "Not enough focus on developing
people-management skills"

EMPLOYMENT CONTACT

www.diamondcluster.com/careers

THE BUZZ
WHAT CONSULTANTS AT OTHER FIRMS ARE SAYING

• "Smart people"
• "Strategic, partnering"
• "Overrated"
• "High priced"

THE SCOOP

Taking a shine to IT

With a total headcount of around 750, DiamondCluster International doesn't stand out for its imposing size. But over the past few years, the firm has managed to develop a sparkling reputation for its marriage of strategy and technology consulting. The firm, based in Chicago, was formed in 1994 as Diamond Technology Partners. In November 2000, after a $930 million merger between Diamond Technology Partners and Barcelona-based Cluster Consulting, the firm was renamed DiamondCluster International.

DiamondCluster serves clients in 10 sectors: consumer packaged goods; financial services; insurance; health care; logistics; manufacturing; public sector; retail and distribution; telecommunications; and utilities. The firm divides its services into three categories—growth, operations improvement and technology—though most of DiamondCluster's engagements incorporate IT in some manner.

An industry indicator

A public company, DiamondCluster is being hailed as a recovery story in the consulting and IT sectors. As the tech services industry began its slow recovery from the economic downturn of the late 1990s and early 2000s, observers began looking to DiamondCluster as a "leading indicator" of the industry's progress. Indeed, the firm suffered from an attrition of revenue in 2002 following a couple of boom years. And if a soft market wasn't bad enough, the firm was plagued by other problems, including overstaffing, residual difficulties integrating Cluster personnel, poor implementation of the firm's strategy practice, and problems with closing a number of important deals. By early 2001, the firm was forced to reduce pay across the board by 10 percent (execs gave up an additional 5 percent), and bonuses vanished, as well. Between March 2002 and March 2003, the firm had reduced its consultant count by more than 36 percent. To further rein in costs, the firm also had to fold its highly regarded journal *Context* in December 2002.

A corporate facelift

DiamondCluster also responded to the situation by undertaking a comprehensive re-branding project. Before the recession, the firm had established a reputation in North America as a niche, Internet-based business with "killer apps." With the burst of the dot-com bubble, industry analysts and the market at large assumed that the firm had fallen out of favor. In November 2002, the firm embarked upon an "archaeological dig," as the firm referred to it, to "rediscover the essence of the firm," and to clarify its direction and unify its message to employees, investors, clients and future business prospects. One of the firm's main goals in taking on the initiative was to avoid being pigeonholed as strictly e-business consultants or traditional systems integrators. Rather, DiamondCluster wanted to attract new clients on the basis of it being a consulting firm that works on "key issues that exist at the intersection of business and technology."

Toughing it out

CEO Mel Bergstein kept a stiff upper lip through the downturn, going for six months without pay himself and pushing "everything out that was not people-related," as he explained in an August 2004 interview with *Consulting Magazine*. Bergstein also reportedly passed out buttons that read "No Whining" to DiamondCluster's remaining staff. The firm essentially "flattened" its structure, placing its most senior staffers in client-facing roles, and reducing the size and number of its committees. Things began looking up as the company reached the end of fiscal 2004 with revenues of $154.8 million, up 16 percent compared to the previous year. Though it still posted a loss of $5.4 million, this was a stunning improvement over the previous fiscal year's $360.1 million loss. Reporting to investors in April 2004, Bergstein stated, "Our business began its turnaround exactly one year ago, and since then utilization has returned to target levels, pricing has improved, our business has returned to profitability, and we have begun hiring again." The industry has taken notice of the turnaround: The Global IT Services Report noted that the firm's strong growth was a good sign for tech consulting as a whole.

Expanding...

While fiscal year 2005 brought signs of recovery to DiamondCluster, it also saw more scaling back. First, the good news: The firm increased its number of first-time clients in 2005 by 41 percent over the previous year. And DiamondCluster raked in $193.2 million in revenues in 2005, up 25 percent from 2004. The North American segment of the business shone, bringing in 73 percent of net revenues during the fourth quarter of the year. The firm also continued to expand, setting up an office in Dubai, designed to serve as a base for serving fixed and wireless telecom clients in the Middle East, with several projects already underway. The firm also opened its first office in India in February 2006.

... and contracting

But in September 2005, the firm announced a restructuring plan in Europe designed to boost profits. The plan included the shuttering of DiamondCluster's offices in Düsseldorf and Lisbon, as well as a downsizing of the Barcelona office. These cuts were expected to reduce the firm's global headcount by 6 percent, but no cuts were planned for North America or the UK. The restructuring was expected to cost the firm $8 million to $9 million during the quarter, but save up to $8 million annually. The plan wasn't all about cutbacks: DiamondCluster also announced that it would be expanding its strategic technology-oriented consulting services to key markets in Germany and the Middle East, with the aim of creating a truly "global" consulting practice.

Change at the top

Effective April 1, 2006, Mel Bergstein stepped down from his position as CEO and was replaced by Adam Gutstein, age 42, who has served as the firm's president since June 2004. Upon Gutstein's donning of the CEO mantle, Jay Norman, currently managing director of the North American and UK practice, took over his role as president and chief operating officer. Gutstein comes highly recommended—in 2005, he was named one of the industry's Top 25 Most Influential Consultants by *Consulting Magazine*.

Raking in the honors

Gutstein's award isn't the only accolade the firm has reaped in recent years. In 2005, the firm was named for the second time as one of the top 10 consulting firms to work for by *Consulting Magazine*, earning high marks for delivering on client commitments, its leadership, culture, compensation and benefits, work/life balance and employee morale. And in June 2005, the firm was honored locally by the National Association of Business Resources, as one of 10 elite winners of the Chicago's Best and Brightest Companies to Work For award. The firm also was honored by the organization as a "best and brightest" company for its use of innovative HR practices.

Diamond engagements

Unlike many other services firms, DiamondCluster doesn't publicize all of its engagements. The contracts it does report reveal a healthy mix of clients from the public and private sectors. One big win for the firm in 2004 was the award of a multi-

Visit the Vault Consulting Career Channel at **www.vault.com/consulting** — with
insider firm profiles, message boards, the Vault Consulting Job Board and more.

VAULT CAREER LIBRARY   **171**

year tech support purchase agreement by the U.S. Department of Justice. The first project under the agreement involves helping the DOJ with its Unified Financial Management System, slated to replace multiple financial management and procurement systems throughout the department. Other public clients, such as California state and local agencies, have tapped DiamondCluster for purchasing agreements. The firm also has worked with the Chicago Transit Authority, unveiling a new touch-and-go electronic fare card it developed for the transportation system in April 2004.

In the private sector, the firm has worked with a major credit card company on a "health check" to look for efficiencies, and has completed engagements with other clients such as a major North American insurance company and a large international bank.

Intellectual sparkle

DiamondCluster really sparkles as a source for some of the industry's most high-powered intellectual capital. The firm gained a following with the 1998 publication of the bestseller *Unleashing the Killer App*, by partner Chunka Mui and e-commerce expert Larry Downes—in October 2005, *The Wall Street Journal* cited it as one of the "five best books about business and the Internet." The firm's insiders have produced other influential business tomes, such as 2001's *The New Market Leaders: Who's Winning and How in the Battle for Customers*, by Fred Wiersema, a DiamondCluster Fellow and renowned business strategist; 2001's *E-Learning: Strategies for Delivering Knowledge in the Digital Age*, by former DiamondCluster consultant Mark J. Rosenberg; and 2002's *The Venture Imperative*, co-authored by former DiamondCluster partner Tim Rohner. DiamondCluster's own research includes an annual Global IT Outsourcing Study, reporting on trends among both buyers and providers of outsourcing services. The firm's white papers on a variety of industry issues have been cited in media outlets ranging from *The New York Times* and *The Wall Street Journal*, to the *Harvard Business Review* and *Sloan Management Review*.

The fellowship of the Diamond

Perhaps the best illustration of DiamondCluster's devotion to intellectual firepower is its "Fellows" program, which taps some of the industry's most innovative thinkers for input on business developments and new ideas. Notable fellows include Pauling Award-winner Alan Kay, former Grateful Dead lyricist-turned-tech-guru John Perry Barlow, and Microsoft researcher Gordon Bell. In January 2004, Vincent Barabba, a former GM, Xerox and Eastman Kodak exec and former director of the Census Bureau, was crowned a fellow. In June 2005, the firm added two more intellectual luminaries to its roster of fellows. One new name, Professor Dan Ariely, of MIT, conducts work focusing on "issues of rationality, irrationality, decision-making, behavioral economics, and consumer welfare," examining topics like online auction behaviors, personal health monitoring and the effects of different pricing systems. The second new fellow, Dr. Eric K. Clemons, is a professor of operations and information management at The Wharton School, where he studies the transformational impacts of information on the strategy and practice of business.

An elite exchange

Since 1999, the firm has held thrice-yearly events known as the DiamondExchange, invitation-only meetings the firm describes as "a multifaceted senior executive program that helps business leaders understand where to use technology for competitive advantage." It helps that the meetings are held in such inspirational settings as Pebble Beach, Calif., and Kiawah Island, S.C. Senior execs from Fortune 1000 companies find themselves mingling at these events with the firm's fellows, sharing perspectives and cutting-edge business research.

GETTING HIRED

Getting the ball rolling

DiamondCluster relies a bit more heavily on experienced hires over campus recruits to fill its ranks, citing the balance as 60 percent experienced hires and 40 percent campus recruiting. One source explains that "most [experienced] hires have at least five years of experience," while another claims that "the firm encourages employee referrals." Nearly half of the experienced hires this past year came to the firm through referrals.

Experienced candidates typically come to DiamondCluster through its web site, employee referrals and, in some cases, via search firms. Resumes are reviewed against the firm's current needs; if there is a match, a recruiter will contact the candidate to begin the interview process. For campus recruits, company representatives will "touch base and get to know first-years through presentations and other events on campus," according to one DiamondCluster employee. The company does the same for second-year students and encourages all students to register and submit their resumes to its online career center as an expression of their interest in working for DiamondCluster.

Wear your critical thinking cap

Potential campus recruits and experienced candidates face a multistage and rigorous interview process in order to work for DiamondCluster. One insider simply calls the whole recruitment process "crazy-intense." Consultants almost universally agree on the company's selectiveness. The process for campus recruits typically includes two on-campus first-round interviews and, for experienced recruits, the process begins with an initial phone conversation with a recruiter followed by a phone or in-person interview with a practice consultant. Final rounds for both campus and experience recruits are held in the Chicago office and consist of three or four interviews—one or two behavioral interviews, one informal case and one case exercise. The formal case is e-mailed in advance to the candidate, while the informal case question is not presented to the candidate until he/she arrives in the office. "In this instance, the candidate gets 45 to 60 minutes to put together a presentation with a recommendation and then 45 minutes to present," one consultant explains. "In this way we are able to test their critical thinking skills in a different context, and also get a view into how well they write and present." Another associate adds that this test is "a critical component of our recruiting process. We're a strategy firm, not a systems implementation shop." The interview process is meant to evaluate a candidate's conceptual and analytical thinking, creativity, adaptability and other skills.

OUR SURVEY SAYS

Culture war?

Insiders give DiamondCluster high grades for being "team-oriented, egalitarian and meritocratic." DiamondCluster associates regularly credit their colleagues for making the company culture stand out and they frequently mention "the people" as one of the most positive things about the firm. "The people are truly the foundation of the firm and the reason why I was attracted," says one consultant. Other employees report that the "culture is the best thing about DiamondCluster; the people care about the clients, our work and each other," adding that there is a high "degree of informality in interacting across levels within the firm." This informal openness allows another insider to "call everyone from a firm data expert to the CTO to get a second pair of eyes to review and Q&A my work." Several consultants disagree, however, saying that the "open and collegial" atmosphere only goes so far and excludes "many of the senior partners," while there seems to be a "lack of respect for lower-level people in the firm."

Most sources, though, have a positive view of the culture, despite some discrepancy in opinion over company policy—specifically how the company's up-or-out policy affects polity. As one insider put it, "although it's up-or-out like most other consulting firms, it's not competitive whatsoever and people genuinely enjoy working with one another." DiamondCluster says that it has also initiated a formal, two-year, on-the-job training program for analysts to team up with more senior consultants and learn the fine points of working with clients and building relationships.

Workhorses

DiamondCluster racks up fewer points in the work/life balance arena and insiders express mixed feelings about the company's workload. Sources specify the "very long and demanding hours," saying that the hours "stretch your limits" and "can be tougher than at other similar firms." One consultant suggests that DiamondCluster "get a grip on hours" with "improved staffing process."

While these complaints may be typical of a famously hardworking industry, in 2005 DiamondCluster's North America segment took in 73 percent of the company's global net revenue—a year in which the firm increased its numbers of first-time clients by 41 percent over 2004. The company's recent success in bringing in new clients may be translating into longer hours for consultants. Many insiders, though, maintain that the workload "varies" from project to project. Sources say that "when at a client site, you're expected to work 8 a.m. to 8 p.m., on average" and "sometimes a project is intense for a couple of weeks, but other times it varies."

Consultants credit DiamondCluster for making an "extra effort" to ensure the 4:1 workweek. A more senior associate says the four days onsite/one day at home schedule works, in general, and that the ratio improves the longer a consultant is with the company. "I have been able to be home for a surprisingly high percentage of the important events in my four kids' school and other activities because the firm understands that those things are important," he reports. The firm notes that it does offer the Flexible Work Arrangements program, designed to provide opportunities to balance consultants' personal and professional lives. Possible options include part-time arrangements, telecommuting, short-term, no-travel arrangements and unpaid leaves of absence.

Growing a career

Sources differ about the strictness of DiamondCluster's up-or-out policy and on how much the company fosters individual growth. Some sources claim that the firm is "strictly up-or-out," estimating that it takes approximately seven years to move up in the ranks to partner after receiving an MBA. However, the general consensus among insiders is that the company has a "mild up-or-out system" where "advancement can be quick if you try hard." One consultant describes the general promotion ladder: "The standard career progression is two years at each level (analyst, associate, senior associate, manager). After becoming principal, time to partner can vary. Consultants with only undergraduate degrees can move into MBA-level positions and are not differentiated." The key to promotion is performance, sources agree. "DiamondCluster is a true meritocracy. While it's true that we recruit a large number of our people from top MBA programs, every person advances based on merit and performance. There are no false barriers to advancement if you prove yourself in the field, where it counts." One insider explains that while the firm's promotion policy is flexible, that leniency only goes so far, saying that consultants have "plenty of opportunities to move through the ranks until the level of partner, where the hurdle becomes very steep. "The path to partner is the mandate," agrees a colleague.

Edging for education

Since DiamondCluster's promotion schedule is heavily based on performance, the firm provides "very good feedback mechanisms...so everyone knows exactly where they stand and have plenty of opportunities to move up if they are willing to continually improve their skills." The company offers "continuous reimbursement for education," "two weeks of pre-work training with practice cases" and quarterly one-week training sessions using "case-based, real-life simulation," in addition to ample opportunities for voluntary training. Several consultants express frustration, though, that after a certain point, "industry- and client-specific knowledge is up to you and your project," and that "time constraints prevent being able to take advantage of [training opportunities]." Another source echoes the same sentiments and states the "need [for] more standardized training, more time to actually take training, and more access to education materials." Insiders say the company is improving its offerings, but that "it is a work in progress."

Monitoring management

Insider opinion of supervisors runs a wide gamut at DiamondCluster. It's "kind of a crap-shoot here," one consultant states. Some sources have had "great luck with supervisors" and find them to be "reasonable, relatively clear with expectations, and enjoyable to work with." Others, however, have had supervisors who provide "very little guidance," theorizing that a "lack of training" at the firm "has resulted in managers with poor management skills." This has been a point of contention for some consultants who say there isn't "enough focus on developing people-management skills" at DiamondCluster, where it appears to them that "people who are very good, natural managers are not rewarded." A senior associate says very good supervisors exist at DiamondCluster, but that "there is an element of managers within our firm which we call 'consultant-killers'" because "the rate of attrition of people that work with them is most likely higher than average." Others appreciate the company's "flat" structure and its "accessible and impressive" partners, but they caution that some partners are "friendlier" than others. In response to such concerns, DiamondCluster explains that it has bolstered its "Career Developer" program, whereby consultants at all levels are assigned to a more senior coach and advocate to help guide their career development.

Benefit bonanza

Insiders justify the plaudits of *Consulting Magazine* and the National Association of Business Resources as far as DiamondCluster's benefits and perks are concerned. One source claims that "the overall benefits package is unmatched." DiamondCluster offers 100 percent health care coverage, which pays for "everything for you and your family" and encompasses domestic partnerships. Employees get at least four weeks vacation per year. Insiders like the company's 401(k) and complimentary employee stock-purchase plan, and note that DiamondCluster pays for a proportion of "cell phone expenses and home ISP" with a "generous" travel expense reimbursement policy. Many employees note the company's "live anywhere" policy as one of its best perks, coupled with the regular "all hands" meetings at DiamondCluster's Chicago headquarters that foster a sense of community among its far-flung staff.

With open arms

Some consultants observe a greater proportion of men at the firm, from top to bottom, and they acknowledge that DiamondCluster has work to do in recruiting women. "I notice women moving up in the organization," one source says, "but they are still relatively underrepresented at the top." The female-to-male ratio is still "pretty low," though consultants see changes in specific instances, like one consultant who worked on a project "where the majority of the team is female. While this is definitely an anomaly, it is hopefully an indicator of progress." Insiders recommend improved work/life balance for mothers to attract women; promotion of more women to partner; and "possibly add one to the board and management team." Another consultant writes of the benefit of better "women representation at recruiting events" and "women-only recruiting events." Insiders feel that "the commitment is there" but they're uncertain if DiamondCluster has "a complete vision for how to recruit and retain" women. The firm notes that one woman serves on its board of directors and that two female partners are on the firm's management committee.

Praising DiamondCluster's commitment to diversity, one source explains that it is a "firm value" to recruit women and minorities, for example, specifically reaching out to "minority- and women-run associations on campuses." Others add that the company's international presence makes it multicultural. "I've never been with a more diverse group of people, in terms of minorities," one consultant says, though another is more specific when he says that the "firm is kind of diverse, but people are mostly white or South Asian." As with women, minority hiring is "getting better" but still has "room for improvement." The firm says that it backs up its commitment to diversity by encouraging consultants to establish "affinity groups." So far, a Women's Forum, GL@D (Gays and Lesbians at Diamond) and an Analyst Group have been established. Other diversity-focused efforts include the firm's sponsorship and participation in a number of national diversity career conferences, including the National Black MBA Association conference, the National Society of Hispanic MBAs conference and the Reaching Out conference.

Act locally

DiamondCluster's community activities focus heavily on the Chicago area. The company "organizes local community events," and participates in efforts like volunteer tutoring, clothing and food drives, and holiday toy drives for Chicago-area children. Consultants in the Chicago area have participated in sports charities and Habitat for Humanity, as well, and in 2005 the company made contributions to the Red Cross after Hurricane Katrina. However, consultants note that most of these community initiatives are "spearheaded by consultants, rather than the firm itself." An insider explains that "those wishing to do community service in their home communities must 'take the bull by the horns' and make it happen," while another laments this fact, adding, "I wish there was a more concerted effort to get more people involved."

"DiamondCluster is a true meritocracy. While it's true that we recruit a large number of our people from top MBA programs, every person advances based on merit and performance."

— *DiamondCluster source*

Visit the Vault Consulting Career Channel at **www.vault.com/consulting** — with
insider firm profiles, message boards, the Vault Consulting Job Board and more.

VAULT CAREER LIBRARY   **179**

Keane

100 City Square
Boston, MA 02129
Phone: (617) 241-9200 or
(800) 73-KEANE
Fax: (617) 241-9507
www.keane.com

LOCATIONS

Boston, MA (HQ)
More than 70 offices worldwide

PRACTICE AREAS

Application Services
  Application Portfolio Management
  Application Outsourcing
  Application Development &
    Integration
  Strategic Staffing
  Testing
Business Process Services
  Business Process Strategy
  Business Process Improvement
  Business Process Outsourcing

THE STATS

Employer Type: Public Company
Ticker Symbol: KEA (NYSE)
President and CEO: Brian Keane
2005 Employees: 10,150
2004 Employees: 9,115
2005 Revenues: $956 million
2004 Revenues: $911 million

UPPERS

- "Stability of an established
  company"
- "Opportunity to move within the
  company to other locations (even
  internationally)"
- Relaxed corporate culture

DOWNERS

- Recent reductions in benefits
- Tough to get ahead
- "Focus seems to be more on profit
  than people"

EMPLOYMENT CONTACT

www.keane.com/careers

THE BUZZ
WHAT CONSULTANTS AT OTHER FIRMS ARE SAYING

- "High-paying"
- "Jack of all trades"
- "Middle of the pack"
- "Branding not clear"

THE SCOOP

A Keane-do attitude

Keane has aimed to connect technology and business since its humble beginnings, in 1965, in an office above a Boston doughnut shop. Keane has remained a family business, despite becoming a multinational public company worth millions; founded by John F. Keane, the firm is now headed by his son, Brian Keane. Employing about 9,000 staffers worldwide, Keane splits its business evenly between business process services—which includes business process strategy, business process improvement, and business process outsourcing—and application services, such as application portfolio management, application outsourcing, application development and integration, strategic staffing and testing.

Keane's public filing in 1970 forced the firm to take a hard look at its finances. In an effort to smooth out the rough spots, the firm developed its Productivity Management approach, a project management strategy that forms the foundation of Keane's application development and outsourcing philosophies to this day.

Keane on growth

Keane experienced its biggest growth spurt in the early 1990s as the company made a series of acquisitions, including GE Consulting Services and PHS in 1993 and AGS Computers in 1994. The firm established its Federal Systems division in 1994, collecting clients in more than 50 federal, state and local government agencies. More acquisitions occurred in the late 1990s, including interactive agency Jamison/Gold in Los Angeles; Parallax Solutions Ltd in the UK; and ANSTEC, Inc., in Washington, DC. The firm's network of branch offices and Advanced Development Centers in North America, the UK and India work closely with Keane Consulting Group (formerly Bricker & Associates), the firm's business consulting division.

Y2Keane

The firm made a name for itself in the late 1990s, as businesses geared up to battle the dreaded "millennium bug." As early as 1996, Keane was on the Y2K case, launching its Resolve 2000 service to help clients plan ahead. By 1999, the millennium market made up 20 percent of the company's business. But once the clock struck midnight on the year 2000, the firm suffered a noticeable drop-off in business, which coincided with a lagging economy. Keane saw some lean years in

2000 and 2001, and responded with a series of layoffs and the sale of its 1,000-person staffing division to Convergys Corp.

Keane in charge

The current Keane in charge of the firm came to the helm with more than just a family name—he has a Harvard MBA and worked his way up. Brian Keane has proved himself through aggressive leadership, stepping up the firm's offshoring efforts and continuing to make strategic acquisitions. The firm boosted its portfolio in June 2005, when it announced its acquisition of Cresta Testing Inc., the U.S. affiliate of UK-based consulting company Cresta Group Limited. The buy was expected to enhance Keane's established software testing service portfolio. In July 2004, Keane acquired Fast Track Holdings Limited, a privately held UK-based consulting firm specializing in the design, integration and rapid deployment of large-scale SAP projects. And in February 2004, the firm signed a letter of intent to acquire IT and consulting services company Nims Associates Inc., based in the Midwest, for $20 million plus a potential $15 million earn-out consideration.

Indeed, 2004 marked a period of turnaround for the firm, as evidenced by stronger earnings than in previous years. For fiscal year 2004, Keane posted revenues of $911 million, up from $805 million the previous year. The firm's bookings were solid through the year, growing to $1.1 billion, a 26 percent increase over 2003. Revenues were almost evenly split between outsourcing and services, with outsourcing making up 51 percent in 2005. In 2005, revenues steadily rose 5 percent to $956 million.

Indian expertise

In August 2005, the firm appointed Richard Garnick as its new president of North American Services. Garnick, a 20-year tech vet, formerly served on the management board at Wipro, an Indian firm that has made a big splash worldwide for its homegrown outsourcing approach. Though Garnick may not have to travel to India quite as often as he did when he was helping the Indian giant build its business, an August 2005 *BusinessWeek* article noted that "India remains central to his formula for success." According to the article, Garnick has aggressive plans for boosting Keane's headcount in India, and may boost the total to 20,000 staffers from its current 2,000. "I want to put the infantry in India. That will give us the foundation to compete with anybody," Garnick said.

Aggressive expansion in India has become par for the course for companies like Keane. The firm made a splash in 2004, when it opened a new state-of-the-art facility in Hyderabad. The expansion followed the December 2003 opening of a new Advanced Development Center (ADC) in Gurgaon, India. The *Boston Business Journal* noted in April 2004 that the company was spending $25 million on its Indian expansion, and an Indian paper reported in November 2004 that the firm planned to increase its Indian headcount to around 5,000 by 2006. But Keane also brings outsourcing closer to home with its "nearsourcing" operation, based in Halifax, Nova Scotia.

The firm's roster of outsourcing clients includes big names like Miller Brewing Company, which renewed a contract with Keane for an additional three years in May 2005. In January 2004, the firm signed a 10-year, $137 million application outsourcing deal with the National Life Group. The firm provides similar services for Schneider Electric in North America.

Help for health care

Keane has a healthy list of clients in the medical world, as well, earning a reputation as a go-to provider of information services outsourcing and turnkey software systems for hospitals. The firm's health care division operates from six branch locations that offer open systems solutions to the entire health care continuum. In February 2005, Long Beach Medical Center in New York tapped Keane to install its patient management solution, EZ-Access Patcom. Later that year, Riverview Hospital in Noblesville, Indiana, and the Medical University Hospital Authority at the University of South Carolina Medical Center elected to use the same technology in their facilities. Additionally, in September 2004, the firm announced that Ernest Health, a start-up rehabilitation provider, was adopting several of its clinical and financial information systems.

Federal dollars

Keane also has made inroads into the public services sector with a series of government contracts. The flashiest such contract thus far was the December 2004 win of an IT services gig with the U.S. Department of Justice, valued at up to $980 million. The award allows the DOJ and other federal agencies to use the full range of Keane's IT support services. In September 2005, the firm made headlines when it was chosen to help upgrade the National Weather Service's Advanced Weather Interactive Processing System in a contract worth around $54 million over 10 years. Raytheon Company, which was awarded the entire contract, tapped Keane as a subcontractor to provide strategic IT, application outsourcing and testing services for the system, which allows more than 100 local weather forecast offices and river forecast centers across the country to generate weather and water forecasts and warnings.

Local government clients include state agencies such as Indiana's Family and Social Services Administration and Michigan's Department of Transportation. In June 2005, the firm launched a redesigned web site for the North Carolina Commissioner of Banks, intended to make it easier for visitors to access regulatory information, news and forms, and to provide electronic payment capabilities that allow financial firms to renew some licenses online.

The firm enjoys strong relationships with public services agencies internationally, too. In July 2005, the state government of Victoria, Australia, engaged Keane subsidiary Kamco for a $367 million deal to deliver an innovative public transit ticketing system for the state of Victoria using a smartcard, a durable plastic card similar to a pre-paid mobile phone card. That same summer, Keane signed and started work on a major finance and procurement system project with Severn Trent Water, one of the UK's largest water authorities.

Backing away from Big Blue

The firm announced in July 2005 that it was backing out of a lengthy relationship with IBM, wherein Keane had provided the firm with staff augmentation services. The arrangement netted Keane $40 million in 2004, but Keane execs said the relationship no longer fit with the firm's strategy of providing application and BPO services to clients.

Home-town heroes

Keane got some home-town kudos in 2005, when *The Boston Globe* named the firm one of the Top 10 All-time Best Performers on its Globe 100 list. Businesses were measured based on how well they increased sales, profits and returns for shareholders in their aggregate performance in these categories over the past 17 years. Keane is one of only three companies that have appeared on the list 16 times since the list's inception 17 years ago. Additionally, in October 2005, Keane was named one of the top 100 employers in Canada on an annual list compiled by Mediacorp Canada Inc., publisher of *Canada Employment Weekly* and other job-search-related publications.

GETTING HIRED

Only the best minds need apply

Keane says it's looking to hire "the best minds in the business and IT services industry." On the firm's web site, you can search current openings and apply for positions online.

Insiders report that the firm's interview process is pretty "standard" and focused on technical know-how. "Interview question were strictly about tech skills," an insider reports. "If they have a slot for you, the interview process is easy. I had one round of interviews followed by a panel interview with the client," says a source. A colleague agrees that "the interview process is easy," and adds that "recruiting will tend to gloss over the position and not give too many details about the job." The source says to expect an interview with recruiting, another with Keane management and a third with the client.

OUR SURVEY SAYS

Friendly teams

Keane boasts a corporate culture that's "relaxed," with an "employee-friendly working environment" and "lots of opportunities," insiders say. "Most people are friendly and work as a team within their groups," says an insider. That said, these groups can be a bit isolated, the consultant notes, as "there is little exposure to activity outside of the project or client you are assigned to."

All about process

A colleague chimes in that Keane is "an extremely process-oriented organization." The benefits of this, the source says, are that "even new hires are able to quickly hit the ground running using corporate documentation," and "there is never any doubt about what the next steps should be for executing the assignment." But the downsides are that "if a situation falls outside the 'process box', it can quickly devolve into the morass of pitting customer satisfaction against corporate process." In addition, "if an opportunity presents itself and is outside the known processes, there is no method to capitalize on it." According to an insider, "Overall, if you like a defined work experience, this is the place. If you're looking for creative opportunities, you'd best look elsewhere."

Bye-bye beach time

Though some insiders argue that Keane offers plenty of opportunity for the ambitious, others complain of challenges when it comes to getting ahead. "There is no career development process in place (in an organization that thrives on process)," an insider gripes. The firm reportedly is big on billable hours and, in fact, in "recent years the trend has been if you are not billing, you are encouraged to seek employment elsewhere (i.e., nobody on the beach)," another source says. Still, the firm does offer training opportunities if they "apply to your job."

A shift in focus

One consultant grumbles that "since 2000, the company has focused more on the stakeholders than the employees." Some recent changes to benefits, sources suggest, convey this impression: The firm reportedly has done away with an earlier perk of offering a condo to employees, and has cut back on tuition reimbursement for undergraduate work in favor of expanding reimbursement for professional certifications. "Yes, by switching to the certificates more money is probably delivered to more people, but it is still a reduction," an insider comments.

But the firm still takes care of its consultants with perks like a 50 percent match on 401(k)s, a 50 percent health club reimbursement and opportunities to buy stock at a discount. As for community involvement, many Keane consultants are active, though the firm leaves that up to personal choice, not making it a part of its firm-wide mission. One a source notes, "Many of the individuals within the organization are involved in the community. A recent article in the company's online publication gave examples of what many were doing. Due to the geographic diversity there isn't an opportunity to push it company wide."

Keane is "an extremely process-oriented organization [and] even new hires are able to quickly hit the ground running using corporate documentation."

— *Keane insider*

Perot Systems

2300 West Plano Parkway
Plano, TX 75075
Phone: (888) 31-PEROT or
(972) 577-0000
Fax: (972) 340-6100
www.perotsystems.com

LOCATIONS

Plano, TX (Corporate HQ)
Offices throughout North America,
Europe and Asia Pacific

PRACTICE AREAS

Applications Solutions
Business Process Outsourcing
Enterprise Solutions
Infrastructure Solutions
IT Outsourcing
Program Management
Strategy and Technology Consulting

THE STATS

Employer Type: Public Company
Ticker Symbol: PER (NYSE)
Chairman and CEO: Peter Altabef
2005 Employees: 17,000
2004 Employees: 16,000
2005 Revenues: $2 billion
2004 Revenues: $1.8 billion

UPPERS

• Excellent training opportunities
• Strong opportunities for
  advancement

DOWNERS

• Can be bureaucratic
• Limited name recognition

EMPLOYMENT CONTACT

www.perotsystems.com/careers
E-mail: recruiting@ps.net

THE BUZZ
WHAT CONSULTANTS AT OTHER FIRMS ARE SAYING

• "Good people, micromanaged"
• "Supportive, hard-working"
• "They bought too many
  companies"
• "Too IT heavy"

THE SCOOP

Humble beginnings

Plano, Texas-based Perot Systems, boasting 17,000 employees and over 400 clients around the globe, was founded by H. Ross Perot Sr. and eight associates over breakfast in June 1988. Entrepreneur and billionaire, Perot began his foray in the consulting world in 1962 when he borrowed $1,000 from his wife and founded EDS, a technology services and consulting company, also based out of Plano. Perot sold EDS to General Motors in 1984 for $2.5 million. Using the money and experience garnered from EDS, Perot launched Perot Systems, bringing aboard associates with industry, technical and management expertise. The initial client list for the fledgling company was culled using the founders' extensive industry contacts and included McGraw-Hill and MCI as its earliest clients. The company went public in February 1999, offering stock at $16 per share.

A steady rebound

Like many tech companies, 1999 and 2000 brought financial woes to the firm. Perot responded to the situation with a series of strategic alliances and acquisitions, including government consulting and IT service providers ADI Technology Corporation and Soza & Co, and has boosted its offshoring work in India for software development and business process outsourcing. Steadily pulling itself up from the slow-down, in 2004 Perot Systems reported an all-time high of $1.8 billion in revenues, which was then surpassed in 2005 by revenues of $2 billion, and the total value of new contracts signed during 2005 amounted to $882 million.

Perot Systems' services can be categorized into four main "solutions": consulting, business process, applications and infrastructure. The solutions include other sub-categories such as enterprise solutions (including ERP with specific expertise in SAP), IT outsourcing, program management, business process outsourcing, revenue cycle outsourcing, and safety program implementation and management for government and private enterprises. Though the company serves various industries—including manufacturing, engineering, construction, homebuilding, financial services, government services, health care (payers and providers), life sciences, pharmacy, transportation and travel/leisure—the bulk of its clients come from the commercial, insurance, government, health care, manufacturing, engineering and construction industries.

Musical chairs

While serving on the board of directors from 1988, Ross Perot Sr. was also chairman of the company from April 1988 to June 1992. He relinquished the chairman position to focus on his presidential campaign in 1992—capturing 19 percent of the vote as an independent candidate—and he remained on the board until 1994. In 2000, he reclaimed the position of chairman, and in the same year, his son Ross Perot Jr., a former chairman of a Perot Systems' venture, HCL Perot Systems N.V., became president and chief executive officer of the company. Perot Sr. remained chairman until September 2004, when Perot Jr. relinquished the chief executive officer post and assumed his father's chairmanship. Perot Sr. remains active in the company to this day. Peter Altabef was promoted to president and chief executive officer of Perot Systems in 2004.

In good health

Perot Systems is an active player in the public sector, especially in the health care industry. In October 2005, the firm created a business unit to bolster its health industry work by focusing on all public sector market segments including the Centers for Medicare and Medicaid Services, the Veterans Administration and the Department of Defense. Commenting on the new group, Albatef stated that it will "enhance our ability to deliver superior solutions that are essential to improving outcomes for both citizens and government at all levels."

The firm's footing in the health care sector was further solidified in 2005. September saw a contract between Perot Systems and Arkansas Blue Cross and Blue Shield to provide inbound call center services, and in October, the company was named one of eight new Medicare Drug Integrity Contractors (MEDICs) by the Centers for Medicare and Medicaid Services. In July, the company acquired Technical Management, Inc., along with its subsidiary Transaction Applications Group, a provider of policy administration and business process services to the life insurance industry for $65 million in cash. Perot Systems bought all of TAG's stock and acquired its 850 employees in the deal, and is working to leverage the group's expertise and status in the industry to earn more insurance-related process and infrastructure business.

So far, 2006 is shaping up to be an equally successful year for the firm in the health sector. In February, the company signed a new seven-year health information management (HIM) agreement with Northern Arizona Healthcare based in Flagstaff, Arizona. NAH has engaged the firm to deliver a comprehensive HIM solution that will bring more accurate and readily available data to Flagstaff Medical Center and the health system. And in January, Perot Systems signed a new outsourcing contract with Triad Hospitals, valued at $1.2 billion, which represents the second-largest new contract signing in the company's history. According to the terms of the contract, the firm will support Triad's clinical and business transformation programs. By automating clinical, financial and administrative processes throughout its network of facilities, Triad hopes to enhance the care delivery capabilities of its hospitals and provide the technology that will foster long-term growth. The deal spans Triad's 49 hospitals and 10 ambulatory surgery centers in 15 states over the course of 10 years.

Getting in with the government

Not all of Perot Systems' public sector deals are focused on the health field. In February 2006, the firm announced that its government sector subsidiary was awarded a Blanket Purchase Agreement by the U.S. Coast Guard with an estimated value of $73 million over a five-year performance period to continue providing LAN/WAN support to its Office of Information Systems and Infrastructure. Under the BPA, Perot Systems will also sustain and increase services including network and system administration, help desk support, training management, Internet/Intranet support, and on-call and administrative support at 59 Coast Guard locations throughout the United States.

And in an effort to boost its work in the government sector, the company acquired the PrSM Corporation in July 2005, an employee-owned safety, environmental and engineering services company, for $7.2 million in cash. PrSM Corporation, reporting 2004 revenues of $7.6 billion, brought in 65 professionals and several existing contracts within the U.S. Department of Energy to the deal. The acquisition allows the Perot Systems government services team to provide a broader framework of safety and quality engineering services to the U.S. Department of Energy and to expand its offerings into other markets such as the U.S. Department of Defense and NASA. Calling the government sector a "priority," Altabef expects the acquisition to help win even more contracts from the U.S. Department of Energy. The company claimed the acquisition of PrSM will be neutral to 2005 earnings but will have a "modest" effect on 2006 earnings.

Advancing in India

In the past few years, the company has forged ahead with its India plans, opening new facilities for its information technology infrastructure operations in Noida and

Visit the Vault Consulting Career Channel at **www.vault.com/consulting** – with insider firm profiles, message boards, the Vault Consulting Job Board and more.

VAULT CAREER LIBRARY   **191**

Bangalore in December 2005. The India team provides real-time IT services such as mainframe, messaging and UNIX engineering services to Fortune 1000 customers in a "follow-the-sun" model that makes the most of resources in every region. The company prides itself on being "three deep"—providing services in applications, infrastructure and BPO—in both India and the U.S., according to Padma Ravichander, managing director of the company's global applications solutions division. Along with its business processing center in Chennai, Perot Systems' India-based business units now have more than 6,000 employees, and the company expects its India workforce to make up one-third of its global workforce by mid-2006.

In May 2005, the business process solutions centers in Chennai received the BS 7799-2:2002 IT Security Certification, indicating that the company has technologies, tools and practices designed to ensure customer data and patient health care information are kept confidential and secure. All of Perot Systems' operations in India are ISO 9001:2000 and BS 7799 certified, in addition to having earned stringent CMMI Level 5 certification for software development processes.

Ongoing outsourcing

Perot Systems had much at stake after dire predictions from research firm TowerGroup in late 2004 about companies opting for IT "in-housing" over outsourcing, especially in the financial services sector. The prediction seemed inevitable in February 2005 when Harvard Pilgrim Health Care announced that it was altering its core administrative system and phasing out its three-year outsourcing relationship with Perot Systems. The contract represented approximately 5.5 percent of Perot Systems' revenue and gross profit. However, Altabef said in a news brief at the time, "We are in a stronger position to manage through this challenge because our signings in 2004 and existing client growth exceeded our previous expectations." This loss followed a previous announcement in October 2004 that UBS Warburg would phase out its own 10-year IT infrastructure management contract scheduled to expire in 2007.

As 2005 wore on, Perot Systems signed numerous contract-extensions and new outsourcing deals that defied the discouraging prediction and added revenue. In November, the firm was awarded a $14 million, three-year contract renewal with Lexington, Kentucky-based CHA Health. The agreement extends a five-year contract between the two companies that began in April 2002 when CHA selected Perot Systems to provide business process outsourcing and technology management services. Additional health care-related outsourcing deals ensued: The firm landed multiple long-term revenue cycle outsourcing contracts with Michael Reese Hospital and Medical Center in Chicago, Prince William Health System in Manassas, Va., and with Seattle-based Northwest Hospital & Medical Center. In May, LifeCare Management Services, LLC, chose the company to provide ongoing data center operations, service desk, project management and strategic consulting support to 21 facilities across the country under a five-year contract. And in December, the company's health care division was still going strong, signing a five-year agreement to deliver project management services and applications support and maintenance to Sentara Healthcare, Inc., based in Norfolk, Va.

The company's largest deal in 2005 was signed in August with Metaldyne, a leading global designer and supplier of automotive industry components. Metaldyne outsourced its network management, service desk and data center operations as part of a 10-year IT services contract. And in another deal in August, the U.S. Department of Education awarded Perot Systems with a $20 million contract to operate, maintain and enhance the Education Data Exchange Network.

Family values

The company strictly adheres to its core values and goals while delivering products and services to its clients. On its web site, Perot Systems promises to "conduct our personal and professional lives in a manner that will bring credit to ourselves, our families and our company at all times." In 2005, the company received the recognition it was seeking, being distinguished in the industry for excellence in service. In January, the firm was named one of the Top 10 Best-Performing IT Services Firms by *Managing Offshore*, a monthly technology newsletter, and NeoIT, an offshoring advisory firm. And in October, *InformationWeek* magazine's annual list of the 500 largest and most innovative information technology companies ranked Perot Systems No. 1 in the IT industry category and sixth overall. (The company placed 52nd in 2004.)

The firm has already earned accolades in 2006, being named one of the Top 10 Best Performing IT Services Firms, as well as one of the top 100 leading service providers worldwide in the 2006 Global Services 100, and has earned a spot on *Forbes'* Platinum 400 Best Companies list. The firm placed No. 4 in the software and services category. Perot Systems was also ranked No. 2 on *Fortune* magazine's list of America's Most Admired Companies for 2006 in the information technology services category.

GETTING HIRED

Superior characters valued

"Character" and "values" are big at Perot Systems, as the firm makes clear on the careers section of its web site. Perot is looking for candidates "of exemplary character and integrity," who are "committed to growth and excellence," and are "driven to deliver superior solutions." Oh, and it also helps if you're "tenacious, flexible and creative," to boot.

Perot Systems advises interested candidates to create a profile at its "New Jobseekers Registration" page. The firm only accepts applications for specific positions, and does not accept general resumes. If your resume doesn't fit the bill for an opening, however, the company says it hangs on to it in a database for access by recruiters for up to two years. Candidates interested in government services positions can use a separate job search engine available on the web site. Some positions require security clearance.

General questions

If your resume matches a position, a Perot Systems recruiter will contact you. From there, the interview process may include a "technical screen" (for technical positions), a team interview and, ultimately, an executive interview with the hiring manager. One insider explains that in his interview process, "Questions were general—what value I could add, my analysis background and where I wanted to go in my career. The lead analyst asked questions about specific experience in past jobs."

Focused recruiting

If you're a student, it's advisable to check with your campus career coordinator for Perot Systems opportunities. Though the firm doesn't provide much guidance online for recent grads and hopeful interns, the firm claims that it is ramping up recent-graduate opportunities and initiated active intern programs last year. For more information, e-mail PSC-collegerecruiting@ps.net. According to one insider, "Perot does not recruit from campuses for full-time work. However, Perot does recruit for internships from universities." In fact, the source says, "Hiring is done through recruiters focusing on professionals in trade journals and web sites." The company also offers specific opportunities to those separating from the military. See the recruiting section of the company's web site for details.

OUR SURVEY SAYS

The latest in high-tech

At Perot, "You get to work with the latest technology and business practices," an insider gushes. Though "the company has gone through several iterations of management over the past five or so years," a consultant describes the firm as "fully competent, with a reasonable degree of variability around the mean from account to account." As for corporate culture, the source adds that "given its legacy from Ross Perot Sr. there is a definite neo-military aspect to the way that Perot operates. Individuals with a military background are generally provided preferential status in organizational restructurings. The culture rewards conformity over risk-taking, and is rather bureaucratic."

Perot gets high marks on its supervisors: The firm has "some amazing project and account managers," a source reports. Experiences vary widely, though, based on teams and projects. As a consultant explains it, "The accounts are fairly autonomous, and in some cases, so are the teams." Consequently, the source says, Perot consultants tend to "behave like the customers for whom they work."

In addition, the source explains, "The hours also vary from account to account." In some cases, the insider says, "I've worked 80-hour weeks if the client expected it, and you don't complain about it if you want to last long in consulting."

A flat structure

The firm's corporate structure can make getting ahead a challenge, a source notes: "The company is very flat. There are opportunities for advancement, but when you are five people away from the CEO, there's not much room before you get to the top."

Benefit-wise, the firm reportedly offers an employee stock purchase plan and an annual bonus of up to 20 percent, "largely dependent on corporate whimsy," an insider quips. Another source grumbles that Perot's "benefits were once great. Today the benefits are barely average. Few tech firms have such washed out benefits."

A ton of training

The firm also offers plenty of "training and education"—in fact, "you will get a ton of it," an insider says. And opportunities for community involvement abound, as "Perot prefers to donate people rather than money," an insider explains. "Time off is frequently given to associates for volunteer activities." In addition, sources tell us the firm is quite diverse. As one insider puts it, "We have someone from every continent, excluding Antarctica."

"You get to work with the latest technology and business practices."

— Perot Systems employee

Visit the Vault Consulting Career Channel at **www.vault.com/consulting** — with
insider firm profiles, message boards, the Vault Consulting Job Board and more.

VAULT CAREER LIBRARY   197

Infosys Technologies Ltd.

6607 Kaiser Drive
Fremont, CA 94555
Phone: (510) 742-3000
Fax: (510) 742-3090
www.infosys.com

LOCATIONS

Fremont, CA (U.S. HQ)
Bangalore (HQ)
Over 40 offices worldwide

PRACTICE AREAS

Application development and
  maintenance
Business process outsourcing
Consulting services
Corporate performance management
Independent testing and validation
Infrastructure management
Packaged application services
Product engineering and design
Systems integration

THE STATS

Employer Type: Public Company
Ticker Symbol: INFY (Nasdaq)
**Chairman of the Board and Chief
Mentor:** Narayana NR Murthy
**Managing Director, President and
CEO:** Nandan M Nilekani
2005 Employees: 45,000+
2004 Employees: 32,949
2005 Revenues: $1.59 billion
2004 Revenues: $1.06 billion

UPPERS

• Lots of room for growth
• Focus on teamwork
• Exciting, rapid growth

DOWNERS

• Promotion can be political
• "Stale layer" of middle
management
• No boundaries between work life
and private life

EMPLOYMENT CONTACT

U.S. Recruitment
Infosys Technologies Ltd.
6607 Kaiser Drive
Fremont, CA 94555
Fax: (510) 742-3092
Campus Hiring
E-mail: campusjobs@infosys.com
Experienced Professionals
E-mail: UScareers@infosys.com
Global Internship
E-mail: intern@infosys.com

THE BUZZ
WHAT CONSULTANTS AT OTHER FIRMS ARE SAYING

• "High quality, low price"
• "Go-getters"
• "Upcoming firm, but will take a
  while to mess with the big boys of
  consulting"
• "Not female friendly"

THE SCOOP

Bill Gates meets Bangalore

Bangalore-based Infosys, sometimes referred to as the "Microsoft of India," rests in the upper ranks of Indian outsourcing giants and receives accolades worldwide for its combination of tech and strategy savvy. Employing over 45,000 staffers in locations worldwide, Infosys offers a mix of tech services, such as application development, business process outsourcing and consulting.

If Infosys is the subcontinent's answer to Microsoft, by extension, Infosys' chairman and "chief mentor," Narayana Murthy, one of the firm's original seven founders, is seen as India's Bill Gates. But Murthy's lifestyle is a bit less lavish than that of his stateside counterpart—according to an article in *Fortune Asia* printed in 2003, Murthy and Infosys president and CEO Nandan Nilekani take home just $44,000 and $42,000 in salary, respectively, and "none of the firm's seven founders receive stock options." "In an age of crooked bookkeeping and executive excess, Infosys stands out as a model of corporate governance," the article contended, citing examples such as the execs' scrupulous reimbursement of the company for their personal calls and their refusal to put family members on the payroll. In fact, Murthy, among India's most powerful business tycoons, still lives in the same three-bedroom house he's shared with his wife for the past 15 years.

A profitable powerhouse

Infosys execs have decided to pour their profits back into the firm's growth, a strategy that's paid off. In 1999, the firm became the first Indian company to list on the Nasdaq. And while other IT rivals were struggling in 2002, Infosys took advantage of its Indian position and began a recruiting and marketing blitz, banking on U.S. companies' desire to save funds by outsourcing. In a dismal year for IT, the firm posted sales of $740 million, up 50 percent from the previous year. The firm's business processing subsidiary, Progeon, launched in 2003, raked in around $80 million in 2004. In November 2004, Infosys and Microsoft announced an enterprise IT transformation initiative, initially investing $8 million jointly to deliver a portfolio of new solutions and services to help clients achieve a simplified, flexible IT environment. In December 2003, the firm announced its intentions to acquire Expert Information Services, an Australian IT services firm, for around $23 million.

During the IT peak, the firm developed strong relationships with big-league American firms like Seattle-based retailer Nordstrom and shoe giant Adidas. Between 2004 and 2005, revenues jumped from $1.06 billion to $1.59 billion, and company execs have forecast revenues of up to $2.13 billion for 2006, higher than earlier predictions. Murthy told *Business Line* that he expects to employ 50,000 people in India and 20,000 in China during the next three to five years.

An outsourcer with a difference

Infosys has been cited repeatedly by industry wonks for its unique strategic approach. The firm doesn't just aim to be the biggest offshore supplier, but also a preferred service and consulting firm, analysts have noted. In an independent survey published by Forrester Research in 2005, Infosys ranked highest in client satisfaction in outsourcing services and was in the top three in consulting services among 11 major global IT service providers.

Storming the States

The U.S. is Infosys' largest market. The company made a splash in the U.S. consulting market in April 2004, forming Infosys Consulting. A subsidiary of Infosys based in Fremont, Calif., the firm is made up of a "dream team" of consultants: Stephen Pratt, who was named CEO of the subsidiary; Romil Bahl, former head of EDS's consulting practice; Pal Cole, former head of global operations at CGE&Y; and Raj Joshi, former CEO of Deloitte Offshore. "This is a wake-up call to our industry: We will offer clients more competitively priced projects, practical ways to increase competitiveness, and a much higher return on their consulting dollar," Pratt stated.

The firm planned to invest $20 million to create 500 U.S.-based consulting positions within the subsidiary, which also has offices in Boston, Dallas and Lake Forest, Calif. As of 2005, the unit has 25 Global 1000 clients. During its first year, the unit recruited more than 100 consultants in the U.S. and was recognized by industry analysts. "Although most of the major Indian outsourcers claim to offer business consulting services, Infosys Consulting is the first official subsidiary created specifically to address this market opportunity in the United States and Europe," IDC analysts declared.

The firm is investing in expansion elsewhere in the world, too. In August 2005, Infosys signed letters of intent to set up software development centers in China, agreeing to invest $65 million over the next five years. The centers are expected to have state-of-the-art infrastructure, including recreational facilities for local employees such as those offered at Infosys' centers in India.

A range of engagements

The firm's recent engagements run the gamut from software development to outsourcing. In September 2005 the firm signed a five-year deal to develop, support and enhance a range of applications for ABN AMRO, the largest multi-million dollar contract ever won by Infosys. In 2005, the firm worked with airline giant Airbus on design, development, software solutions and more for its Airbus A380 model. Infosys' RFID solution was adopted in April 2005 by Kids Headquarters, the world's largest children's apparel company. And in December 2004, the firm announced the successful delivery of a new software application for Victoria, Australia's Department of Infrastructure, designed to help the department manage its public bus services contracts.

Sweeping the awards

The press has taken notice of Infosys' rapid rise. *Wired* magazine ranked the firm No. 9 on its Wired 40 list for 2005, up two places from its 2004 ranking at No. 11. *Business 2.0* ranked Infosys in eighth place on its B2 100 list of the world's fastest growing tech companies. The firm even managed to upstage eBay and Apple in the rankings. The firm also placed high on *BusinessWeek*'s annual Information Technology 100 list, coming in at No. 10, ahead of rivals Tata, Wipro, and even Accenture and IBM. Back at home, Infosys has topped India's *Businessworld*'s Most Respected Companies list since 2001.

Reshaping the globe

Nilekani, who became president of the firm in 2003, enjoys a high profile on the world's stage. In fact, it was a conversation between Nilekani and *New York Times* scribe and bestselling author Thomas Friedman that inspired Friedman's 2005 book, *The World Is Flat: A Brief History of the Twenty-First Century*. Nilekani pointed out to Friedman that, in an age of virtual communication, "the playing field is being leveled," with countries like India now able to compete for work in the knowledge industry worldwide.

An unsettling situation

Despite its worldwide accolades, the firm hasn't been entirely immune to scandal. In May 2003, Infosys settled a sexual harassment suit filed by a Fremont, Calif.-based employee against former U.S. director Phaneesh Murthy. Under the terms of the out-of-court, $3 million settlement, Infosys reserved the right to take its own legal action against Murthy (no relation to the company's chief mentor), and the scandal led to bad blood between the firm and its former employee. Phaneesh, who maintained his innocence in the matter, was not held financially liable. He has now found success with a new software firm.

In October 2004, Murthy and another plaintiff reached a settlement before a new sexual harassment case went to trial. Infosys refused to contribute to any of the $800,000 settlement—half was paid by insurers and half came from Murthy himself.

A clear corporate conscience

Nilekani and his Infosys colleagues are also renowned as corporate do-gooders. In an interview with *CNETAsia* published in November 2004, Nilekani outlined his corporate philosophy, declaring, "The softest pillow is a clear conscience." According to Nilekani, "No corporation can sustain its progress unless it makes a difference to its context. Thus, a core value of Infosys is a strong sense of social responsibility." Infosys' philanthropic arm, Infosys Foundation, was founded in 1996 "with the objective of fulfilling the social responsibility of the company by supporting and encouraging the underprivileged sections of society," according to the company. The foundation's initiatives include projects in health care, "social rehabilitation and rural upliftment," education, and arts and culture. Under a large rural education program, the foundation has set up 5,500 libraries in India's government schools. The firm also contributed both financially and with hands-on help following the devastating tsunami in Southeast Asia at the end of 2004.

Educating the masses

Education is also a big deal to Infosys—not just for philanthropic purposes, but also because the firm is hungry for well-trained new talent to fill its swelling ranks. Infosys' global internship program, InStep, is the largest institutionalized internship program of its kind in India. InStep brings talented students from schools around the world—including universities such as Carnegie Mellon, Harvard, Wharton and London Business School—to India. In 2005, 100 interns participated in the program, which allows participants to gain hands-on experience on real projects with the firm.

In July 2005, the firm launched Campus Connect, an initiative aimed at partnering industry and academia. The initiative is meant to help schools prepare students for high-tech jobs through seminars and faculty workshops, allowing access to Infosys course materials online, and working with colleges to help them align their curriculum with industry standards. In February 2005, the firm opened a Global Education Center in Mysore, India, inaugurated by India's prime minister. The center, which can accommodate 4,500 trainees at once, is one of the largest of its kind in the world. Infoscions can come to the center for training on technological and managerial skills, while the Infosys Leadership Institute, on the same campus, helps to "groom and develop" the firm's future execs.

GETTING HIRED

Info, please

Infosys maintains an info-packed careers section on its web site, featuring employee testimonials, details about benefits and training, and a job search engine covering positions worldwide. Students can visit the site for the large list of schools from which Infosys recruits.

The firm also maintains a separate site devoted to its InStep program, an internship program for undergrads and grad students worldwide. The hands-on Infosys immersion program runs year-round, with typical assignments ranging from eight to 24 weeks. Participants receive a monthly stipend along with airfare to the location of their internship, usually in Bangalore, though positions also come up occasionally in the U.S., UK, Japan and Canada. In India, the firm says, interns receive accommodation in a furnished apartment, free food and transportation, and a chance to explore India during "internship excursions."

Puzzling it out

As the firm has grown, a source tells us, interviewers put "more emphasis on case analysis [and] academic credentials." According to a colleague, Infosys' interview "used to be one of the toughest entry-level interview processes in its home nation, India—that's how I got in a two-hour, at-length discussion on technology, puzzles and engineering. Infosys was heavy on puzzles and analytical ability for entry level positions." The source adds, though, that the "tech boom (rather the outsourcing boom) diluted that to the extent that they did away with the interview process altogether. The results showed—and getting some sense back, [the] interview process was again formalized. Results are better now." These days, the insider says, the firm looks for "individuals with extremely strong technical skills."

OUR SURVEY SAYS

Under construction

Infosys' corporate culture is evolving as rapidly as the company itself, sources suggest. As one consultant puts it, "Imagine living in a building where construction is still going on, and the building management keeps adding new tenants in scores. That, in a nutshell, is Infosys in its growth pangs from a small (but nevertheless great) to a huge organization." For the most part, this growth has been positive, insiders suggest, creating a culture of "transparency" and "winning through teamwork," along with "individual contributions and accountability."

But another insider grumbles that there's a "large difference" between the "stated culture" and the real one. "The stated culture is an intention which is noble and idealistic; unfortunately the middle management is a stale layer, inept at implementing such a culture." The scene at times can be "very Dilbertesque," the source adds.

Still, Infosys is a "meritocracy," says an insider. The firm offers "plenty" of opportunities, a colleague adds, "provided you can 'keep everyone happy'" and "play politics." It's mostly a "'figure out where you want to go yourself' phenomenon," another source chimes in. Hours "depend heavily on your project (and what you want to prove to your managers)," says an insider. But a co-worker reports that "your life belongs to Infosys," and "no one would even think twice about calling you on your personal number at 12:00 a.m. for a very trivial issue."

Mini India

As for diversity, currently Infosys resembles "a mini India spread across the globe," a source says, though "the top guys are working to change that." The firm reportedly has initiatives in place to promote opportunities for women.

Infoscions receive a bonus that's tied to revenues, a source reports. It's "not the highest salary package, but competitive with the model of the future," the source elaborates.

"Imagine living in a building where construction is still going on, and the building management keeps adding new tenants in scores. That, in a nutshell, is Infosys in its growth pangs from a small (but nevertheless great) to a huge organization."

— *Infosys consultant*

Visit the Vault Consulting Career Channel at **www.vault.com/consulting** — with
insider firm profiles, message boards, the Vault Consulting Job Board and more.

VAULT CAREER LIBRARY   **205**

Getronics NV

290 Concord Road
Billerica, MA 01821
Phone: (978) 625-5000
www.getronics.com

LOCATIONS

Billerica, MA (North America HQ)
Amsterdam (HQ)
Offices in over 30 countries
worldwide

PRACTICE AREAS

Application Services
Communication Services
Security Services
Technology Transformation Services
Workspace Management Services

THE STATS

Employer Type: Public Company
Ticker Symbol: GTN (Euronext
Amsterdam)
Chairman and CEO: Klaas Wagenaar
2005 Employees: 27,000
2004 Employees: 21,026
2005 Revenues: €2,593 million
2004 Revenues: €2,38 million

UPPERS

• Commitment to training
• Ample opportunities for
  advancement

DOWNERS

• "Tight" financials equal limited
  raises
• Lots of changes at the top

EMPLOYMENT CONTACT

us.getronicsjobs.com
E-mail: us.recruiting@getronics.com

THE BUZZ
WHAT CONSULTANTS AT OTHER FIRMS ARE SAYING

• "Successful at network support"
• "Will work a task through until it is
  completed to satisfaction"
• "Seem to be improving"
• "Low morale"

THE SCOOP

Getting to Getronics

The Amsterdam-based Getronics NV is a €3 billion company providing a variety of information and communication technology services (ICT) to such mega-clients as 3Com, Barclays, Cable and Wireless, the European Commission, HSBC, Morgan Stanley, Novartis and Shell. Getronics works in a number of different industries, with primary expertise in finance, government, telecommunications, retail, transportation and manufacturing. Today, more than two-thirds of the company's revenues, which totaled €2,593 million in 2005, come from customers in Europe and the Middle East.

The firm's history dates back to the incorporation of Groeneveld, Van der Pol & Co.'s Elektrotechnische Fabriek N.V. in 1887, forming a company that installed controls and technical equipment for the shipbuilding and utilities industries. After a number of acquisitions, mergers, name changes and strategic divisions, the company emerged a century later as Geveke Electronics NV in 1985, then Getronics NV in 1988. In 1999, Getronics acquired U.S.-based Wang Laboratories, the star-crossed networking and telecom giant, for €1,42 billion. The purchase catapulted Getronics into the upper echelon of international IT service providers.

Powerful partnerships

Getronics maintains partnerships with three of the world's leading technology companies. The company has served as one of a select few global service partners with Dell, undertaking nearly 1 million managed services actions annually on Dell's behalf. Getronics is a Microsoft Gold Certified Partner for enterprise systems and has developed enterprise scale business solutions based on Microsoft enterprise technology for years. Getronics and Cisco have partnered to deliver IT solutions from initial design to installation and management, and the company was the first to develop Cisco-related Global Voice Access and Global Security Specializations. And in February 2006, Getronics signed its largest-ever financial services deal when it was selected by Barclays to enter a strategic partnership. Getronics will be responsible for providing desktop and application management support to over 30,000 users, the majority of which are UK-based. The five-year contract, valued at €200 million, will be handled mainly in the firm's UK offices, with support from its Spain and Budapest operations.

On a Wang and a prayer

Although the 1999 Wang Laboratories purchase boosted Getronics' position as a viable competitor in the IT game, the acquisition nearly sent the company into bankruptcy. While attempting to repay the debts, Getronics suffered heavy annual losses for years, dropping as much as €924 million, or 26 percent, from 2002 to 2003. The company's corporate leadership appeared equally troubled when chairman and CEO Peter van Voorst and CFO Jan Docter resigned in February 2003 to make way for two recovery experts, Klaas Wagenaar and Axel Rückert. In December of the same year, Wagenaar replaced Rückert as chairman and CEO. With Wagenaar at the helm, Getronics set off on a course to reverse its long-term adversity, cutting costs, divesting unprofitable subsidiaries, and restructuring services and product lines. In September 2004, Getronics launched its streamlined platform of seven principle services: IT Security; Converged Communications; Enterprise Content Management; IT Mobility; Storage, Server & Network Integration; Application Integration & Management; and Network & Desktop Outsourcing.

Pretty in PinkRoccade

In March 2005, Getronics enhanced its UK operations by acquiring 95.2 percent of rival IT services provider PinkRoccade NV, based in Voorburg, Netherlands. Later that month, the merged company announced its new management team, including UK chairman Stuart Appleton and new UK COO Clive Hyland, former UK CEO of PinkRoccade. The impact of the acquisition remains unclear. In 2005, Getronics' revenues were €2,593 billion, up 23 percent from the year before. Sales from service products jumped 41 percent to €2,18 billion, some 84 percent of the company's total business, while product revenue fell 27 percent to €411 million.

In 2005, Getronics introduced plans to cut roughly 600 jobs in the Netherlands and the UK, along with restructuring plans that would reduce the number of offices in the Netherlands from 70 to 15. In addition, the firm announced in January 2006 that it would sell its Italian business activities to an Italy-based ICT services company. According to the firm, "ongoing challenging market circumstances" in Italy and the postponement of a large government outsourcing project originally awarded in June 2005 rendered the firm's Italian operations financially unviable.

Getronics getting into outsourcing

These transitions were partially a result of increased interest from international clients in using inexpensive offshore and near-shore resources, something Getronics is responding to by setting up delivery centers in Hungary and Mexico, which staff some 500 employees. The firm also signed several significant outsourcing deals in 2005 and 2006. In January 2006, the firm finalized a five-year deal with Mercator Verzekeringen, in which Getronics will take over the majority of Mercator's computer infrastructure and existing ICT contracts. In December 2005, DSM selected the firm for an outsourcing agreement to manage its 20,000 workplaces and ICT infrastructions worldwide, establishing its position as DSM's single global service provider. The three-year, €40 million contract encompasses over 40 countries and reinforces Getronics' partnership with DSM, for which it has been providing ICT support since 2002. Also in December, Getronics and Wegener, a large publisher in the Netherlands, announced their intention to sign a three-year outsourcing agreement. According to the terms of the contract, Getronics PinkRoccade would provide workspace management services, becoming Wegener's strategic partner in servicing its 4,300 workplaces in over 80 locations, as well as the related ICT infrastructure.

GETTING HIRED

A day in the life

Getronics maintains separate career web pages for many of the countries the firm covers. On the U.S. page, candidates can read "Day in the Life" profiles for an inside look at workdays at the firm. In addition, Getronics offers a "Career Coach" section detailing tips on everything from building a resume to acing an interview (a useful section for any job seeker). There are even tips on managing your work/life balance after you land that Getronics position.

Though the firm says it "rarely" hires recent grads just out of school, it does offer some intern and co-op options (the former typically are unpaid, while the latter offer some pay). The firm lets interns know that they should "expect to spend very little time photocopying"—students are "treated like a team member from day one," working on significant projects. Interested students are invited to search the firm's job database for opportunities, or e-mail the firm directly with their resume and other information about what they're looking for.

General to particular

A source tells us that, after receiving a phone response to a resume sent to the firm, an interview was set up. The meeting consisted of "questions very general in nature, such as 'Where do you see yourself in five years?' and 'What are your best and worst attributes?'" the source says. "In the second interview the questions were more of the same, but a significant increase in detail was required in order to provide an accurate and complete response." By the third round, the source adds, the questions were more technical and customer service-oriented.

OUR SURVEY SAYS

Stuck in the middle with you

A rapidly changing company like Getronics naturally has a corporate culture that's also on the move, insiders suggest. As one source puts it, "I have survived vast changes in corporate culture," from "cultures that portrayed the employee as No. 1 to cultures where the employee did not seem to mean much at all." The source adds, "Currently the culture is somewhere in the middle. Employees are well cared for but can be gone at the drop of the hat."

Carpe diem

Still, says an insider, "With new projects coming up, there is a decent chance for advancement into new positions that are being created based on the projects." A colleague agrees: "Everything is an opportunity with Getronics. It just depends on how well you are able to capitalize on each opportunity when it presents itself." Another source tells us that "it was hard to get in the door here, but now it's like family."

A lot of these opportunities are supported by Getronics' commitment to training, insiders say. "Business education has been achieved by setting and attaining realistic goals through in-house training programs and experienced mentors," one source tells us. "Each employee has a built-in support group regardless of which rung of the corporate ladder he might be standing on at the moment." The source also praises the firm's "virtual university," adding, "employees are encouraged to take advantage of this resource to enable them to further their professional development. The opportunities are there. Getronics wants each and every employee to succeed."

As for compensation, since "things have been tight," an insider says, "compensation increases are rare to none. If there is one, it is usually 1 to 3 percent." Staffers enjoy an in-house gym and full-service cafeteria.

Visit the Vault Consulting Career Channel at **www.vault.com/consulting** —with
insider firm profiles, message boards, the Vault Consulting Job Board and more.

VAULT CAREER LIBRARY   **211**

Wipro Ltd.

Doddakannelli Sarjapur Road
Bangalore, Karnataka 560 035
Phone: +91 (80) 844 0011
Fax: +91 (80) 844 0256
www.wipro.com

LOCATIONS

Bangalore (Corporate HQ)
Over 50 offices worldwide

PRACTICE AREAS

Business Process Outsourcing
Consulting
Infrastructure Management
IT Services
Product Design

THE STATS

Employer Type: Public Company
Ticker Symbol: WIT (NYSE)
Chairman and Managing Director:
Azim H. Premji
2005 Employees: 42,000
2004 Employees: 29,500
2005 Revenues: $1.8 billion
2004 Revenues: $1.3 billion

UPPERS

• Wide exposure to diverse areas of
  the IT industry
• "Fair and healthy" promotion
  system

DOWNERS

• Only true believers in outsourcing
  need apply
• Huge organization

EMPLOYMENT CONTACT

www.careers.wipro.com
E-mail: manager.career@wipro.com
U.S. Recruitment: (732) 394-8255

THE SCOOP

Dominating the scene

Indian tech services giant Wipro Ltd. employs over 42,000 associates scattered over 35 countries. Financially, the company has seen earnings and revenues grow at double-digit rates spurred by increasing demand for cheap, fast IT services, and given its secure position in the outsourcing market. Its outsourcing arm, Wipro Technologies, claims to be the fourth-largest IT services provider in the world in terms of market capitalization. In June 2004, *BusinessWeek* magazine included Wipro on its list of top 100 technology companies globally.

The company has over 421 clients, of which 140 are Global 500 companies, an increase of 24 percent from 2003. The client list includes big-ticket names such as StorageTek, Sun Microsystems, Morgan Stanley, General Motors, Cisco and Nokia. The company claims 90 percent of its customers contract with Wipro across multiple service lines.

Cooking oil heir does good

In 1966, at the age of 21, Azim Premji, a Stanford graduate with a degree in electrical engineering, took over Wipro from his father when the senior Premji died suddenly. Heir to the cooking oil company, Premji cultivated the $2 million firm by diversifying into other commodities—including soap—and adding computer development, software and services to transform it into a $1.76 billion IT services organization with customers across the globe. While a majority of the company's business comes from IT services, it has retained its computer hardware unit, lightbulb business and a diagnostic equipment venture with GE Medical Systems. The company maintains its cooking oil and soap ventures to this day.

As chairman and managing director of Wipro Corporation, *Business India* named Premji Business Man of the Year in 2000, and *The Economic Times* named him the Business Leader of the Year in 2004. Worth more than $6 billion, in November 2004, *The Financial Times* included him on its list of the top 25 billionaires who have done the most to bring about significant and lasting social, political or cultural changes. In addition, *Time* magazine listed Premji in April 2004 as one of the 100 most influential people in the world.

Shuffling leaders

In July 2005, Wipro shifted P R "Sekar" Chandrasekhar from his position as the head of Wipro's European Operations to the chief executive of Americas and Europe. Under his leadership Wipro's European operations have bloomed, especially in strategic consulting. Explaining Chandrasekhar's promotion, Premji stated, "Our clients work with us across multiple geographies and having a common head for Europe and the Americas will align us better with this trend." Sekar called North America Wipro's "largest market."

In June 2005, Wipro lost a significant and influential executive when Vivek Paul left to become a partner at the Texas Pacific Group, a private investment firm. Paul led Wipro Technologies from California for six years and helped improve Wipro's performances in R&D services, IT outsourcing and business process outsourcing (BPO). He was also instrumental in developing the company's training strategy.

Partnerships around the world

Wipro has become one of the largest BPO services providers in the past two years, providing help-desk support and customer service functionality to a broad range of customers. While building up its strengths in the outsourcing marketplace, the company strives to put together a team of consultants that can compete with the likes of IBM and Accenture. The company has allied itself with major players such as Microsoft and SAP, devoting over 5,000 employees to specifically deliver Microsoft solutions. In September 2005, Wipro became the first Indian IT service provider to be awarded Gold-Level status in the Microsoft Windows Embedded Partner program.

In December 2005, Wipro announced a global partnership agreement with SAP to begin offering Business One, SAP's business management solution for small and mid-size enterprises. Under this agreement, Wipro will offer full lifecycle implementation services to subsidiaries of large enterprises in the U.S., and will jointly explore further opportunities for SAP Business One. The company also trains and certifies consultants in the Business One technology solution.

The firm also announced a partnership with the New York Stock Exchange in February 2005, in which it will enable its new eGovDirect.com[sm] software, a filing system to assist companies listed on the NYSE manage and submit their corporate compliance information. The password-protected web site acts as a secure platform between companies and the NYSE, allowing an easy exchange of information. It also acts as a benchmarking tool that lets companies compare their own corporate governance structure against that of other NYSE companies.

Building up muscle

Wipro also continues to expand its service offerings. In 2002, it strengthened its U.S. consulting arm and became a player in energy consulting by acquiring American Management Systems for $26 million. An $18.7 million acquisition of NerveWire in April 2003 added financial software to the company's product offerings. And in December 2005, Wipro expanded into the payments market with its $28 million acquisition of mPower, based out of Princeton, New Jersey.

With revenues of around $18 million, mPower focused on payments and had a joint venture, MPACT, with MasterCard International. The acquisition gave Wipro a 100 percent stake in MPACT, resulting in a strategic partnership with MasterCard. mPower also maintained an offshore facility in Chennai, India. The mPower deal brought in 300 employees and deep expertise in payments to help expand Wipro's Financial Solutions business. "The payments industry is an area where we expect to see rapid growth in the near future," said Sriram Srinivasan, a vice president at Wipro Technologies.

To increase its products lines in the wireless LAN and Bluetooth space, Wipro acquired the Austrian firm NewLogic in December 2005. The $56 million deal gave Wipro 120 specialists, intellectual property cores for complex wireless applications, and radio-frequency designs. Wipro also now has access to 25 patent filings. "In the product engineering space, ownership of IPs is a key asset for building services revenues," said Ramesh Emani, president of Wipro's Product Engineering Solutions unit.

"No one-trick pony"

Branching out "from the traditional confines of BPO, Wipro filed 22 invention disclosures in 2004 and set its sights on globally outsourced research and development projects. As the company tackles rising visa costs and transition in the BPO arena, it's betting that project engineering services will be the next big thing for Indian IT companies. In an interview with *Outlook Money*, an Indian newspaper in September 2005, Pratik Kumar, executive vice-president at Wipro, declared that Wipro is "no one-trick pony." According to Kumar, in 2005, enterprise solutions contributed over 57 percent of revenues, while BPO brought in 11 percent. With a 10,000-plus R&D engineers' pool, Wipro claims to have the largest third-party R&D house worldwide, and is setting its sights on globally outsourced research and development projects.

The company has continued to sign contract renewals and new deals, including the five-year, multi-million dollar contract signed with TUI UK in late 2004. Part of TUI AG, the largest travel company in Europe, TUI UK contracted with Wipro's remote infrastructure practice for desktop support for around 10,000 desktops, 300 servers, L1/L2 helpdesk, monitoring and messaging services across 800 locations throughout the United Kingdom. And in January 2006, the firm signed a global service contract with General Motors to integrate, develop and implement software solutions to GM facilities around the world.

Points for performance

In August 2004, research group IDC gave Wipro high marks for its IT services, ranking the company ahead of IBM and Accenture. "Wipro's strengths lie in it being one of the largest players in the offshore market to offer a full breadth of services including application development, reengineering, package implementation, IT infrastructure and support, product design and development, and BPO," IDC said at the time.

Forrester Research ranked Wipro a "strong performer" in the global delivery of infrastructure management in its December 2005 scorecard. Forrester evaluated Wipro's strategy and current offerings against eight Indian vendors and five global vendors providing global delivery infrastructure management services. Wipro received high marks in the areas of vision and productivity improvements, offshore/nearshore staff and infrastructure revenues.

Investing in people

Wipro claims to have over 2,000 domain consultants and 500 technology consultants who specialize in e-business and package applications. Of the 42,000 employees on its payroll, more than 5,000 are spread out across North America, Europe and Japan. Over 10,000 employees work on a per-contract basis.

To keep its forces up-to-date, united and strong, the company invests in serious training for all of its employees. The company claims its staff of 70 full-time instructors provides 240,000 man-days of training annually. The "World Campus" initiative allows up to 1,000 associates to take courses simultaneously.

The firm's educational efforts extend beyond Wipro's ranks, as well. Premji's Azim Premji Foundation is a not-for-profit organization devoted to providing over 1.8 million children with quality education. His personal foundation works alongside the company's Wipro Cares initiative to plan to implement community service programs.

GETTING HIRED

At home around the world

The careers section of Wipro's web site is heavily geared toward India, though the firm does provide a job search engine covering positions worldwide. You can also register to have job alerts e-mailed to you as openings arise. On an FAQ page, Wipro says it's looking for candidates who are "focused on customer satisfaction," "self-confident enough to provide leadership and direction to customers, equally at home in Europe, the U.S., Japan, or India," and have a "single-minded dedication to be the very best they can be."

Entry-level candidates have the best chance at Wipro if they have some sort of computer engineering or other technical degree. When we checked, the firm had a section on its site for "freshers," or those just out of school, but it had no job opportunities listed at the time. Likewise, the campus recruiting pages had no events listed.

Insiders report going through two rounds of interviews, split between technical and HR. Those "freshers" can also expect a written exam and a group activity or discussion on top of the interviews, sources say.

OUR SURVEY SAYS

The wide world of Wipro

Wipro is a great place to amass tech experience, insiders tell us. "Working in Wipro provides a wide exposure to technologies. One can learn a lot of diverse things if one wishes," a source says. The firm's culture is "exciting" and "challenging," another insider reports.

Wipro staffers are given a boost by the firm's "very fair and healthy promotional system," which "gives credit" to employees who perform, a source notes. "If you stick to your work and have a sincere, honest attitude, you will be rewarded well."

CGI Group Inc.

1130 Sherbrooke Street West
5th Floor
Montreal, Quebec H3A 2M8
Canada
Phone: (514) 841-3200
Fax: (514) 841-3299
www.cgi.com

LOCATIONS

Montreal (Global HQ)
More than 100 offices in 17
countries worldwide

PRACTICE AREAS

Application Management
Business Process Services
Systems Integration and Consulting
Technology Management

THE STATS

Employer Type: Public Company
Ticker Symbol: GIB (NYSE),
GIB.SV.A (TSX)
President and CEO: Michael Roach
Founder and Executive Chairman:
Serge Godin
2005 Employees: 25,000
2004 Employees: 25,000
2005 Revenues: $3.1 billion
2004 Revenues: $2.45 billion

UPPERS

- Not too "political"
- Flexible work hours

DOWNERS

- Can be hard to get ahead
- Lots of changes in recent years

EMPLOYMENT CONTACT

www.cgi.com/web/en/careers/working
_at_cgi.htm

THE BUZZ
WHAT CONSULTANTS AT OTHER FIRMS ARE SAYING

- "Good folks over there"
- "Growing fast"
- "Highly politicized"
- "Lacking"

THE SCOOP

Sticking to its guns

Founded in 1976 by Serge Godin and André Imbeau, CGI Group is Canada's largest—and one of North America's largest—independent IT and business process service (BPS) firm serving both businesses and governments. The firm's business is divided between its IT and BPS divisions; BPS includes outsourced management and processing of a company's business functions and represents close to 16 percent of the company's total revenues. CGI and its affiliates employ close to 25,000 professionals and have over 100 offices serving clients in 19 countries. Initially a private company, CGI went public in 1986. Godin and Imbeau maintain leadership positions within the company, with Godin in the lead as executive chairman, and Imbeau as executive vice president and chief financial officer. In January 2006, Michael Roach became the president and CEO.

Growing, growing, growing

In the past few years, CGI has invested aggressively in its growth by signing outsourcing contracts, creating partnerships, acquiring companies and opening new offices in the U.S., Europe and Asia. Since going public, CGI has made over 65 acquisitions.

The group's long list of partners includes industry giants such as Microsoft, BEA, IBM, Oracle and Sun Microsystems, while its client roster runs the gamut across industries and boasts such gems as Air Canada, American Express, AT&T, Bank of Canada, the Commonwealth of Virginia, the Government of Canada, J.P. Morgan Chase, Merrill Lynch, Prudential Financial, the U.S. Department of Health and Human Services, the U.S. Department of State and the Vodafone Group.

And the CGI's most recent acquisitions are leading the firm in a positive direction. In May 2004, the firm acquired roughly three-quarters of the employees from American Management Systems (AMS), a business and IT consulting firm, and renamed it CGI-AMS. This wholly owned U.S. operating subsidiary seems to be making strides, as it acquired privately-held, New York City-based consulting and systems integration firm MPI Professionals in August 2005. Founded in 2001, MPI specialized in project management, compliance, convergence, risk management and straight-through processing for the financial services sector, with a specific focus in capital markets. With revenues of $17 million, MPI employed 80 senior-level professionals. The next month, CGI-AMS reeled in Silver Oak Solutions, a government and commercial sector management solution firm.

Creating jobs

The firm had solid financial results in fiscal year 2005, with revenues and net income consistently higher than 2004 figures. The divestures helped maintain a strong balance sheet, along with new contracts. With its extra dough, CGI used $101.5 million to buy back over 14.8 million Class A subordinate shares at an average market price plus commission of $7.82 Canadian ($6.82 in U.S. currency). Additionally, the company, through CGI-AMS, invested $6 million in October 2005 to open a software development and systems integration facility in Virginia's Russell Regional Business Technology Park in Russell County. The investment is estimated to create 300 new jobs within 30 months for the coalfield region.

Bigger is better

CGI spent 2005 busily augmenting its client list and trying to sign more long-term contracts than it did in 2004. In February, the company started off the year with a bang, landing a contract with the World Anti-Doping Agency for a four-year IT contract to host the highly confidential infrastructure on all international and national athlete profiles worldwide. In March, the City of Montreal awarded the firm with a two-and-a-half-year business process and integration contract valued at $9.6 million. In June, CGI signed a 10-year end-to-end IT outsourcing contract valued at $30.5 million from Uni-Select Inc., a North American distributor of aftermarket auto parts. The deal also brought in 23 Uni-Select professionals to CGI. In addition, the firm signed a two-year project with Quebec's Ministère Du Revenu in October—valued at $17.4 million—to adapt and integrate the IT and accounting systems related to the Quebec Goods and Services Tax. And finally, in November 2005, the Housing Trust Fund Corporation of New York, a division of Housing and Community Renewal, selected CGI for a five-year, $44-million BPS contract.

CGI-AMS also had a strong year, scooping up large and multi-year contracts with a variety of government agencies and commercial businesses. The Centers for Medicare & Medicaid Services, a U.S. Department of Health and Human Services agency, agreed to a contract valued at $14.5 million in June 2005 for CGI to develop and support its Payment Reconciliation System. In the same month, Kentucky joined the growing list of public sector clients using CGI-AMS solutions. The group had signed with the City of Dallas, Texas; Baltimore County, Maryland; Baltimore

County Public Schools; the State of Utah; San Bernardino County, California; and the City of Austin, Texas, earlier that year. And finally, in July 2005, CGI-AMS sold a Proponix solution, its hosted, Web-based, fully integrated trade finance platform to Union Bank of California, the fourth-largest commercial bank in California.

Sticking with CGI

CGI considers contract extensions a key part of its growth strategy. As such, despite its efforts to sign new clients, CGI has not forgotten its existing relationships, renewing many of them in 2005. Not surprisingly, some of the company's longest-standing clients are located in its Canadian home town. CGI's relationship with the Department of National Defence of Canada extends back over 15 years. Clearly satisfied with the firm's work, this long-term client cemented its relationship once again when, in April 2005, the governmental agency signed CGI to another three-year contract valued at $13 million.

Contract extensions continued to be a running theme for the firm in 2005 and 2006. Canada's Yellow Pages Group Co. extended its contract with CGI for another seven years in late January 2005, and the Canadian Payments Association renewed for another 10 years in March—a contract valued at roughly $20 million. In October, Alberta Health and Wellness expanded its 2001 contract for four more years for $52 million. CGI started off 2006 on the right foot in February, when Aviva Canada, a property and casualty insurance group, extended its IT contract through 2011, bringing in $16.6 million.

The firm's clients aren't limited to Canadian borders, however. In May 2005, CGI-AMS signed a multi-year, $33 million contract with Los Angeles County—another long-term client since 1986—to supplement its existing agreement to implement the county's financial system. The Columbus Metropolitan Housing Authority also re-signed with the firm in June 2005, renewing its 2000 contract for a two-year deal valued at over $22 million. And finally, in July, expanding on a 2004 agreement valued at $109 million, John Hancock Life Insurance signed a separate seven-year IT outsourcing contract valued at $166 million.

Scaling down

While the company keeps its eyes open for new partnerships and acquisitions, it is also trying to stay lean and focused. Michael Roach, CGI president and CEO, stated in March 2005, "As part of our ongoing business practice, we are continually assessing our operations to ensure that we are in line with our strategy." At times, he continued, "the interests of our clients and professionals are best served through our decision to divest." In October of that year, Everlink Payment Services Inc., a Canadian electronic transaction switching service provider, acquired CGI's electronic switching assets for $24.4 million. As part of the transaction, 39 CGI professionals joined Everlink Services and the company turned over its Relay and CyberGateway switching solutions.

This divesture follows another transaction in March 2005 in which Garda World Security Corporation, a provider of security and cash handling services in Canada, acquired the principal assets of Keyfacts Entreprises Canada Inc., CGI's wholly-owned subsidiary. Valued at $3 million, Keyfacts provided information search and retrieval services for investigative purposes in Canada. The subsidiary had total revenues of approximately $14 million in 2004. In that same month, a data processing provider, Open Solutions Inc., paid CGI $24 million in cash for its U.S. Services to Credit Unions business unit and the CyberSuite product line. The unit provided core processing, loan origination, and Web hosting solutions for approximately 180 credit unions in the United States. The group reported revenues of approximately $16 million in 2004.

GETTING HIRED

Become a member

If you want to get on board at CGI, first get the lingo straight: The firm calls its people "members, not employees," according to CGI's web site. Among the firm's basic criteria for entry is an "EEE skillset," which the firm describes as a combination of education (ideally with certifications and/or post-grad study), expertise (in matters of industry verticals, project management and the consulting environment), and experience (the kind that "demonstrates success," of course). The firm's site allows CGI wannabes to search for open positions, and offers tips on what the firm looks for in resumes and cover letters.

Straight shootin' recruitin'

A consultant tells prospective "members" that CGI's "recruiters are straight shooters," with a "no-nonsense approach." While getting in is "not an easy process," the source says, it's "worth it if you get the offer."

One insider describes the experience of applying as a consultant: "I had one day with four interviews. I was interviewed by a recruiter, who asked me very basic questions about my resume, college and work experience. I also [was] interviewed by a junior staff employee…A mid-level staff person told me about the project where I was supposed to perform work, asked my about my experience in systems, and also asked me if I would enjoy working on systems. Finally, I met with a senior employee, who talked about [the firm] in general, and talked about his background." The source adds that "the interviews were not very technical, probably because I was applying for a functional position and I had strong subject matter expertise."

Another source describes an even more laid-back interview process, after being recruited through a contact on the "inside". "There were the traditional questions on my technical knowledge and experience. His questions after this were more focused on how I could handle difficult situations," the source says.

OUR SURVEY SAYS

A "very dynamic environment"

More than one consultant tells us that CGI is a "good place to work." According to an insider, the firm "does not seem to have the hierarchy that one would see in such firms as the former 'Big Five'. That is, people don't need to cower in fear [of] managers and vice presidents. The office doesn't seem too political." "There have been a lot of changes over the last few years, but the ship is definitely headed in the right direction," a colleague notes. While the firm is "every bit as professional as any other IT consulting firm," the source adds, "we tend to not take ourselves as seriously as other like companies." Another consultant notes that, "as an outsourcer, CGI is a young company," adding that the firm boasts a "very dynamic environment." It's also a social group, the consultant states, where "co-workers are open to share their experiences in a mutually beneficial attitude," and "people usually go out in small groups for lunch."

Young and old

As for the work itself, an insider says, "Some projects are very 'young,' filled with recent grads. Some are very 'old,' filled with other government contractors and ex-military types. The projects can vary widely depending on industry group, client, manager [and] co-workers."

CGIers put in some long weeks, but they're balanced out by shorter ones, sources suggest. "The hours are supposed to be 45 hours a week, but hours a week depend highly upon the client, deadlines and client deliverables. For some clients, CGI-AMS employees may work 60 hours a week, while for other clients, it is 40 hours a week," says a consultant. A Canadian source, however, notes that "official hours of work are 37.5 hours [per] week."

Flex time

An insider praises the fact that the firm is "very supportive of flexible work schedules. For example, several employees have been able to leave work at 3 p.m. to coach high school teams or pick up children from soccer practice." In addition, CGI "also allows for part-time work, though employees who can work part-time are very strong performers, who have done very well and have strong technical skills and institutional knowledge."

Supervisors come in all stripes at CGI, a consultant tells us: "Some are stricter and tougher than others. Some managers may simply give employees manuals, while other managers may walk staff through the software designs." Overall, though, the source adds, "expectations are reasonable."

Positioned for success

Insiders indicate that CGI doesn't follow a strict up-or-out promotion path. This, says a source, "has positive and negative implications—employees may get stuck in non-management positions for years. Other employees, however, may get opportunities to be 'team leads' within the first few years of employment." Another source lauds the firm's "very well structured personnel review process and disciplined execution of it." "Since CGI is a young company, opportunities for advancement are quite present. If you meet or exceed expectations, you only need to position yourself to get the visibility required," a consultant says.

Perks pay off

CGIers are mostly satisfied with salaries, which are described as "much better than market average, especially for college hires." A source notes that "raises depend drastically on the economy and on CGI's health." As for benefits, the firm reportedly offers a share purchase plan, tuition and transportation reimbursement, "great moving and relocation packages," and a "year-end bonus up to 15 percent upon meeting objectives." Some consultants see CGI's telecommuting option as a mighty perk, too.

Women at CGI see the firm's flexibility as a big bonus. "They are really flexible with part-time mothers and full-time parents who need to leave at [a] certain time for child care priorities," says a source, who cautions that "it's really all dependent on your manager, which can be a really unfortunate situation if you have a bad one." The firm is also reportedly quite diverse, a requirement built into the firm's government contracts, an insider suggests.

Visit the Vault Consulting Career Channel at **www.vault.com/consulting** —with
insider firm profiles, message boards, the Vault Consulting Job Board and more.

V/\ULT CAREER LIBRARY   **225**

101 Park Avenue, 26th Floor
New York, NY 10178
Phone: (212) 557-8038
Fax: (212) 867-8652
www.tcs.com

LOCATIONS

New York, NY (U.S. HQ)
Mumbai (Corporate HQ)
Offices in 35 countries

PRACTICE AREAS

Business Process Outsourcing
Consulting
Engineering & Industrial Services
IT Infrastructure Services
IT Services
Product Based Solutions

THE STATS

Employer Type: Public Company
Ticker Symbol: 532540 (Bombay
Stock Exchange), TCSEQ (National
Stock Exchange)
CEO and Managing Director:
Subramaniam Ramadorai
2005 Employees: 59,000
2004 Employees: 40,900
2005 Revenues: $2.24 billion
2004 Revenues: $1.56 billion

UPPERS

• Staffers take pride in the firm
• Opportunity to move around in
  practice areas and locations
• Lots of training and room for
  growth

DOWNERS

• Hierarchical employment structure
• U.S. staffers can be at a
  disadvantage
• Some compensation frustration

EMPLOYMENT CONTACT

www.tcs.com/0_careers/hotjobs.htm

THE BUZZ
WHAT CONSULTANTS AT OTHER FIRMS ARE SAYING

• "Giant player with good strategy"
• "Diverse"
• "Demanding and no work/life
  balance encouraged"
• "Too big"

THE SCOOP

All in the family

Fakir Chand Kohli, the grandfather of Indian IT services, founded Tata Consultancy Services in 1968. While overseeing the corporate operation of Tisco (now called Tata Steel Limited), a company owned by Indian giant Tata Group, he realized the potential in providing IT solutions to clients. Kohli developed TCS's business model around his realization and, as such, TCS claims to have pioneered the offshore delivery model for IT services. From the start, the firm's Mumbai office accepted documents flown in from all over India. Workers punched data into cards, turning jobs around in seven days. Soon, the firm began offering this service to other companies, many of them outside India. One of its first U.S. jobs was archiving the crime database for the Detroit Police Department. Over time, TCS migrated from data entry to code writing and applications maintenance.

TCS was founded as a separate company within the Tata Group. The Tata Group is India's second-largest software exporter (trailing only behind Infosys), with business interests in seven sectors: engineering, materials, energy, chemicals, services, consumer products and information systems/communications. The Tata family of enterprises comprises 93 companies. The information systems/communications sector, of which TCS is a part, includes 12 companies owned by Tata.

No small potatoes

TCS has a solid worldwide presence, with offices in 34 countries across 5 continents. It maintains 55 offices in North America, supporting over 9,000 employees. The firm's revenues display its steady growth, reaching $2.24 billion in 2005, up from $1.56 billion in fiscal 2004. The company claims seven of the Fortune Top 10 companies on its client roster, and expects to break into the Top 10 consulting firms in the world by 2010. Clients include AT&T, Boeing, British Airways, British Telecom, Canadian Depository for Securities, Citibank, Compaq, Dell Computer Corporation, Eaton Corporation, Fidelity Investment and Ford. In 2004, General Electric alone accounted for 16 percent of TCS revenues.

Coming out

Born and bred in India, Tata Consultancy Services was the subcontinent's first global billion-dollar software company, accounting for 2 percent of India's exports and 15 percent of its IT services segment. The company was a privately held entity until June 2004 when it went public on both the Bombay Stock Exchange and the National Stock Exchange of India after two years of preparation. The initial public offering of 55.45 million shares was the largest in Indian stock market history at the time. Shares rose more than 40 percent on the National Stock Exchange and over 20 percent on the Bombay Stock Exchange. Ratan Tata, chairman of Tata Group, said the company had "underestimated the enthusiasm" of the investors. The IPO raised $1.2 billion for the company and provided TCS with a stronger base to compete with India's other powerhouse IT companies.

Financial growth

Tata is continually looking for ways to expand its client roster and projects. In 2004, the company added 8,000 employees and boosted its client roster with 52 new companies, many of which were from the financial sector. In November 2005, TCS purchased 100 percent equity in Comicrom, a Chilean banking and pensions business process outsourcing company, for $23 million. A privately held company with 1,257 employees, Comicrom provided BPO services to banks, insurance companies, pension funds and government agencies. With revenues of $35.5 million in 2005, the company boasted a 57 percent market share of the check processing business in the country and counted 70 percent of the country's banks on its client list. The acquisition allows TCS to focus on vertical, platform-specific BPO opportunities. It also boosted TCS's regional staff to over 2,000 and its client base to over 100.

In October 2005, TCS acquired Sydney-based Financial Network Services, an Australian core banking solutions vendor, in its first major international acquisition. The deal, which totaled $26 million, strengthened TCS's portfolio of banking and financial services products and provided the company with an established global customer base. Prior to the acquisition, TCS had implemented FNS's Core Banking Solution in three of India's major banks, including the State Bank of India. In September, TCS bagged a five-year application maintenance project from ABN AMRO worth $250 million. TCS agreed to implement the Centralised Core Banking Solution in 1,000 branches of Central Bank of India in June 2005. The contract, signed before TCS acquired FNS, included FNS products. TCS also agreed to redesign and deploy a bank-wide Corporate Network for an additional 1,367 locations, by designing, building and maintaining the bank's data center, disaster recovery center and facilities management services.

A family reunion

As part of a large corporate conglomerate, TCS has the advantage of being able to use its Tata siblings to its advantage. Tata Teleservices, a telecom service provider, kept things in the Tata family by outsourcing its IT infrastructure management to TCS in September 2005. The strategic partnership is valued at $250 million over five years and gives customers access to services from both companies. And in July, TCS expanded its financial operations by merging with Tata Infotech Limited. Tata Infotech employed over 3,600 consultants and had strong operations in the U.S., UK and Australia serving Fortune 500 clients in banking, financial services, insurance, telecommunications and retail. Tata Infotech also offered e-learning, hardware design and contract manufacturing services.

Making new friends

Compared to other major Indian IT companies, TCS's exposure in the U.S. has been fairly limited. To combat this, the firm has pursued aggressive globalization tactics and has successfully allied itself with U.S. businesses to expand its portfolio and service offerings. The partnerships also help TCS deal with the backlash that Indian companies often face when entering IT services in the U.S.

TCS partnered with Hyperion to deploy performance management and business intelligence software to its clients. Under the partnership, signed in January 2005, TCS built an internal Hyperion Center of Excellence in its Bangalore Delivery Center featuring a lab for research, proof of concept, prototyping and advanced training. The Hyperion-TCS partnership offers quicker access to its 100 global customers, and is a "cornerstone in our aggressive growth strategy for the Business Intelligence Practice," according to TCS's Santosh Mohanty, head of the business intelligence practice.

Other partnerships forged in 2005 include a November contract with SAP in which TCS agreed to design and build tools around SAP platforms. In June and July, TCS signed with QAD and Cognos, respectively, to deliver the companies' software solutions to clients. TCS also partners with QAD on system design and implementation. The firm also landed a contract extension with BEA Systems to deploy BEA products to clients. Since 2000, TCS has provided global support and IT services expertise for BEA customers, such as integration, migration and development of BEA-powered solutions. BEA, in turn, has provided TCS with its enterprise infrastructure software platform for TCS products such as Quartz, Apollo, eTreasury and IIMS.

Microsoft match-up

In an effort to deliver IT solutions to global clients more effectively, TCS and Microsoft announced in May 2005 that they would be implementing the Microsoft Connected Services Framework—a server-based software solution that allows telecom operators and service providers to create and collect communication services across multiple networks and devices. The solution is intended to reduce cost, enhance operational efficiency and boost revenues.

Capitalizing on this teamwork, China's Sino-India Cooperative Office selected TCS and Microsoft in June 2005 to work with the Beijing Zhongguancun Software Park Development Co., Ltd., Uniware Co., Ltd., and Tianjin Huayuan Software Park Construction and Development Co., Ltd., to establish a software joint venture company to provide IT outsourcing services and solutions. As the majority shareholder, TCS intends to build the venture as a role model for the growing Chinese software industry.

Heightening high-tech endeavors

TCS also strengthened its radio frequency identification (RFID) offerings by opening an RFID Technology Center in Chicago in June 2005. The center was established to house offsite teams, as well as to test and benchmark RFID products. The company claims the center has the capabilities to assist organizations in connecting the disparate RFID components. TCS entered the RFID marketplace with its dedicated RFID practice staffed by core technology and business experts drawn from various industries. In March 2004, TCS announced a partnership with Oracle to support its Sensor Based Services for RFID initiatives. In August 2005, Virgin Atlantic chose TCS and Oracle to tag critical parts used in aircraft maintenance and repairs.

Not just outsourcing

The company devotes a good portion of its energies to non-outsourcing activities, as well. In its Tata Research Development and Design Center, products developed target the software development lifecycle and include modeling and code generation tools. The research center is also involved in the areas of language processing, formal methods and research on artificial intelligence and decision support.

GETTING HIRED

Wanted: globetrotters with zeal

On its web site, TCS maintains a detailed FAQ outlining its hiring practices and policies, along with job listings sorted by global region. "Consultant selection," the firm explains, "is a planned operation involving aptitude tests, auditions, an interview process, and the recommendation of the institute concerned." The firm lists a number of attributes it looks for in would-be TCSers, including domain knowledge, knowledge of IT, reasoning ability, analytical ability, creativity, communication skills, emotional maturity, initiative, people sensitivity, situation sensitivity, drive and determination, a "willingness to trot the globe at short notice" and a zeal for excellence. "If you have these attributes," TCS says, "you can be certain we are looking for you."

Same-day results

One consultant recruited straight out of college says the campus hiring process is "very easy." A colleague reports, "During the campus recruitment, I had a written exam which tested quantitative and qualitative abilities, as well as critical reasoning and psychometric analysis. Those passing this test were then interviewed the same day or the next. I had my interview around 10 a.m. and got my selection result around 4 p.m." The source adds, "My interviewers were a senior employee (maybe with four to five years of experience) and a senior manager (someone with over 10 years of experience). Two specific questions I can remember are: 'Will you be able to move to different locations if your work requirements demand so?'; and 'What programming languages do you know?'"

Another consultant hired with a master's degree explains, "We had a written aptitude test (fairly easy to pass) and a round of interviews. Since I came from a non-computer science background, the interview was restricted to a few questions about my master's-level project. A personality assessment was included." This was followed by a technical test after the offer letter was granted, the insider says.

A colleague states that "the technical interview will be more focused on your bachelor's project work and some tricky questions from your engineering basics. If you are to exhibit some [of your] innovative works…you are sure to get a job at TCS. The insider adds, "When I was in the technical round, I displayed some of my work that I did in [the] design field (mechanical engineering) and the interview was a cakewalk for me."

OUR SURVEY SAYS

TCS pride

TCS is defined by its hard-charging style, as well as for its reputation for ethics, sources say. "I am proud to be a TCSer," says a source. "As everyone knows, the company is governed by its ethics and Tata culture, like any other Tata group company." According to a co-worker, insiders take pride in the firm's "strong vision." "Ask any TCSer what his motto is; he will for sure say this: 'Top 10 by 2010'. It personally gives you a feel of greatness. The company is really keen on achieving it, and is fiercely competing with its global industrial peers like IBM, Accenture and Capgemini." The source also enjoys the feeling of working in a "socially conscious" company—though this "may be a brand-building strategy," the insider says, "for me, as I was directly involved in one such initiative, [it] felt emotional."

But another insider observes that the firm's corporate culture "varies from very driven to absolutely not caring," depending on management. "I have worked with managers who used to work for the love of it and used to motivate the teams very well. I have also worked for managers who were totally incompetent, but survived because the organization would not get rid of deadwood."

India oriented

Culture may also vary depending on how far one operates from the firm's home base, insiders suggest. A consultant warns that, "overall the work culture can be tough for UK or U.S.-based employees...All the systems are geared for Indian or India-based associates. U.S. associates can have a tough time in getting access to corporate network or filling your appraisal."

Another source notes that corporate culture depends on the client, too, since the firm is big on onsite work. "Some of the offices are much better [than] others. The culture and opportunities depend on a lot on the client...For example, GE project teams have much better skill sets and work culture compared to other clients...But the organization is very hierarchical and getting to meet the senior management is very difficult (or should I say impossible?)." A colleague agrees that TCS "is very hierarchical. Associates are expected to concur and agree with whatever superiors say. Any differing opinion is perceived as a challenge."

The pros and cons of flexibility

As for workload, an insider notes that "hours were quite flexible when I worked in India as well as in the U.S. The commitment to get the job done on time was always there and most of the employees honored that." But a colleague gripes that "employees are expected to work 60 to 80 hours a week." Furthermore, the source grumbles, "Generally work is not defined; [the] concept of roles is missing. For example, a sales manager is responsible for marketing, sales, execution, billing, recruitment, logistics and everything else. And he (not many 'shes') is expected to do all these in his personal time."

All over the world

Globetrotters can benefit from TCS's international spread, a source suggests. "TCS provides the best learning opportunities for someone starting out from college," the source elaborates, adding that since the firm has "projects all over the world," consultants can "expect to travel to a foreign country within one to two years of joining it. I was fortunate to be sent to a non-English part of Europe where the local operations take care of providing apartments free of cost." A colleague chimes in: "No other company in the world allows you to serve clients in various parts of the globe as TCS does…Young recruits get to travel to [various sites] sooner than at any other company. In my case, it took exactly two years, but on an average, guys with 18 months of experience venture out to travel abroad."

In addition, the source reports, TCS offers the chance to try on different jobs and areas, as "there is always an opportunity to work in different industrial sectors like Telecom, BFSI, Retail, etc. If you [are] bored of working in one domain for more than a year or two, you can very well opt to hop to another domain. I started my career in telecom and I'm now in finance." As for getting ahead, a consultant says, "Opportunities for advancement are tremendous for those who really cater to the exact requirements…[For] the last few years, performance measurements have been strengthened and only the best [are] advanced appropriately."

Passing the buck(s)

TCS does have some reputation for stinginess among insiders when it comes to compensation and reimbursement. "Salaries are negotiable," a source says, advising newbies to "negotiate hard and get everything in writing. After joining there is not much scope of increase." Bonuses are "not well defined," the source adds, and stock options generally have been limited to the executive level. As for time off, an insider reports that "U.S. associates get two to three weeks of vacation; Indian [associates] get four weeks." The source adds that the "insurance policy used to be horrible. It's improved slightly, thought it's still awful." For many money-related issues, a consultant says, "Every decision is 'case by case' and executives love to play passing games—Operations to HR to Accounts to Operations. Even buying a $100 software [program] can take months, and claiming your bonus can take a year (if you are persistent). For some strange reason, HR and Accounts rule and are part of every decision."

"No other company in the world allows you to serve clients in various parts of the globe as TCS does...Young recruits get to travel to [various sites] sooner than at any other company."

— *TCS source*

Visit the Vault Consulting Career Channel at **www.vault.com/consulting** —with
insider firm profiles, message boards, the Vault Consulting Job Board and more.

VAULT CAREER LIBRARY   235

Fujitsu Consulting

333 Thornall Street
Edison, NJ 08837
Phone: (732) 549-4100 or
(800) 882-3212
Fax: (732) 549-2375
us.fujitsu.com/consulting

LOCATIONS

Edison, NJ (HQ)
17 offices in 12 states

PRACTICE AREAS

Application Management
Business & Technology Architecture
Business Process Management
Call Center Operations
Information Management
Outsourcing
Packaged Applications
Staff Supplementation

THE STATS

Employer Type: Subsidiary of Fujitsu
Limited
Ticker Symbol: 6702.T (Tokyo Stock
Exchange)
Chairman and CEO: John T. Rose
2005 Employees: 3,300
2004 Employees: 3,000
2005 Revenues: $44.5 billion
(Fujitsu Limited global revenues)
2004 Revenues: $45 billion
(Fujitsu Limited global revenues)

UPPERS

- "Opportunity to work with new
  clients/people"
- "Interesting work"
- "Flexible work hours"

DOWNERS

- "No information about the various
  career streams available"
- "They expect you to work
  extra...but don't belly-up to the
  bar"
- "Employees are replaceable and
  treated as such"

EMPLOYMENT CONTACT

www.fujitsu.com/global/about/
  employment
E-mail: FC.Communications@
consulting.fujitsu.com

THE BUZZ
WHAT CONSULTANTS AT OTHER FIRMS ARE SAYING

- "Strong support of university
  programs"
- "Amiable executives and strong
  product offerings"
- "Vendor-reliant"
- "Weak outside Japan"

THE SCOOP

The prodigal son

A trusted provider of management and technology consulting to business and government, Fujitsu Consulting is the North American consulting and services arm of the $44.5 billion Fujitsu Limited. The parent organization is headquartered in Tokyo and employs more than 150,000 worldwide.

Today's Fujitsu Consulting was originally founded in 1973 under the name DMR Group, Inc., which was acquired, along with Trecom, by the Amdahl Corporation in 1995 and 1996, respectively. Amdahl merged the two groups, retaining the DMR name. Along came Fujitsu in 1996, making its move into consulting services by acquiring Amdahl and its DMR division. The consulting group was officially rebranded to Fujitsu Consulting in 2002. Today, the group, headquartered in Edison, N.J., with a staff of 3,300, provides IT governance, information management, legacy systems modernization and application outsourcing services.

Pulling its weight

Fujitsu Consulting seems to be pulling in its share of profits for the mighty parent. In the first half of 2005, the firm's services group, of which Fujitsu Consulting is a part, posted revenues of $8.9 billion, a 2.3 percent increase from the first half of 2004. Performance was flat in Japan, but the overseas groups posted an 8.2 percent growth, accounting for 30 percent of the total revenue for the subsegment. For fiscal year 2005, the company saw profits of $1.2 billion for the services group, a 43 percent increase from 2004's $837 million. The first half of 2005 alone showed income for services up $345 million, a 187 percent increase from the first half of 2004.

Creative problem solvers

On its web site, the firm describes itself as "the people who show up in the middle of the night to fix a problem you didn't know you had or didn't expect to solve. We even go one step further by applying imagination and creativity to tap into your staff's competencies to make sure the problem doesn't recur." Others recognize this strength and award Fujitsu Consulting with accolades. In 2004, *KMWorld* named Fujitsu Consulting one of the top 18 vendors in knowledge management, and the company won the CRM Consultant "One to Watch" award at *CRM Magazine's* CRM Leader Awards in 2003.

Fujitsu's services platform is built around Macroscope, a trademarked integrated IT and business methodology that helps assess client needs. The analyst group Gartner recognized the strategic methodology as an industry leader in 2002. In November 2005, Fujitsu Consulting announced the addition of Microsoft's Visual Studio 2005 Team System to enhance Macroscope's project delivery capabilities.

The firm launched another new program in September 2005—Fujitsu Advanced Claims Processing Utility—a product developed in conjunction with FileNet Corporation. The program combines enterprise content management with business process management services and is designed to expedite property and casualty claims processing, reduce claims payout and administrative costs, and improve customer service and retention.

Becoming a full-service provider

Fujitsu Consulting has grown over the years in the tried and tested way. It has acquired smaller companies to enhance its service offerings, and established non-exclusive IT relationships with market leaders to expand its product lines. In addition, the firm maintains market and alliance relationships to provide it with unlimited access to solution packages and advance notice of changes, as well as in-depth knowledge to support clients' system integration and IT consulting needs. Some of these partners include SAP, Microsoft, Documentum EMC, Interwoven and Oracle.

In terms of acquisitions, 2005 was a big year for Fujitsu. In March, the firm acquired Cendera Technologies, a Dallas-based professional services company. The addition of Cendera enhanced Fujitsu's business process outsourcing capabilities, especially for telecommunications outsourcing, the company said at the time. Fujitsu Consulting acquired all of Cendera's assets along with its veteran staff of telecommunications software developers and operational support systems specialists. According to the terms of the agreement, Fujitsu retained all Cendera employees.

In May of that same year, Fujitsu announced its acquisition of Minneapolis-based BORN in an all-stock deal. Acquiring BORN, a business and technology consulting firm, extended its delivery capability in several markets including Minneapolis, Denver, Dallas, Milwaukee and Atlanta. BORN's staff of 400 professionals helped increase Fujitsu Consulting's headcount in North America, and added expertise in areas such as enterprise resource planning, Microsoft solutions, enterprise data management and application integration. Analyst group Gartner smiled on the deal and stated, "Consulting, development and integration services is increasingly becoming a scale market in which larger vendors that offer multiple service lines have a competitive advantage. Being a full-service provider is key to making it into the top 10 rankings in North America."

Calling all arms

Fujitsu works with clients in both the public and private sectors. In the public sector, the firm has developed an integrated set of services to help U.S. government agencies design complex business cases to justify IT capital investments. In early September 2005, the Federal Emergency Management Agency asked Fujitsu Consulting for additional call center capabilities to handle calls from the victims of Hurricanes Katrina and Rita. The firm scaled up its operations and responded to more than 1 million calls in 80 days of operation.

At its peak, the call center employed more than 1,200 staff, operating 16 hours per day, seven days a week, and managing up to 30,000 calls per day. "Making a call center of this scale operational on such short notice is unprecedented," said Jerry Crowley, general manager of Call Center Operations, in November 2005.

Lending advice

Fujitsu Consulting houses a think tank that produces case studies and reports. The studies are often client-based, looking at specific business problems clients face and examining Fujitsu's solutions. Other reports and whitepapers, however, take a more industry-wide stance. One of the think tank's most recent reports, written in 2004, focused on the role of a firm's CIO and protecting the organization's information health by balancing IT spending to ensure that IT does not impinge upon business performance. Quite often, the report said, the risk of an IT project is assessed not so much by critical failures related to new technologies, but by the little hiccups and increased need for hands-on work with anything untried and untested.

GETTING HIRED

Mature audiences only

Fujitsu Consulting seems to favor experienced hires, foregoing campus recruitment in pursuit of referrals and applications from people already in the workforce. "I can say that we actively recruit using our existing employees to find new people," one insider states, while another admits, "I got hired through a reference; not sure how else the firm works on that aspect."

While several Fujitsu insiders felt that they were "not at liberty to discuss" the hiring process, one source explains how he had "six interviews over two months," including an interview with a "resource manager" that "consisted of sitting and listening to him talk about himself."

OUR SURVEY SAYS

Keeping it local

Sources are generally positive about the atmosphere at Fujitsu Consulting, declaring that despite the group's mergers and growth through the 1990s and early 2000s into a "large multinational" firm, "the basic tenets and work ethics have remained the same" in individual offices where "we still operate pretty much as a local team." Insiders describe the advancement policy as open and flexible, and say that "promotions are provided on the basis of demonstrated competency against a standard set of criteria used throughout the organization. Anyone can request a promotion review at any time and these are undertaken by a group of senior consultants (in the case of middle or junior people) or the management team (for senior people)."

A less-than-satisfied source, however, says that the firm survives on exaggeration and marketing" and "they expect you to pad your resume" to make consultants look good to clients, while "they don't pay well enough to attract outstanding employees." Others insist that "training is minimal and consists of computer-based training" and that the company needs to "improve employee training conditions."

Family matters

Insiders give Fujitsu Consulting high grades for travel, workload and overall work/life balance. Average workweeks for some insiders can be 37.5 hours, and others find travel requirements to be almost nonexistent. "Travel for me has been very minimal," a consultant tells us, "typically less than a day or so every two or three months. And most of those have been short, commuter-length trips for meetings." This is an important factor for consultants with family and other interests outside of work. Insiders say the company has an "understanding of family versus work balance" and is "very good about recognizing the need for me to spend time with my family, and that family is more important to me than work."

Benefits and more

Benefits and perks provided by the company include the basic "matching pension contributions, standard medical, extended medical and group life insurance." A consultant notes that although Fujitsu provides "good long-term disability coverage," the retirement savings plan seemed "pathetic." According to a colleague, the firm also holds "monthly meetings where lunch is provided at a nice hotel," and employees get four weeks of vacation per year, "regardless of years" worked at the company.

Fujitsu Consulting participates in some community activities, including the nationwide "United Way campaign," as well as "some very local ones (food banks, etc.)."

PA Consulting Group

123 Buckingham Palace Road
London
SW1W 9SR
Phone: +44 20 7730 9000
Fax: +44 20 7333 5050
www.paconsulting.com

LOCATIONS

London (HQ)
Operations in over 35 countries

PRACTICE AREAS

Business operations consulting
Decision sciences
Information technology and systems
  integration
Market analytics
People and organizational change
Program and project management
Sourcing for value
Strategy and marketing
Technology and innovation - product
  & process development
Zanzibar Managed Service

THE STATS

Employer Type: Private Company
President & CEO: Bruce Tindale
2005 Employees: 2,750
2004 Employees: 2,600
2005 Revenues: $581 million
2004 Revenues: $580 million

UPPERS

- "Supportive and friendly culture"
- "It's not so large that you get 'lost' in it"
- Employee-ownership scheme proves profitable

DOWNERS

- "Sometimes not a lot of time to stop and reflect"
- "Tendency to place billing hours over personal development"
- "Long hours and high pressure"

EMPLOYMENT CONTACT

www.paconsulting.com/join_pa

THE BUZZ
WHAT CONSULTANTS AT OTHER FIRMS ARE SAYING

- "Strong brand in Europe"
- "Smallish specialist firm"
- "Not focused"

THE SCOOP

Born in the UK

Founded in 1943, the London-based PA Consulting Group is a global leader in the field of management, systems and technology consulting, with offices in more than 35 countries and a staff of around 3,000. PA's consultants earn more than a paycheck for their services: The privately-held company is owned entirely by its employees. The company has experience and a proven track record within a number of different industries, including energy, financial services, government services, health, international development, life sciences, manufacturing, postal, retail, telecommunication, transportation, travel and tourism, and water. IT plays a big role in the firm, contributing over 40 percent of the firm's overall revenue, with applied technology contributing an additional 14 percent of global revenues.

Shaking things up

PA Consulting Group started off 2006 on a new foot. In October 2005, the firm announced some major structural shifts within the firm's senior management. The changes, which took effect in January 2006, placed Andrew Hooke, former head of the Government Services Group, in the role of chief operating officer. Hooke will work alongside CEO Bruce Tindale to implement the firm's growth strategy. Equally significant changes occurred in the management of the government services, IT consulting, technology, strategy and industries, and business transformation groups. The firm also appointed Barbara Thomas Judge, non-executive chairman of the UK Atomic Energy Authority and one of the first women to be appointed as Commissioner for the Securities and Exchange Commission, to its roster, naming her non-executive director. Commenting on these changes in October 2005, executive chairman Jon Moynihan stated, "We believe that these changes will bring added vigour and insight to the leadership of the company, help us to continue down the road to success, and in particular lay further foundations for a smooth transition between generations."

Venturing above and beyond

In an effort to expand its technology base and offer new services and solutions for its clients, as well as to provide career and financial opportunities for its consultants, PA has embarked on several "PA ventures." These investments, which become wholly owned subsidiaries and specialist companies of PA Consulting Group, are businesses in which the firm invests its own capital to exploit its own intellectual and technological know-how.

PA's latest business venture, Aegate, is hard at work creating a next-generation approach to patient safety by supplying authentication services for pharmaceutical products at the dispensing point. Simply put, Aegate "promises to bring resolution to the vast worldwide problem of fake medicines," according to PA's web site. In April 2005, PA invested roughly $26.8 million in the business to develop and roll out its solution, "Authentication at the point of dispensing™". The new company is already making a name for itself: In October, it received the 2005 Frost & Sullivan Best Practice Award for Entrepreneurial Company in recognition of its "unique and commercially attractive solution to combat pharmaceutical counterfeiting and fraud and secure patient safety." The company is now planning to roll out its solution in the U.S., UK and Belgium in 2006, and in order to realize the market potential of the program, named Gary Noon, a veteran of the pharmaceutical industry, to CEO of Aegate in November 2005.

PA launched another strategic venture in February 2006 called Zanzibar Managed Service, a new eProcurement solution for the UK public sector. PA Shared Services Limited—a PA subsidiary—will be delivering Zanzibar under a five-year contract signed with UK government department OGCbuying.solutions, together with three international consortium members

Selling out

UbiNetics, a PA venture that emerged in 1999 out of the company's Wireless Technology Practice, has also created some recent headlines. UbiNetics produces new goods for wireless communications and has rapidly become a world leader in 3G test and measurement products, and in next generation multimode 2G/3G/HSPDA cellular software and technology. It also supplies semiconductors and handset devices to several global telecom operators. In May 2005, the Test and Measurement division of UbiNetics was sold to Aeroflex Inc. for $84.5 million, and in July 2005, PA sold the other half of the business—Volume Product Technology—to CSR Plc. for $48 million. Commenting on the sale in a September 2005 *Financial Times* interview, Moynihan said, "When it gets to the stage that we can't add any value to it, that is the time to go. We don't want to hold on to a venture for the sake of it." PA has no further interest in the operations of UbiNetics, but retains a residual interest in the holding company, UbiNetics Holding Limited, and in another PA venture, Cubiks, a specialty HR consultancy that it sold off in April 2004.

Heading to the beach

In May 2005, PA announced that it would be providing technical assistance in research and business development to the Caribbean Hotel Association (CHA). The research will focus on the development of sustainable tourism performance indicators for small, medium and micro enterprises (SMMEs). Additionally, the firm will concentrate on strengthening the CHA, developing business models for National Hotel Association and SMMEs. PA is also offering its technical services to the Caribbean Tourism Organization by advising on ways to improve the research capacity of its member organizations and conducting a variety of studies on topics such as air transportation models, cruise tourism impacts, soft adventure market and community tourism. Since 1998, PA has been a member of the Caribbean Alliance for Sustainable Tourism's Governing Council, working on various projects to promote "environmental management" in the hotel sector. As a result of such projects, Jamaica boasts the world's first four hotels to be Green Globe 21 certified. Additionally, Jamaica now leads the world in Green Globe 21 certified tourism businesses, including a commercial hotel chain with all its affiliated hotels. PA has also assisted Dominica in becoming the only country to benchmark Green Globe 21.

GETTING HIRED

Jobs across the globe

PA's web site lists current openings worldwide and accepts online applications. Candidates may only apply for a maximum of three jobs, and the firm cautions that "submitting multiple applications would be counter-productive."

PA's extensive online careers page explains that the firm's selection process may vary slightly depending on role and country. Some things are consistent, though, including PA's use of role play and group exercises, a partner interview, technical interviews and specialized verbal, numerical and personality tests.

PA, as in "psychometric assessments"

For the personality assessment, the firm gives a test known as the PAPI (Personality and Preference Inventory), developed by ex-PA venture company Cubiks (links for more information are available on the site). The verbal "reasoning for business" test asks candidates to "interpret and draw inferences from business-oriented data and then solve problems related to this information," the firm explains on its web site, while the numerical assessment "has been designed to determine how well an individual can work with numbers, and involves questions based on data presented in a variety of forms including graphs, diagrams and statistical tables."

The firm's recruitment and interview process is "efficient and rigorous," and recruiters pay particular attention to applicants from Cornell, MIT and UCLA, insiders suggest. According to one consultant, "I went through the graduate recruitment process. This consisted of a first interview with psychometric tests, followed by an assessment day which included a second interview, a presentation and a group exercise."

OUR SURVEY SAYS

Lots of room for growth

The "P" in "PA" might as well stand for People, according to insiders. "The people are the best thing about PA," says a consultant. The firm boasts "a very professional and open culture," a colleague comments. As another insider puts it, the firm requires "competitive and hard work," but offers "lots of scope to grow personally." In the words of another source, "Having worked alongside competitor organizations, I struggle to see why people would choose to work for them over PA."

While "the firm expects people to work hard," the work/life balance situation has "definitely improved," and PA is "making proactive steps to improve the lot for all of its consulting staff," sources tell us. Consultants report logging between 45 and 60 hours of work per week, with three to four days of travel, "as you would expect in consulting." Still, a source reports, "Travel requirements are varied: Some people travel a lot, others are on assignments close to their office." And another insider notes that the firm is "flexible with specific life events, e.g., marriage, young children, etc." In addition, says a colleague, "PA is very good at giving people opportunity—you don't have to constantly seek line approval."

Meritocracy abounds

Unanimously, sources describe PA as a "meritocratic." Says one insider, "PA promotes people who are ready to operate at the next rank above, when they are ready. It is not an up-or-out policy. You can expect to advance as quickly as you are feasibly able to demonstrate your capabilities; typical duration from graduate ranks to partner [is] 10 to 15 years." Another source agrees: "If you have the right skills, you can progress (rather than it being based on age or time served). There is a strong emphasis on also having the necessary experience to support skill sets to prevent people being promoted faster than is beneficial for them and the company." According to another consultant, "If you want to do well and are good, you can move fast. If you consistently underperform, you will be encouraged to leave."

Reaping rewards

PA's unusual compensation scheme is highly attractive to its go-getter consultants. As a source explains, "We are employee-owned, so all of us own stock in the firm awarded through our bonus. This is based on asset valuation, so it grows in value if we make profits, which we consistently do. This investment significantly outperforms the markets. In addition, we have a successful venture business linked to our consulting business; as ventures are created, we (as shareholders) are awarded stock in them and reap the rewards when they are sold. This has offered very substantial additional returns to shareholders (i.e., us, the employees) over the last few years."

As for other perks, the firm reportedly shines in training, offering an "excellent core consulting skills program." In addition, says an insider, under a "recently instigated scheme," employees are now encouraged to take time off for community volunteering efforts. This adds up to about "three days of voluntary service through a registered charity," but "allocation of the hours is driven by individual requests," sources add.

While the firm has been running "a major diversity initiative over the past year," results are only slowly coming to pass, insiders suggest. PA is "committed" to hiring and retaining women and minorities, a consultant says, but "this is not fully reflected" in their numbers at the senior levels just yet.

4201 Lexington Avenue North
Arden Hills, MN 55126-6198
Phone: (651) 415-4401
Fax: (651) 415-4891
E-mail: info.us@btsyntegra.com
www.btconsulting.com

LOCATIONS

Arden Hills, MN (U.S. HQ)
Fleet, UK (HQ)
Offices in 25 countries worldwide

PRACTICE AREAS

Consulting
Customer Relationship Management
Enterprise Security
Financial Trading Systems
Message Management Platform
Systems Integration

THE STATS

Employer Type: Subsidiary of BT Group
Ticker Symbol: BTY (NYSE)
President: Tim Smart
2004 Employees: 5,000
2005 Revenues: $1.5 billion
2004 Revenues: $1 billion

UPPERS

- Flexible placement options
- "The company has a clear plan on gaining market share"

DOWNERS

- Euro-centric
- "We sometimes have difficulty competing in pure price plays"

EMPLOYMENT CONTACT

www.btconsulting.com

THE BUZZ
WHAT CONSULTANTS AT OTHER FIRMS ARE SAYING

- "Global reach"
- "Large, well known"
- "Telecom only"
- "Weak player"

THE SCOOP

Return to the brand

Now part of the global BT Global Services brand, BT went by BT Syntegra until September 2004, when the company decided to switch the focus back to the global brand. BT, formerly known as British Telecom, has positioned itself in the market to become more than just another telecom company. Once it gained widespread recognition as a company with a broad reach in global IT and network services, the firm decided that it no longer needed a separate brand under which to offer its IT consulting services.

Financially, the company has done well in recent years. BT Global Solutions reported a 17 percent increase in revenues during the 2005 financial year to $5.7 billion. BT reported revenues of $1.5 million, or 25.8 percent of total Global Services revenue. According to the company's annual report, BT's 14 percent growth in 2005 reflected the new contracts won in 2004. Its specialties include consulting, customer relationship management, enterprise security, financial trading systems, message management and systems integration. Its industry base is broad, including energy and utilities, government, retail and manufacturing, travel and leisure, health care, financial trading systems, financial services, communications, and air and logistics.

Traversing the globe

BT's solutions find their way around the globe and in a wide variety of industries. The company's CRM and e-commerce service for leisure attraction operators appear in scattered institutions, including the British Museum, the Tate Britain, Madame Tussaud's in New York, Las Vegas and London, and the Lincoln Park Zoo in Chicago.

In July 2005, the firm signed a contract with Regions Hospital in St. Paul, Minn., to transform its staff communications processes. Through its Team Communications offering, BT provided the hospital with business and technical consulting services, and implemented a wireless communications system in a trauma unit and a medical surgery unit. According to Regions staff, the instant communications system helps increase patient safety by allowing nurses to call additional assistance for a patient in need or crisis without leaving the patient's bedside to search for help. The system also reduces wait time between a nurse's call and a physician's response. At the time, Chris Turnquist, vice president of sales for BT stated, "We place a great deal of focus

Visit the Vault Consulting Career Channel at **www.vault.com/consulting** — with insider firm profiles, message boards, the Vault Consulting Job Board and more.

VAULT CAREER LIBRARY   **249**

on how our customers can operate more efficiently through more timely and effective communication." Regions Hospital is now working with BT to expand the communications system into 20 additional patient-care areas, including general medical surgery units, the Surgery Center, the Burn Center and the Emergency Center. The hospital estimates that 1,200 total staff across shifts will be using the communications system when the roll-out is complete.

Corporate communication

BT also lands many projects on the world's stock trading floors, thanks to its ITS collaborative trading system (used in over 50 countries), global remote monitoring service, and other offerings from its sibling BT groups. In February 2005, the New York Mercantile Exchange signed with BT to implement these services in an effort to upgrade its trading floor.

That same month, Seoul-based Korean Inter Dealer Broker and ICAP, the world's largest interdealer broker, contracted with BT to install voice trading technology on its floors. Bond brokers using BT's ITS pV405Hi turrets and pV42i speakers can listen to up to 12 or more individual open-line voice channels and respond to market opportunities as soon as they happen. Commenting on the deal, Mick Williams, BT's general manager of financial services for Japan and Korea, claimed, "With Korea's financial markets going through a period of transformation, the country is positioned to become a significant financial centre in Northeast Asia. Using BT's voice trading technology—designed specifically for the trading room—KIDB-ICAP is well placed to take advantage of the developments in the Korean market as it evolves and grows."

BT also offers customers its message management platform to manage corporate e-mail. An open software platform, MMP can be integrated with a variety of systems to maintain consistent environments and rules across networks.

Government connections

The company has always had a strong public sector practice and 2005 was a good year for solidifying its government relationships. Most recently, in November, the firm signed a 10-year strategic partnership agreement with Registers of Scotland to deliver strategic IT services to improve the agency's internal processes, as well as to enhance its product and service offerings to meet growing business demands. The firm also extended its existing contract with the UK Ministry of Defence, establishing a $10 million deal in March to design, build and operate an extension to the Ministry's Land Systems Reference Centre. The LSRC tests Defence

Communication Information Systems to ensure that new and existing technology can work together in the field successfully. The new extension will also enable the LSRC to test the increasing amount of new technology and equipment developed by and for the armed forces.

In February 2005, BT landed an 11-year strategic services partnership contract worth more than $52.2 million with the Northern Ireland Housing Executive, the UK's largest housing authority. Under the agreement, BT will implement and support a new IT infrastructure for the NIHE. And in January, BT was awarded a three-year contract extension with Her Majesty's Customs and Excise to supply, operate and manage the Customs Handling of Import and Export Freight service. Under the extended contract, worth $48.8 million, BT will operate the service until 2010. BT designed and built the initial service in 1989 and continues to support and operate it all year round.

GETTING HIRED

Global opportunities

There are a variety of ways to get on board at BT—but first you'll need to navigate the firm's somewhat confusing careers page on its web site. If you're looking for U.S. opportunities, you may follow links on the firm's site for "U.S opportunities," though this link kicks you over to the BT Global site, which is oriented toward applicants in the UK and elsewhere in the world.

If you're interested in spending two years in the UK to launch a career in IT consulting, take a look at the firm's two-year graduate program. The program, which "allows recent grads to combine training, hands-on project work and international experience in the areas of their choice," is designed for grads with less than two years of industry experience. Participants are based in one of the firm's four main UK locations: Fleet, Sunbury, Newcastle or Leeds. Applications can be submitted and tracked on BT's web site.

For MBAs, the firm takes applications online, while also participating in business school events. The firm assures candidates that "every application is treated the same, wherever it originated." Minimum criteria are a strong academic background, a minimum GMAT score of 650, a minimum of six years of "proven management experience (not including internships)" before graduate studies, and evidence of promotion and responsibility in previous business roles.

A lengthy process

According to an insider, candidates can expect to face a "lengthy interview process," with "approximately five to seven interviews in a two-visit scenario." Once the firm selects applications, it brings in candidates to participate in a phone interview, after which they are invited to visit the firm for a more in-depth discussion. Assuming this goes well, prospective BTers are then invited to an "assessment center," where they may face tasks such as selection testing (including verbal/numerical reasoning or behavioral tests), case study exercises, group exercises and yet another interview.

The firm also offers opportunities for undergraduate placements—for two to three months in the summer, or six to 12 months for "industrial placements." Again, the firm requires applications to be submitted online for these opportunities.

THE BEST OF
THE REST

Affiliated Computer Services, Inc.

2828 North Haskell Avenue
Dallas, TX 75204
Phone: (214) 841-6111
Fax: (214) 821-8315
www.acs-inc.com

LOCATIONS

Dallas, TX (HQ)
More than 750 offices around the
world in nearly 100 countries

PRACTICE AREAS

Business Process Outsourcing
Information Technology Outsourcing
Systems & Integration

THE STATS

Employer Type: Public Company
Ticker Symbol: ACS (NYSE)
CEO: Mark King
2005 Employees: 55,000
2004 Employees: 43,000
2005 Revenues: $4.35 billion
2004 Revenues: $4.1 billion

UPPERS

• "Family friendly"
• Team-oriented culture

DOWNERS

• "Bottom-line driven"
• Numerous organizational ups and
  downs

EMPLOYMENT CONTACT

www.acs-inc.com/career/index.html

THE BUZZ
WHAT CONSULTANTS AT OTHER FIRMS ARE SAYING

• "Working its way up"
• "Diverse"
• "Need to affiliate more"
• "Snobby"

THE SCOOP

Pioneering BPO

Affiliated Computer Services, Inc., has built a huge name for itself in a relatively short period of time. Since its founding in 1988, ACS has amassed a client roster of top commercial and government organizations, specializing in business process outsourcing, information technology outsourcing and systems integration. In fact, ACS claims to have pioneered the concept of providing BPO services on a grand scale. Headquartered in Dallas, Texas, ACS posted $4.35 billion in annual revenues in fiscal year 2005, and employs over 55,000 people worldwide.

ACS is the brainchild of Darwin Deason, who rallied a number of IT professionals in the late 1980s to create a firm designed to work with clients on IT outsourcing projects and systems and integration services. ACS's first clients were in the financial industry, followed by engagements in the communications, education, energy, government, health care, insurance, manufacturing, retail and transportation sectors.

A new King

The firm saw a shift in its top ranks in October 2005 when then-CEO Jeff Rich left to pursue other business opportunities. Rich, who had held the CEO position since 1999, departed with a $4.1 million payout and a contract to do future business with the company. Mark King, who had been serving as president and COO, was named the new CEO, retaining his presidential role as well. An employee of ACS since its founding, King continues to work closely with founder Deason, who serves as chairman of the board.

Gobbling them up

The firm expanded rapidly in the 1990s, building itself up through a series of strategic acquisitions. In 1996, the firm bought Genix Group for $135 million, creating the fourth-largest outside provider of data processing services in the nation. Other acquisitions during the decade included BRC Holdings Inc., a developer of computer and management systems for health care organizations and local governments; Boston-based Unclaimed Property Services, a division of State Street Corp.; and Medicaid software and services specialist Consultec. By early 2001, the firm had consumed around 50 companies.

Visit the Vault Consulting Career Channel at **www.vault.com/consulting** – with
insider firm profiles, message boards, the Vault Consulting Job Board and more.

VAULT CAREER LIBRARY   255

Slowed spending

While ACS changed direction in the 21st century, selling off some units in order to balance its business portfolio with commercial and government clients, it didn't stop its spending spree entirely. In August 2001, the firm acquired both the business processing unit of National Processing Co. for $43 million and IMS Corporation, a Lockheed Martin subsidiary, for $825 million in July 2001. In June 2002, ACS purchased FleetBoston's Financial Corp. education services unit for $410 million as part of a plan to expand into the business of student loan processing. The company began 2003 with the purchase of CyberRep, a provider of customer care and customer relationship management services, for an undisclosed amount. Meanwhile, the firm enjoyed financial favor while racking up long-term, multi-million dollar contracts with high-profile customers like Blue Cross, American Express, Motorola and the Department of Education. Also in 2003, ACS made an interesting swap with Lockheed Martin, with the two firms agreeing to sell separate IT services units to one another. Lockheed picked up ACS' federal government tech services business for $658 million, and ACS bought Lockheed's commercial information technology business for $107 million.

The firm's 2004 acquisitions included Patient Accounting Services Center, a provider of billing and collections services to the health care industry, Truckload Management Services, a processor of online document management services for the trucking industry, and BlueStar Solutions Inc., which oversees e-mail messaging systems. In mid-2005 ACS completed its purchase of Mellon Financial Corp.'s HR consulting and outsourcing business for $405 million. Also in 2005, the firm made a few more acquisitions, including the $32 million purchase of LiveBridge, a global customer services company, and the $104 million purchase of the Transport Revenue division of Ascom AG, a Swiss communications company.

To Fiji and beyond

Along with its acquisitions-driven growth, the firm has spread its workforce to far-flung places around the globe. In November 2003, ACS opened an outsourcing services center in Fiji as part of a larger plan to expand operations in the Asia-Pacific region. And in spring 2005, the company announced plans to open a new global services center in Tianjin, People's Republic of China, with an initial workforce of around 200. The center would support business process outsourcing and information technology services.

Pulling off profits

ACS pulled off a profitable 2005, posting revenues of $4.35 billion, up 13 percent from 2004, excluding revenues associated with 2004's divestitures. The firm continued its winning streak in 2006, announcing second quarter revenues of $1.35 billion, up 31 percent compared to the same quarter the previous year. During the quarter, the firm set a record for new business, signing $251 million in annually recurring revenue.

Rumors began to swirl in late 2005 and early 2006 that ACS might be put up for sale. In January 2006, the firm broke its silence on the matter, announcing that its "unsolicited discussions" with a group of private equity investors angling to buy the firm had been called off. However, the firm said, it was still considering ways to enhance value for shareholders. A few weeks later, ACS announced a plan to borrow money to buy nearly half of its outstanding shares, delighting investors who sent ACS stock skyward. In February 2006, the firm filed papers with the Securities and Exchange Commission indicating that it planned to cut up to 1,700 jobs and reduce operations in one of its Mexican near-shore services center. According to the documents, the positions to be cut were mainly in "offshore processors and related management." The firm said it also planned to cut costs by selling a corporate jet.

Under the gun

ACS has seen its share of legal headaches through the years. According to a February 2006 article in the *Edmonton Journal*, ACS was charged by the Royal Canadian Mounted Police with offering "secret commissions" to two Edmonton traffic officers in a scheme involving a traffic photo ticketing system. According to the article, ACS has a $3.2 million-per-year contract with Edmonton that includes an annual fee and bonus for photo tickets issued that catch speeders and red-light runners. The case is set to go to trial in Canada later in 2006.

In another scuffle, the firm faced an investigation by the Securities and Exchange Commission in early 2004 for its contract procurement practices in Florida. A report compiled by the Inspector General of Florida revealed that ACS was paid $7 million in total fees during the 2002-2003 contract period, with $1.4 million of the fees from performance-based payments. ACS, which vowed to cooperate with investigators, said the report also "identified examples of possible false job placements and wage manipulation which could have resulted in certain performance-based payments."

Visit the Vault Consulting Career Channel at **www.vault.com/consulting** — with insider firm profiles, message boards, the Vault Consulting Job Board and more.

VAULT CAREER LIBRARY   257

State-of-the-art in Medicaid

The firm's federal business has been on the wane in recent years, and the firm divested a good portion of this business in 2003, including contracts with the U.S. Air Force.

But ACS retains a solid relationship with many states, helping them handle the tech side of programs such as Medicaid. The firm is the largest government program pharmacy benefits administrator in the nation, serving 26 states and the District of Columbia. ACS made headlines in January 2006 when it signed a 20-month, $11.6 million contract amendment with Louisiana's health department to expand its Personal Care Services operation, which helps state residents request long-term home care. And in October 2005, the firm signed an $82.5 million contract with the State of New Mexico Human Services Department for full fiscal agent services, covering administrative duties such as Medicaid system management.

An Rx for outsourcing

The firm's recent IT outsourcing wins include a December 2005 contract with DriveTime Sales and Finance Corporation valued at $4.8 million. The firm will help install new loan servicing and collection technology for DriveTime. An even bigger win came in August 2005, when ACS was tapped by GlaxoSmithKline, the second-largest pharmaceutical company in the world, to provide remote server management and monitoring services under a deal valued at more than $100 million. The firm has worked on IT projects with GSK since 2003.

ACS has been making similar headway with its business process outsourcing contracts. In February 2006, the firm was awarded a three-year BPO contract to provide call center services for Johns Hopkins Health Care. The firm inked another $56 million BPO contract in January 2006 with Aetna, an ACS client since 1999, covering document preparation, imaging, storage, management and retrieval services for medical, dental, disability and other types of claims. Another BPO win came that same month, when the firm announced a three-year contract to process student loans with KeyBank National Association.

Buck's benefits

ACS provides HR and benefits consulting services through subsidiary Buck Consultants. In February 2006, the firm signed a contract with the Pension Benefit Guaranty Corporation (PBGC) to continue providing benefit consulting and administration services, as it's done for the past 15 years. In January 2006, Buck was tapped to provide actuarial and consulting services for the State of Alaska's retirement plans.

Tickets to ride

ACS also derives a healthy portion of revenues from innovative solutions for transportation through its recently acquired Transport Revenue group. In January 2006, the Metropolitan Transit Authority of Harris County (MTAHC) in Houston, Texas, tapped ACS to install a new contact-less ticketing system for the area's bus and light rail transportation network, a contract worth $14 million. The firm has deployed similar solutions using "smartcard" technology in international locations, including one up and running in Lyon, France, and another on the way in Zurich, Switzerland.

Making the lists

ACS continues to top who's who lists in its field. In January 2006, the firm was named by *Global Services* magazine to the No. 1 slot on the 2006 Global Services 100 list of top performing BPO providers, up from No. 2 the year before. The firm also was ranked at No. 6 in *Global Services'* listing of the best performing infrastructure services providers for 2006. For the seventh year in a row, ACS made *Forbes'* 2006 list of the Platinum 400, which ranks America's "best big companies"—those with revenues of over $1 billion. The firm came in No. 8 in its industry, and 248th overall. *Forbes* also named ACS to its 2005 Best of the Web list in the BPO category for the fifth consecutive year. *Software* magazine placed ACS at No. 20 in its 2005 ranking of the world's top software and services providers.

GETTING HIRED

Getting affiliated

ACS hopefuls should start with a visit to the firm's web site, where they can browse available jobs by title, category, division, keyword and location. Applicants can build a profile and post a resume online. The firm also offers internship opportunities for students enrolled in a college program (undergraduate or master's) working toward a degree in business, computer science, management information systems or computer engineering, with a minimum GPA of 3.0. These internships typically run from May through August.

Visit the Vault Consulting Career Channel at **www.vault.com/consulting** — with
insider firm profiles, message boards, the Vault Consulting Job Board and more.

VAULT CAREER LIBRARY   **259**

Most insiders report going through at least two interviews to land a job at ACS. One source says "there were two panels," noting, "I interviewed with one panel of four or five people for approximately one hour and the other panel of four people for approximately one hour. I had to fill out some questions prior to the interview that pertained to the specific job. The questions were typically general in nature. They asked things like strengths and weaknesses and situational questions."

Another insider reports, "I had two interviews with the company, one offsite over lunch, and one onsite to gauge my technical skills. The offsite interview was informative about the company; the onsite one was to see my fit with ACS." A colleague adds that interview questions "focused on tangible, practical aspects of the job and how my skills would apply to getting it done. I was expected to give examples of successful projects in the past and my role in identifying and overcoming challenges to my job."

OUR SURVEY SAYS

Corporate camaraderie

Insiders suggest that, in a company of ACS's size, corporate culture can vary widely. As one consultant puts it, "Because it is so large and diverse, it is hard to sum up what the entire culture is. But for the small part of the company that I see, it strives to keep employees well trained. My local management staff is wonderful to work for; they are very family-friendly, but I don't know if that is true in other ACS jobs." Another source reports that "the corporate culture is very much a form of camaraderie and direct management willing to work with you as opposed to against you." In another office, an insider explains that staffers enjoy a "positive, relaxed atmosphere, with a business casual dress code and reasonably flexible work hours." The same source adds that "there is a team environment overall, which aids in meeting tough deadlines." But another staffer gripes that the firm is "bottom-line driven," cautioning that "employees are told to reduce costs regardless of the effects on current clients, services or product offerings. There have been at least five reorganizations within the last 18 months or so."

Putting in the hours

An insider describes the hours at ACS as "the typical 8 a.m. to 5 p.m. Monday through Friday, with extra hours at night or on the weekend to finish projects occasionally." Another source grumbles that "it is expected that employees work well over 40 hours each week, given the short supply of resources."

As for advancement at ACS, an insider says, "It seems it used to be based on favorites," but under newer management, it now "seems based on experience and who you know. However, for those employees who work really hard, the opportunity is there."

Ajilon Consulting

210 West Pennsylvania Avenue
Suite 650
Towson, MD 21204
Phone: (410) 821-0435 or
(800) 626-8082
Fax: (410) 828-0106
www.ajilonconsulting.com

LOCATIONS

Towson, MD (HQ)
More than 64 offices throughout
the U.S., UK, Australia, Europe and
Canada

PRACTICE AREAS

Application Development & Integration
Application management &
maintenance • Data warehousing
• EBusiness • Systems
transformation
Infrastructure Management
Desktop • Help-desk • Server
IT Quality Management
Performance & usability testing •
Process improvement • Software
quality assurance & testing
Supplemental IT services
IT staff augmentation

THE STATS

Employer Type: Subsidiary of Adecco
Ticker Symbol: ADO (NYSE)
President and CEO: Roy Haggerty
2005 Employees: 10,000
2004 Employees: 10,000
2005 Revenues: $2.5 billion
2004 Revenues: $1.27 billion

UPPERS

• "Low management overhead"
• "Helpful in providing new
  opportunities for their consultants"

DOWNERS

• "Lack of job security"
• "They do very little to create
  corporate culture"

EMPLOYMENT CONTACT

Visit the Career Center section of
Ajilon Consulting's web site,
www.ajilonconsulting.com, for job
search and resume submittal links

THE BUZZ
WHAT CONSULTANTS AT OTHER FIRMS ARE SAYING

• "Hard-working"
• "Techies"
• "Body shop"

THE SCOOP

Many names, much experience

Ajilon Consulting was founded in 1969 and has been a subsidiary of Adecco, an HR solutions company, since 1987. Formerly known as Adia Information Technologies and Comp-u-Staff, the company renamed itself Ajilon in 1996 to reflect its "agility" in providing IT services. The North American IT consulting division adopted "Consulting" to its name in May 2002 to differentiate itself from other Ajilon divisions providing managed services worldwide.

Headquartered near Baltimore, Md., Ajilon Consulting provides specialized IT consulting services to an extensive client list that includes over two-thirds of the Fortune 100 companies. Its services include application development and integration, IT quality management and testing, infrastructure management and supplemental IT services. The national district offices are comprised of district managers, account managers, technical recruiters and administrators who provide client and consultant support. The Global Solutions Centers deliver customized project solutions for clients that increase performance and efficiencies.

Leading the expanding pack

Ajilon has boosted its ranks through a series of strategic acquisitions, the most recent of which being the MYTA Corporation in April 2002. Ajilon also acquired IMI Systems, Inc., in April 2000, and Software Quality Partners and Computer People Inc. in 1999. Leading the firm's consulting operations is Roy Haggerty, who joined the company as President & CEO in 1990. The company currently has 10,000 employees and 64 locations worldwide.

Works well with others

Ajilon has been successful in partnering with other companies to break into new markets or expand its product offerings. In 2005, Ajilon buddied up with Comcast Business Services to jointly offer telecommuting technology over broadband designed for both employees and administrators. In February 2004, Ajilon joined Hewlett-Packard's .NET Solutions Partner Program to provide e-business, systems transformation and data warehousing solutions to HP's small and medium business customers. Ajilon also launched two services in 2003: a software usability evaluation service designed to trim months off of usability testing projects, and a value management service that incorporates ITCentrix's Value Accelerator software. In Canada, Ajilon has assisted consulting peer Accenture on a program for Canada's

Citizenship and Immigration agency designed to keep closer tabs on individuals entering and leaving the country.

Not just offshore, near-shore too

Like other tech consulting firms, Ajilon has not ruled out offshore opportunities to save clients money and to boost efficiencies. While it has a development center based in Russia, the company has looked closer to home by setting up centers in Toronto and Montreal, in addition to its domestic centers in Nashua, N.H., and Raleigh, N.C. The 17,000 square foot Montreal facility mainly offers help desk and infrastructure management support, while software development, software quality assurance and testing, infrastructure support and application management are offered by the other centers. Over 200 IT professionals are staffed at the Canadian centers. Initial near-shore clients included a provider of advanced integrated circuit solutions, as well as the Canadian branch of a major fast food chain.

A cool place to be

In August 2005, Ajilon was named one of 60 Cool Places to Work in Michigan because of its compensation plans, career path programs, and real life benefits to employees. Sponsored by *Crain's Detroit Business*, the *Grand Rapids Business Journal* and the Michigan Department of Labor and Economic Growth, the award measured overall teamwork, camaraderie, personal growth, flexible work hours, fun, ethics and values. Ajilon was selected as one of the Best Places to Work in Southeast Michigan by the same group in 2003.

Quality assurance, guaranteed

Ajilon also gets positive reviews from its customers. One thing that differentiates Ajilon from its competitors is that in 1995, the firm became the first U.S. IT services company to acquire the ISO 9001 certification. In May 2004, the firm announced that it had received high marks overall in its first year of quarterly customer satisfaction surveys, which were implemented as part of the ISO 9001 standards. Of the 248 customers who responded to the initial survey, more than 90 percent reported high levels of satisfaction with the firm. The firm's consistent customer satisfaction is also evidenced by its coveted Q1 status with Ford Motor Company, which remains in good standing after Ajilon completed renewed requirements for continuous improvement in quality standards. Ford acknowledged Ajilon's recertification in September 2005 with a Q1 plaque and flag, which are now permanent fixtures in the firm's Detroit office.

Paying it forward

Ajilon makes an effort to be involved in various community events. In order to reach out to women in technology—still a male-dominated field—the company sponsored the 7th Annual 2005 Women in Leadership Technology awards gala in Houston. The event honored Houston's most influential women in technology and gave Ajilon the opportunity to formally commit to advancing women in the field. Ajilon also co-hosted a Capitol Hill event in April 2005 after the 6th Annual Hoop Dreams Congressional Reception, to raise funds for academic college scholarships for Washington, DC, public high school students.

Many of the employees give back to their communities and participate in Ajilon's Charitable Donations Program, which provides funds to support charities that are important to employees. The firm also adopted a military pay differential in April 2005 for its employees serving in the armed forces in the Reserve or the National Guard. Retroactive to September 11, 2001, current, past and future salaried employees who take leave to serve or train in the military continue to receive the portion of their Ajilon salary that's over and above what they get from the military.

GETTING HIRED

Getting a foot in the door

Ajilon garners its roster from a variety of sources, primarily online job advertisements and employee referrals. "Everyone I know of has been referred by other employees," one source reports. (Ajilon regards referrals very highly, evidenced by finder's fees they pay consultants for bringing in new talent.) First, the firm examines a prospect's potential to serve a specific client. Above all, an insider notes, applicants "must first fit a client need. There is an internal screening process to ensure potential consultants are 'team' oriented."

The interview process—a combination of interviews with both the firm and its clients—generally follows three steps: first, an interview with HR; then, a technical screening; and finally, an interview with the potential client. A successful interviewee lays out the process: "After they have received your resume, you are then called in to the office for a formal interview. They then recruit you to various consulting positions that are available. If there is an open consulting position that you are suitable for, they will set up an interview with that company." The firm's hiring process boils down to a client's acceptance of the potential consultant. An Ajilon employee reports being "interviewed by clients via telephone. Got accepted...Ajilon did not conduct any interview. Just asked a few basic questions. Very laid back interviewing technique. If clients approve we are in!" Another consultant echoes the same sentiment, saying, "If a client wants you, the company hires you."

OUR SURVEY SAYS

A client-defined culture

When Ajilon's consultants say the clients they serve define the firm's culture, they aren't using metaphorical politicking. One consultant laments the fact that the firm does "very little to create corporate culture," a fact largely attributed to consultants working at client sites. An insider reports that "as a consultant on the client side, there is not much exposure to the company's culture (except via e-mail)." And a number of sources note the lack of communication between the firm and its consultants. One states that the firm is "not always in touch with what's going on with consultants in the field." Another consultant says of his relationship with other Ajilon workers, "My contact is limited to less than five in-person meetings per year and less than 10 on the phone." Additionally, one source notes that the number of company events has "dramatically decreased."

However, not all Ajilon consultants are complaining; they appreciate Ajilon's "low stress" environment. Employees note that despite operating mainly from a distance, the company has a reliable and efficient support structure. "Ajilon is the epitome of one hand washing the other. They show phenomenal supportiveness of their staff and strive hard to keep their frontliners engaged and active." Another consultant appreciates that "'respect for one another' is highly valued."

Never far from home

Despite spending most of their time offsite, Ajilon consultants rarely have to travel overnight away from home. As on source reports, "All assignments have been an easy commute from my house." Ajilon is conscientious about accommodating its consultants by matching them to clients nearby, whenever possible. "As a single parent, I can't travel at all," one insider says. "Ajilon has recognized this and not challenged it. I have never been asked to travel, which is good." Commuting to client sites located near one's district office isn't always a bowl of cherries, though, especially for one Philadelphia-based consultant, who observes that "they aren't compassionate about the travel time required for such a large district area."

Tied to client satisfaction

As with work/life balance and day-to-day culture, opportunities for promotion are defined more by clients than by executive decisions at Ajilon. "Since I work at a client site, my promotions are tied into client satisfaction," one insider says. "It's my impression that promotion and salary raises are slow and small based on the client's economic environment. The firm's promotion policy is not clear to me, i.e., I don't know what criteria to meet to get promoted." However, promotions to middle management are based on internal decisions. As one source explains, "there is opportunity for moving into mid-management positions in addition to normal consulting duties."

Some consultants bemoan the lack of job security as an Ajilon employee. Staffers report that the company is "slow to find more positions when an employee is on the bench" and offer "no commitment for future work after a current assignment is complete." Insiders wish upper management would be more proactive about maximizing its human resource strengths. "The firm should identify and sponsor the best consultants and utilize them to a higher potential," one insider says, while another notes that "it's all too easy to get stuck at an account for far too long a time."

"Hard ceiling"

Salaries are also primarily tied to a client's happiness and financial status, and most Ajilon employees are relatively happy with the pay levels, which are competitive up until the senior level. "The firm's low-cost provider stature forces a hard compensation ceiling," a source explains, "but the range is adequate except for the most senior." Another agrees, reporting that "there is ample range in technical salaries to permit good compensation for those that choose not to pursue management or sales, to a large degree. Senior personnel run into a hard ceiling." Ajilon's vow to keep costs low for its clients occasionally rankles consultants, however, especially when overtime work is left off the bill. "Sometimes I have more than 40 hours of work in a week," says a disgruntled consultant, "but I am only allowed to charge the client for 40 hours."

Plenty of perks

Ajilon consultants are largely supportive of the firm's benefits package, which includes medical and dental insurance, disability, 401(k) and the occasional sporting event. Consultants are especially fond of "recruiting perks," where the company pays handsome bonuses to workers who recommend qualified potential new hires. Employees also speak highly of training opportunities, particularly to courses offered through Ajilon's "Virtual University" and other "training pertaining to my job." However, as one consultant reports, "no training is provided unless it is free or from an accredited college, and a course that pertains to a current career position. If you wanted to expand [your] knowledge to be more marketable, you have to pay for that yourself."

A point of contention has arisen following the cessation of tuition reimbursement. As one source explains, Ajilon "offered a tuition reimbursement program, which I was very happy with because it was helping me get my master's degree. But they 'changed the rules' and made it very hard for me to continue getting this benefit." The firm further clarifies this issue, stating that it does reimburse for training, tuition and degree programs as long as the courses relate to the consultant's position and IT career path.

High supervisory marks

They may not see each other very often, but Ajilon consultants think highly of their supervisors and directors. "I see my supervisor once a year for performance ratings which have been provided by my clients," offers one consultant, while another praises his bosses because they "are very easy to work with" and "don't get in the way." One Ajilon consultant appreciates that his bosses "are very open and honest with what is going on in the marketplace. They also give you great input into what projects they submit you for." Staffers are grateful for the largely helpful and responsive management, as for many, supervisors are the only link between a consultant and the company. "I am very loyal to my district manager," says one employee. "Other than that, I have no relationship with the company."

Skills-based diversity

Ajilon consultants give their firm high marks for diversity. As one insider states, "Based on my exposure in my current position, diversity is alive and very healthy in my workplace." Another offers equally high praise: "My firm does a great job with recruitment and retention of women and minorities." Ajilon employees are convinced of the company's willingness to hire the most qualified consultants for client work, regardless of gender, skin color or sexual preference. "The company hires people who are billable," one source reports. Another contact adds that "competence is the driving factor [in recruitment], not political correctness." And although there are many more men than women in the IT division, respondents stress that appearances are more reflective of industry-wide demographics than prejudicial treatment. "Bottom line is that you can't equalize opportunity for gender or race if the ratio of candidates is grossly off-balance," one source says. The same consultant continues,

"I've met only a few women from Ajilon. All were very competent." The same goes for minorities. One minority insider states that he has "been treated extremely well by everyone at Ajilon."

Giving back

Ajilon's charitable giving is a two-way street, with decisions shared by employees and top brass alike. "Every year the firm chooses a few charities that we are encouraged to participate in or donate to," says one staffer. "We are also given the opportunity to submit to the firm a charity that we think would benefit from donations." In addition to allowing workers to submit recipients for the firm's charitable donations, Ajilon publicly recognizes its workers that make significant contributions. "They...highlight various people in newsletters," an insider reports, and the firm matches employee contributions to various charities. This year, Ajilon was actively involved in toy and blood drives, as well as the United Way, the Salvation Army, local community charities and Hurricane Katrina relief efforts.

Visit the Vault Consulting Career Channel at **www.vault.com/consulting** — with
insider firm profiles, message boards, the Vault Consulting Job Board and more.

VAULT CAREER LIBRARY **269**

Alliance Consulting Group

Six Tower Bridge
181 Washington Street, Suite 350
Conshohocken, PA 19428
Phone: (610) 234-4301
www.allianceconsulting.com

LOCATIONS

Conshohocken, PA (HQ)
10 offices throughout the U.S. and
one office in Hyderabad, India

PRACTICE AREAS

Application Services
Development • Integration •
Testing • Support
Information Management
Business Intelligence • Master
Data Management
Package Enterprise Solutions

THE STATS

Employer Type: Division of Safeguard
Scientifics
Ticker Symbol: SFE (NYSE)
President and CEO: Anthony Ibargüen
2005 Employees: 826
2004 Employees: 646
2005 Revenues: $94 million
2004 Revenues: $93.1 million

UPPERS

• Independence and autonomy
• Very experienced co-workers from
  varied backgrounds

DOWNERS

• Few long-term positions available
• No unifying firm culture

EMPLOYMENT CONTACT

See the Human Resources section of
the company's web site to search
open positions and to contact the
company

THE BUZZ
WHAT CONSULTANTS AT OTHER FIRMS ARE SAYING

• "Good reputation"
• "[Needs to] diversify and grow"

THE SCOOP

Background check

Alliance Consulting Group provides business intelligence and information management solutions to clients in the pharmaceutical, financial services, manufacturing, health care, and retail and distribution industries. Located in Conshohocken, Pa., a few miles northwest of Philadelphia, the firm specializes in data warehousing and business intelligence; master data management solutions; application development and integration; infrastructure and application testing and maintenance outsourcing; and package enterprise solutions. Alliance Consulting employs over 800 consultants, a mix of core full-timers and specialized independent contractors.

Loyal client networks

The company claims a roster of Fortune 1000 companies as clients, including DHL, Fidelity Investments and Wyeth. On its web site, the company brags, "our biggest clients now were our biggest clients then," referring to its 11-year history. Alliance's top 10 customers accounted for approximately 54 percent of total revenues in 2004, an increase of 25 percent in 2003. One customer alone accounted for 11.2 percent of Alliance's total revenues in 2004.

In 2005, Alliance expanded its existing accounts and added new service offerings, posting revenue growth throughout the year. After struggling with the economic slowdown after the tech bubble burst and the loss of several key figures and its headquarters location in the September 11 terrorist attacks, the group is finally turning around, operating at profitable levels since mid-2005. In late 2005, Alliance successfully landed a number of data management projects with several pharmaceutical companies, in which the consultancy will track and analyze top prescribers, sales data and drug safety trends to comply with FDA regulations.

Creating the Alliance

Safeguard Scientifics Inc., a company with a history of investing in small up-and-coming firms, acquired Alliance Consulting for $55 million in December 2002. At the time of the acquisition, Safeguard had two wholly owned subsidiaries, Aligne and Lever8, which offered similar services as Alliance. Safeguard merged the two companies into Alliance to form the firm in its current state. As Alliance's majority shareholder, Safeguard Scientifics owned 98.9 percent of the consulting group as of December 31, 2004.

At the forefront of the firm is Anthony A. Ibargüen, who moved from his position as managing director of Safeguard to become Alliance's CEO and president in 2004. A former IBM employee, Ibargüen was also a managing director of Internet Capital Group (Nasdaq: ICGE), an Internet holding company, and president and COO of Tech Data Corporation. No stranger to IT consulting, he led the effort to acquire Alliance back in 2002.

Looking to India

In October 2004, Alliance acquired Mensamind, Inc., a software development company based in Hyderabad, India, with offices in Chicago, to add offshore capabilities to its current service offerings. An ISO 9001:2000-certified company, Mensamind has also achieved SEI/CMM Level 5 certification since merging with Alliance. After the acquisition, Mensamind was renamed Alliance India and its senior executive team formed the core of Alliance's Global Delivery Center for Excellence, established to respond to client needs. Alliance executives touted the acquisition as a way for the company to offer more flexibility in the outsourcing sector. Rao Tummalapalli, co-founder of Mensamind, is currently Alliance India's managing director.

Having a heart

Alliance prides itself on its corporate citizenship, encouraging its employees to take an active role in community service initiatives. After Hurricane Katrina devastated most of the Southeastern U.S., Alliance organized its employees into volunteer groups and agreed to match employee donations to the Red Cross to contribute to the relief effort. The firm also sponsors charity golf events to help raise money, such as the 17th Annual Madden Golf Classic to support Huntington's Disease Society of America, in addition to organizing networking events, educational initiatives and internship programs to support the IT community.

Alliance also has strong ties to the Naandi Foundation, a nonprofit dedicated to eradicating poverty and improving the standard of living of marginalized or less privileged people. Through Naandi's "Support Our Schools" program, Alliance India is in its second year of supporting a school, donating money and volunteer time to provide basic amenities and improved educational resources.

GETTING HIRED

Want to work there?

Ranked in the Inc. 500 among the top 10 fastest growing private companies in America, Alliance offers job seekers an accessible search engine on its web site to peruse its current openings. The company claims to promote a largely entrepreneurial culture where employees are encouraged to "always, always tell us if we're doing it wrong...we can take it, even if it hurts." The site specifies openings for full-time employees, as well as for independent contractors.

Alliance's hiring process is simple and straightforward. According to an insider, the process includes—in this order—a review of the candidate's resume, a phone interview, an in-person interview and, finally, an interview with the client.

Seeking seasoned professionals

When Alliance staffs specific projects, it looks for experienced hires who will hit the ground running. "We generally don't hire straight out of college [or] MBA programs in the projects I work on," says one insider. "Our model is that we basically come onto a customer site and take over the management of some piece of their work/application, and our sales pitch is that we can take over and run the projects/maintenance/support cheaper than the customer could do for itself, so that the customer can free up its experienced people to work on other things…We can't afford to give positions like these to people who don't know what they're doing." Consequently, Alliance generally prefers experienced people who can work "without a great deal of oversight…no matter what level they're operating at."

OUR SURVEY SAYS

Mixed signals

Overall, Alliance gets positive marks on its culture. One insider says the company employs "good people" and supervisors that "do not micromanage," while another lauds the "independence" that the company promotes. Alliance is said to go to a "great deal of trouble to understand its customers' business model and culture and to make sure the people it supplies to the customer are people who will fit in there." One source adds, "I've been in this business a long time and I've never seen anyone go to the lengths this company does to understand the customer and see what needs to be done to support them. I haven't seen anything even remotely showing that same dedication to the customer."

Alliance culture, then, tends to be determined at the customer site and influenced by project managers who have autonomy "to run our own projects as we see fit, which is something I very much like, but I don't know if that's representative of the whole corporation" according to one source, who adds that "the people I deal with are very permissive, open-shop...it's pretty much open. No one stands on ceremony."

However, it's hard to say how people feel about working at the firm, in general; while the culture may have a pleasant feel to it, others express some trepidation over their future at the firm and their career path. One source notes that there is some "uncertainty" at the firm, while another more explicitly explains that "there are no advancement opportunities for technical consultants other than in sales and marketing."

Standard issue

In general, consultants describe the benefits at Alliance as being "pretty much the standard stuff." The firm offers consultants and full-time employees medical, dental and vision coverage, flexible spending plans, short- and long-term disability, life insurance, a matching scholarship program and a college savings plan, 401(k), a fitness discount program and a credit union. One consultant adds vacation and comp time as particularly attractive perks.

"I've been in this business a long time and I've never seen anyone go to the lengths this company does to understand the customer and see what needs to be done to support them."

— *Alliance insider*

Visit the Vault Consulting Career Channel at **www.vault.com/consulting** — with
insider firm profiles, message boards, the Vault Consulting Job Board and more.

VAULT CAREER LIBRARY   **275**

Appian Corporation

8000 Towers Crescent Drive
16th Floor
Vienna, VA 22182
Phone: (703) 442-8844
Fax: (703) 442-8919
E-mail: info@appian.com
www.appian.com

LOCATIONS

Vienna, VA (HQ)
Boston, MA
Dallas, TX
Minneapolis, MN
New York, NY
San Francisco, CA
Washington, DC
Ottawa

PRACTICE AREAS

Business Intelligence
Business Process Management
Data Warehouse & Data Marts
Enterprise Identity Management
High-Speed Analytics
Knowledge Management &
   Collaboration
Personalization
Web Services & Application
   Integration

THE STATS

Employer Type: Private Company
President and CEO: Matthew Calkins
2004 Employees: 165
2004 Revenues: $25 million

UPPERS

• Young, fast-paced organization
• Tons of training

DOWNERS

• Government-focused
• Limited time off

EMPLOYMENT CONTACT

Appian Corporation
ATTN: Recruiting - New Candidates
8000 Towers Crescent Drive
16th Floor
Vienna, VA 22182
E-mail: jobs@appiancorp.com
www.appian.com/AboutAppian/
Careers/careers.html

THE BUZZ
WHAT CONSULTANTS AT OTHER FIRMS ARE SAYING

• "Up-and-coming"
• "Fraternity"
• "Limited areas of expertise"
• "No life outside work; forced 'fun
   time'"

THE SCOOP

Little shop of honors

Appian Corporation seems to be the little company that took growth hormones. From its founding in 1999 through 2004, the Beltway-based Appian saw triple-digit revenue growth overall, along with a healthy workforce explosion, that landed the private company on *Inc.*'s top 500 list for 2004 as one of the fastest growing businesses nationwide. Software innovation—which earned the company recognition and awards—and strategic business partnerships have helped Appian land business with some big brand names like Federal Express, General Motors and Home Depot, as well as with many branches of the federal government, which supply much of the company's bread-and-butter work. The U.S. Army and U.S. Navy have also used Appian to help soldiers access up-to-date deployment information, training schedules and other data.

The company today has offices in Minneapolis, Dallas, San Francisco, Boston, New York and Ottawa, but it is in Washington, DC, that Appian has emerged as a prominent employer. In 2005, the *Washington Business Journal* ranked Appian one of the 50 best places to work in the region, based on employee opinions of management, working conditions and environment, and company culture. Appian provides consulting and professional services for business process management (BPM), data warehousing and business intelligence, and in the general field of knowledge management (KM) for which *KMWorld* named it one of the 100 Companies that Matter in Knowledge Management in 2005.

Knocking your SOX off

In 2002, President George W. Bush signed into law the Sarbanes-Oxley Act, partly in response to the accounting failures of Enron, WorldCom and other large corporations. Among its many provisions for in-house oversight, SOX, as the act is occasionally referred to, required large publicly-traded companies to tighten internal controls. Appian, which already employed its Appian Enterprise BPM system to create compliance control software, rolled out a number of its own SOX solutions in early 2005.

The compliance control package, which allows companies to integrate and monitor multiple data storage, communication and infrastructure systems, manages and tracks the steps required of corporations to ensure compliance with SOX by auditing trails and identifying potential problems before they become Enron-like debacles. Canadian lumber giant Tembec, signing a significant contract with Appian in late

Visit the Vault Consulting Career Channel at **www.vault.com/consulting** — with
insider firm profiles, message boards, the Vault Consulting Job Board and more.
VAULT CAREER LIBRARY   **277**

2005, selected the firm's Sarbanes-Oxley solution based on its ability to give executives real-time actionable insight into key financial processes and activities.

In 2005, Appian formed several strategic partnerships to extend the reach of its solution to different markets. In January, it teamed up with iWay Software to allow its customers more flexibility in adapting existing software to Appian Enterprise. In March, the firm partnered with MDY Advanced Technologies on a new product certified under Department of Defense standards for electronic records applications. The solution involves integrating MDY's FileSurf enterprise records management software with the Appian enterprise suite. Appian also allied itself with MorganFranklin Corp in June 2005 to work on Web-based compliance management solutions. The companies will collaborate to provide commercial and government clients with solutions to maximize their strategic business processes, improve data management, enhance productivity and ensure compliance with regulatory laws.

Government cheese

When Appian first launched Appian Enterprise, the suite was deployed by the U.S. Army and Navy to access information, schedules, contact lists, health information and more. But in 2005, the firm adapted its solutions for government agencies to conform with compliance regulations. In September, it released a program to help agencies fall in line with the Office of Management and Budget's (OMB) Circular A-123 regulation, which had been recently revised. Appian's solution enables federal agencies achieve timely, cost-effective compliance with the documentation, financial reporting, internal controls testing requirements and tight deadlines mandated by the OMB's guidelines. Around the same time, the firm released a program to help agencies comply with the Freedom of Information Act.

GETTING HIRED

The Appian way

For consultant positions, candidates are required to boast prior software consulting experience, "ideally in a BPM, Portal, DM or EAI-related setting." You should come equipped with a bachelor's degree in a quantitative major, such as engineering, economics or computer science, along with a "demonstrated interest" in business and technology. The firm is also looking for applicants who are "articulate, intelligent, and independent thinking," with a record of academic achievement and strong communication, problem solving and design skills.

The firm also recruits from top colleges and universities, accepting resumes from all majors and concentrations. During the 2005-2006 academic year, Appian scheduled recruiting events at Carnegie Mellon, Columbia, Cornell, Dartmouth, Duke, Georgetown, Harvard, MIT, Princeton, Rensselaer Polytechnic, Tecnológico de Monterrey - Campus Monterrey and Estado de Mexico, University of Maryland, University of Pennsylvania, University of Texas at Austin, University of Virginia (UVA) and Yale. Students whose schools are not on the list are encouraged to send resumes and cover letters (stating their major and GPA) directly to Appian at jobs@appiancorp.com.

Meet the chiefs

An insider tells us the interview process consists of two rounds, with a first round of meetings with two senior consultants, and a second round of meetings with the firm's CFO and CEO. The CEO "always sits in on every second-round interview," the source says, which "ensures that he personally signs off on everyone joining the organization." Interviewees can expect a "couple of brain teasers," though the firm offers "mainly behavioral interviews." All final rounds are conducted at the firm's headquarters in Vienna, Va., the source adds.

OUR SURVEY SAYS

Fast, young and bright

Appian, an insider tells us, is a "very fast paced," "young organization," chock full of "extremely bright employees recruited from top schools in America." Opportunities are "given to those who ask for them and have proven successes," and "loyalty is cherished," the source adds.

Cruising and learning

The firm's emphasis on training is clear. During a yearly week-long Caribbean cruise for all employees, a source reports, staffers attend "Appian Business School for specific subjects in technology, art and other areas of interest like etiquette." In addition, "new employees go through a grueling two-week training called Appian Academy which educates employees about technology, business, strategy and product features. Graduates of Appian Academy finish with a final project and presentation."

Appian consultants reportedly work around 50 hours per week. Salary packages include "a revenue-sharing scheme for all employees," and "high percentage-based salary raises are provided if performance is excellent." The source adds that "vacation time is limited to two sick days a year, 10 personal days," and the aforementioned one-week cruise, though "unpaid personal leave, with special permission, is also available."

Opportunities are "given to those who ask for them and have proven successes."

— *Appian employee*

Visit the Vault Consulting Career Channel at **www.vault.com/consulting** — with
insider firm profiles, message boards, the Vault Consulting Job Board and more.

VAULT CAREER LIBRARY   **281**

Aquent

711 Boylston Street
Boston, MA 02116
Phone: (617) 535-5000
Fax: (617) 535-5005
www.aquent.com

LOCATIONS

Boston, MA (HQ)
70 offices in 17 countries

PRACTICE AREAS

Application Development
Infrastructure Support
Marketing Technologies
Project Management
Quality Assurance
Sales Channel Management
Supplier Relationship Management
Web Development

THE STATS

Employer Type: Private Company
CEO and Director: John Chuang
2005 Employees: 500
2005 Revenues: $335 million
2004 Revenues: $287.6 million

UPPERS

- "Flexible work hours"
- "Employees don't slog hours as at other consulting firms"
- "Results oriented"

DOWNERS

- "Slow growth"
- "Not enough junior people"
- "Compensation"

EMPLOYMENT CONTACT

it.aquent.com/FindJobs

THE SCOOP

Hands across the water

At its founding back in 1986, the three-man operation known as Mac-Temps, headed by John Chuang, basically provided typesetting services. Today, the $335 million company—now known as Aquent—staffs 10,000 IT professionals working in Web development, marketing technologies, application development and infrastructure support. The company places application developers and testers, tech writers, network designers, database architects and administrators, and computer operators.

But Aquent seems to have shifted its focus to building up its marketing division in response to an international hiring spike in the marketing, communications and creative services industries. This isn't to say that the company has abandoned its computer-oriented roots, but as Aquent enters its 20th year in 2006, it has spent some time abroad buying up creative service and marketing sector placement agencies, especially in Australia. By mid-2005, the Boston-headquartered private company had purchased or merged with 16 such agencies around the Pacific Rim, including five large firms in the Land Down Under alone. The buying spree reflected the company's deliberate goal to consolidate and grow in foreign markets. "You kiss a lot of frogs to find your prince," Aquent executive Greg Savage told *AdNews* in September 2005. "We would only buy a business if it brought us a strategic opportunity—like getting into Perth or dominating the Melbourne market."

This shift in focus is evident in both foreign and domestic markets, as Aquent sets its eyes more on staffing marketing specialists with large corporations. To that end, in July 2005 Aquent merged with Corporate Project Resources, Inc, (CPRi) a $25 million interim marketing staffing firm specializing in placement services for Fortune 500 companies. The merger resulted in the formation of a new Aquent division - Aquent Marketing Staffing—based in Chicago. Company officials announced that Aquent Staffing opened an office in Washington, DC, in addition to its existing offices in Chicago, Atlanta, Dallas, Detroit and New York, anticipating that marketing staffing will drive company growth through 2006. The new division touts access to 50,000 graphic designers, Web designers, copywriters and other interim specialists around the world.

Where IT's at

Aquent's 2005 shopping spree for marketing firms came two years after a protracted attempt to merge with a competitor, IT consulting firm Computer Horizons, in a $150 million takeover bid. Computer Horizons initially rejected Aquent's offer and the

Visit the Vault Consulting Career Channel at **www.vault.com/consulting** — with insider firm profiles, message boards, the Vault Consulting Job Board and more.

VAULT CAREER LIBRARY   **283**

deal became labeled a hostile takeover attempt. Later that year, Aquent managed to get dissident directors elected to Computer Horizons' board and it faced defeat in court where it attempted to block Aquent's takeover. In November 2003, though, Aquent withdrew its bid, saying Computer Horizons had become a different company from the one it intended to merge with earlier that year.

The failed merger made big news at the time and, in the ensuing two years, the company seemed to turn its attention to other, growing areas, such as outsourcing management and marketing, and integrating marketing and IT with a Web-based project management solution called Robohead, which launched in 2004. When Aquent issued Robohead3 in May 2005, the company claimed that a number of Fortune 500 companies were using it, though the company does not reveal the names of its clients.

Over the years, Aquent's IT division, working in dozens of cities, has provided staffing and solutions in project management, quality assurance, application development, supplier relationship management and channel solutions for telecom, pharmaceutical, aerospace and petroleum companies. Aquent's technology solutions have included the building of a multilingual Internet ordering system, a Web-based hedge fund management system incorporating spreadsheets and reports, and a supply management portal to a suite of Web applications.

GETTING HIRED

Finding a fit

Aquent itself only reports a 500-member staff, a low figure compared with the thousands of workers the company places. Applying for a job begins with registering on Aquent's web site which presents a broad range of opportunities, from full-time positions to contract and freelance hiring. Potential applicants can create an account by registering on the site and posting a resume and personal information that remains forever searchable by Aquent agents. Candidates have two application options: either applying to a specific job opening or simply joining the database.

An insider explains, "Each candidate's resume is compared to the job requirements. Candidates must pass a technical interview, a management interview and a recruiter screening to receive an offer. Technical interviewers are selected on the basis of their ability to identify good hires in the past." Sources tell us that candidates interview with both the company and the client.

OUR SURVEY SAYS

Individual preferences

Employee attitudes differ regarding the level of independence granted to Aquent consultants. One consultant raves about "the atmosphere, the freedom and the job," while another lauds the "extremely intelligent and visionary senior management" for creating "a culture that encourages individuality."

Other sources, however, see leadership in a different light, noting, in particular, a lack of communication from higher-ups. One source grumbles that there is "little guidance from management" and "no training to speak of." A consultant requests "more communication from Corporate. I never hear from them," while others yearn for more oversight from superiors, including one consultant who says, "Management needs to take a bigger role in enforcing process and guiding the way we use technology." Another worker notes that "as an onsite consultant, I sometimes miss business meetings or other communications."

Moving forward

Individual ambition remains the benchmark for promotion, says one insider. Though "very selective about new hires," there are "no other barriers except how fast the organization can grow. Promotion is up to the individual. If he/she wants to advance, there are means of doing so." Promotion policies at Aquent, though, do not get the thumbs-up across the board. Some insiders complain about an "unsatisfactory promotion potential," while at the same time, the company "tends to keep middle managers whose contributions to the company do not warrant their salaries."

In broader questions of movement, some employees have voiced concerns about what they perceive as the firm's "lack of direction." One consultant recommends the company develop a "better definition and implementation of a growth plan, where the employees feel they are a part of it."

Work perks

Aquent receives high marks on its employee benefits. Insiders note the firm's "good health care, dental and eye care," in addition to "six holidays" and "four weeks paid vacation." A senior consultant appreciates the firm's "paternity leave, software discounts and training." The company also offers life insurance, a 401(k) and company matching program, and profit-sharing for senior managers. Additionally, Aquent is "very flexible about work hours," a source reports. Consultants enjoy the "opportunity to learn new technology" and the "professional, friendly environment that encourages each person to gain further education to not only help the company, but for yourself."

Aquent's united way

The company encourages its employees to be involved in local communities and holds charity campaigns to benefit the United Way and other local causes. One consultant notes the "career day-type activities in local schools" as one of Aquent's community outreach efforts. Another source says that the "company matched hurricane relief donations this year" in the wake of Hurricanes Katrina and Rita.

"Promotion is up to the individual. If he/she wants to advance, there are means of doing so."

— Aquent consultant

Visit the Vault Consulting Career Channel at **www.vault.com/consulting** — with
insider firm profiles, message boards, the Vault Consulting Job Board and more.

VAULT CAREER LIBRARY   287

Atos Origin

5599 San Felipe, Suite 300
Houston, TX 77056
Phone: (713) 513-3000
www.atosorigin.com

LOCATIONS

Houston, TX (North America HQ)
Brussels (Corporate HQ)
Paris (Financial HQ)
Offices in 40 countries worldwide

PRACTICE AREAS

Consulting
Managed Operations
Systems Integration

THE STATS

Employer Type: Public Company
Ticker Symbol: ATOS (Euronext Paris)
Chairman and CEO: Bernard Bourigeaud
2005 Employees: 46,254
2004 Employees: 46,584
2005 Revenues: €5,459 million
2004 Revenues: €5,302 million

UPPERS

• "You can become everything you are qualified for"
• "Not too much pressure on work"
• "Good flexibility in moving around"

DOWNERS

• "Few benefits"
• No feeling of corporate unity
• Uncertain promotions and bonuses

EMPLOYMENT CONTACT

North America headquarters and Recruiting Center: (866) 875-8902
To search job openings, go to www.atosorigin.com/en-us/Careers/
Job_Openings/default.htm

THE BUZZ
WHAT CONSULTANTS AT OTHER FIRMS ARE SAYING

• "Focused"
• "Implementers"
• "Good for limited projects"
• "Quiet"

THE SCOOP

So many mergers in so little time

Atos emerged in 1997 when French IT services firms Axime and Sligos, themselves products of earlier mergers, united as one. Origin was the Dutch subsidiary of Royal Philips Electronics, which merged in 1996. Atos and Origin joined ranks in 2002 to form a solid unit. In August of 2002, Atos Origin acquired the UK and Netherlands businesses of KPMG Consulting and, in January 2004, bought IT services company SchlumbergerSema from Schlumberger for €1.28 billion, nearly doubling its staff at the time.

Quick to shine

Despite its relatively brief existence, Atos Origin has become Europe's largest publicly traded IT consultancy, with a staff of over 46,000 providing consulting, systems integrations and managed operations services to clients in 40 countries across the globe. Atos Origin serves clients in numerous industries, including automotive, chemical, financial services, high tech and electronics, oil and gas, pharmaceutical, public sector, retail, telecom, transportation and utilities. The firm's clients include European and global industry giants such as ABN AMRO, BNP Paribas, BP, Euronext, Fiat, Lucent, Shell and Unilever.

The gold medalist of IT services

In July 2005, Atos Origin, the current Worldwide Information Technology Partner of the International Olympic Committee, penned a contract extension to serve as the IT systems integrator for the 2010 Winter Games in Vancouver and the 2012 Summer Games in London. The firm had also served in that role for the 2004 Athens Summer Games and at the time of the announcement was already preparing IT services for the 2008 Summer Games in Beijing. In June 2005, Atos Origin unveiled its expansive testing program for the 2006 Winter Games in Torino, which had been in the works 18 months before the scheduled opening ceremonies on February 10, 2006.

Refocused and united

In order to better serve the company's 100 key clients, from whom it derives more than 65 percent of total revenues, Atos Origin consolidated its consulting arm under a new division: the aptly named Atos Consulting. The division serves the company's major clients in telecom, manufacturing, financial services and public sectors with 2,500 consultants globally. Atos Origin also streamlined its card payment and Internet processing businesses into a single organization—Atos Worldwide—and created two internal organizations, Global Consulting and Systems Integration, and Global Managed Services, to better control and coordinate work by business line and to ensure positive future development of services. The reorganization appeared to be paying dividends with a steady stream of new orders, including the company's largest outsourcing contract ever: the take-over of a substantial part of KarstadtQuelle's IT infrastructure, an eight-year contract worth €1.2 billion.

Spreading its wings

Atos Origin announced plans in July 2005 to expand its commitment to the Asia Pacific market, looking to double headcount by the end of 2005 and multiply the region's contribution to its revenues from 4 percent to at least 10 percent by 2008. The company employs about 2,000 people in its Asia Pacific region, and is looking to recruiting in India to double that figure. The firm's Asia Pacific headquarters in Singapore employs 300 people, a number it looks to boost by at least 100 percent within three years. CEO Bernard Bourigeaud said that his company is quite active in China and is looking to expand its credit card processing in the Asian market where, unlike in North America and Europe, no clear-cut market leader yet exists. He explained that Atos Origin is "hoping to develop this market in Asia out of Hong Kong, where we have a state-of-the-art data center, India and mainland China." Atos Origin plans to develop India as its offshore base and utilize China as a platform from which to develop further business in the region.

Why go it alone?

To better utilize current technology, Atos Origin maintains partnerships with leading technology firms around the globe to gain access to proprietary technology belonging to other companies. The firm claims that combining with various organizations will allow it to provide the ideal solutions for its clients who seek the "best of breed" in their various industries. The firm uses application infrastructure software company BEA Systems, Inc., for essential parts of its systems integration services utilized in enterprise Web applications. Atos Origin is also an accredited reseller of HP hardware and software systems, while in return all Atos Origin customers receive global break-fix capability from HP. Atos Origin also collaborates with Microsoft to improve the world of IT security and identity management, and in the oil and gas industry, it has teamed up with Oracle for more than a decade. In addition, the company has working partnerships with software engineer PeopleSoft, business and ERP software provider SAP, and eBusiness applications software maker Siebel Systems, Inc.

GETTING HIRED

Step by step

Atos Origin has a three-step hiring process: online application, pre-screening and interview. The company encourages experienced workers to apply through its web site by searching through its posted jobs, completing a standard application form and posting their resume. Applicants can indicate if they're looking for full- or part-time work, the length of assignment they desire and their salary expectation. Atos Origin then invites candidates in for one or more interviews, and perhaps a skills assessment, depending on the particular assignment.

OUR SURVEY SAYS

Atomized Atos Origin

Atos Origin's corporate culture seems to make little impression on its consultants in the United States. Insiders say "there is no real structure to the company in the U.S." and "there is no corporate culture beyond any given project." This may not always have been the case, insiders contend, implying that corporate belt-tightening put a cinch on costs associated with fostering a sense of camaraderie. "There have been attempts at creating esprit de corps," says one insider, "but when there was a need to create better news on profitability, all nonbillable travel was cancelled and along with it went [those] attempts. Now we do conference calls after work hours to bring the staff up to date on the latest things happening." This lack of face-to-face bonding time can have a severing effect on Atos Origin consultants when they spend most of their time with clients. "I'm always at the customer site and I have little knowledge of my firm," says one insider.

American isolation

On a larger scale, a couple of consultants note that while Atos Origin has a global presence, there is no sense of unity within the company as a whole, and this can impact their work. Atos Origin employs 1,200 people in North America, according to its web site, just 3 percent of its global workforce of over 46,000, which may go beyond giving American consultants the impression of working for a separate, isolated company. In America, one source says, "few people have ever heard of Atos Origin, so you have to constantly explain the size of the company worldwide. However, doing so only inflates people's expectations of what the company can

Visit the Vault Consulting Career Channel at **www.vault.com/consulting** — with
insider firm profiles, message boards, the Vault Consulting Job Board and more.

V/\ULT CAREER LIBRARY   **291**

actually do. In the end, that expectation cannot be delivered upon and everyone is disappointed."

Atos Origin consultants in the U.S. note the difficulty they have in communicating with overseas branches of the firm. "Getting help from other geographic areas is difficult at best; feeling a part of a global consulting company is impossible here," says an America-based insider. A second source echoes this sentiment, noting a "lack of cooperation between different service lines."

Compensating factors?

Compensation and benefits seem to be a sticking point for a number of consultants. One Europe-based insider says that Atos Origin provides "few benefits" while other insiders remark on restricted salary growth between 2002 and 2005, when Atos Origin took over the European offices of KPMG Consulting. There have been "bonuses for some, but hardly any salary increase for many" since 2002, the consultants say, adding that improved "compensation, training and paying more attention to people" could make Atos Origin a more enticing place to work.

Other consultants grumble that Atos Origin doesn't cultivate its workforce or advance its employees' careers. They say "it's not clear what promotion for technical specialists is" and "opportunities for advancement are generally nonexistent," while "annual reviews were also nonexistent." Another consultant thinks the annual reviews were used to justify "why people received little or no bonus dollars and why salaries were generally not increased." This could all be changing, though, as the firm began to implement annual reviews in 2005.

Flexibility pays off

Atos Origin insiders are more enthusiastic about work hours and travel requirements. On its web site, the firm spells out its attitude toward work/life balance: "Many countries promote flexibility so our people can fine-tune the balance between work and the rest of their life." And Atos Origin consultants seem greatly appreciative of the firm's efforts to realize this benefit. One source explains, "I usually don't have to travel far unless I want to," while another tells us "the work hours vary by project but are generally kept at the 'sane' level." One insider remarks that you don't "feel too much pressure" working for Atos Origin, and praises the company for its "flexibility."

"The work hours vary by project but are generally kept at the 'sane' level."

— Atos Origin source

Visit the Vault Consulting Career Channel at **www.vault.com/consulting** — with
insider firm profiles, message boards, the Vault Consulting Job Board and more.

VAULT CAREER LIBRARY   293

Bull

300 Concord Road
Billerica, MA 01821
Phone: (978) 294-6000
Fax: (978) 294-7999
www.bull.com/us

LOCATIONS

Billerica, MA (U.S. HQ)
Paris (HQ)
Worldwide presence in over 100
countries

PRACTICE AREAS

Application Services
Consulting & Systems Integration
IT Infrastructure Consulting
IT Infrastructure Products
Outsourcing
Servers

THE STATS

Employer Type: Public Company
Ticker Symbol: BUL (Euronext Paris)
Chairman and CEO: Didier Lamouche
2005 Employees: 7,458
2004 Employees: 7,531
2005 Revenues: €1,173 million
2004 Revenues: €1,541 million

UPPERS

• Good name in Europe

DOWNERS

• Still rebuilding after economic
  slow-down

EMPLOYMENT CONTACT

www.bull.com/us/careers/index.html

THE SCOOP

Bull's market

Headquartered in Paris, Bull is an international IT group with a presence in more than 100 countries. With revenues of €1,173 million in 2005, the firm has 7,500-plus employees and more than 100,000 customer installations worldwide. North America makes up only a sliver of the firm's overall revenues—just 5 percent in 2005. The rest of the pie is divided among France (47 percent), other European countries (33 percent) and elsewhere. Bull enjoys a high profile in Europe, and it's taking advantage of the rapid change in the region: Seven of the 10 countries that recently joined the European Union have tapped the firm for help in upgrading their customs and tax systems.

Bull's clients predominantly come from the defense, finance, health care, manufacturing, public and telecommunication sectors. The company's Products and Systems segment focuses on large servers that offer a combination of power and flexibility in Linux, Windows, Unix and legacy environments. In North America, Bull's operations are divided into two separate divisions: Bull Products & Systems (BP&S) and Bull Services & Solutions (BS&S). The company has spread sales and support systems in key geographic areas across America, and the U.S. is also home to Bull's large systems R&D facility and its Technical Assistance Center (TAC), provider of first-call maintenance for Bull clients worldwide. Bull also maintains large data centers in the Boston area, Minneapolis and Phoenix through BS&S, which provides systems integration and outsourcing services to clients throughout the U.S.

Helping a bull find its footing

As the firm struggled to regain its footing in the wake of the tech downturn in the early 21st century, its home country stepped up to help. In January 2005, the firm received a restructuring payment of €517 million from France. The aid was tied to a profit-sharing agreement requiring Bull to pay the French State 23.5 percent of its consolidated profits before tax exceeding €10 million for an eight-year period.

A new horizon

In early 2006, the firm unveiled "Horizon 2008," a strategic plan that sets forth a number of goals, including accelerating the growth of the services business to transform it into the major source of the group's revenues and enhancing operational efficiency. The firm also addressed its management ranks, with Bull appointing a new general manager in charge of services, Jean-Pierre Barbéris (in March 2005); a new chief financial officer, Philippe Lederman (May 2005); and a new chief information officer, Guy Gautron (June 2005). By the end of the year, the firm was showing a profitable trend. But while French offices saw early results, the firm said its Italian facilities trailed a bit due to "recent deterioration of the economic climate" in the country.

In November 2005, Bull launched a major new ad campaign promoting the firm as the "Architect of an Open World." The campaign, unveiled in France, Germany, Italy, Spain and the UK, as well as in Brazil and the Czech Republic, was meant to demonstrate how Bull can help organizations "break free from past shackles by breaking down the barriers in their information systems and opening them up in total security," the firm said.

Bullish on Poland

In March 2006, Bull acquired Polish consulting firm AMG.net, a 150-employee firm with roughly €6 million in revenues for 2005. The buy, part of Bull's larger strategic goal of strengthening its position in Eastern and Central Europe, established a major Bull competence center in telecom and media for the region.

Today, Bull maintains partnerships with many of the world's leading IT firms—including IBM, Intel, NEC, NCR, EMC, STK, BEA, SAS, Oracle and Microsoft—providing the company with access to cutting-edge technology to help develop customized solutions.

Choosing Bull

The firm had some contract wins to report in 2005. At the end of 2005, Bull scored a systems integration coup—the biggest in the firm's history. Along with Lockheed Martin, the firm was tapped to deliver a new address recognition system for the French postal service. The advanced optical system is expected to begin handling 65 million letters daily in 2007. In September, the Belgian Interior ministry chose Bull to help renew its IT equipment using its NovaScale servers. Also in 2005, the Brazilian federal police force awarded the firm a contract to deploy a system to control and authenticate biometric passports.

Streamlining IT for the public sector? That's BS!

BS supplies end-to-end business intelligence solutions to state and local U.S. governments, with a presence in 29 states and 150 agencies across the country. BS distributes its services to the public sector through the BS *Know*ledge Framework, an information management infrastructure that consists of the industry's most complete combination of people, products, processes, tools and technologies devoted to public sector agencies.

BS focuses on three public sector markets: Health & Human Services, Justice & Public Safety and Tax & Treasury. The company has aided states such as Michigan, Minnesota, Illinois, New York and Utah in managing their Medicaid and medical assistance programs efficiently and accurately. In 2001, Bull's health sector won "Laureate" status to the Illinois Department of Public Aid for its implementation of the nation's largest server-based Medicaid data warehouse and decision support system, developed and maintained by BS&S.

BS&S data warehousing solutions have aided the entire tax compliance cycle for its various government clients, including screening and selecting candidates for audit, conducting the audits, and managing and tracking the entire audit process. For example, in Michigan, BS developed an integrated information technology solution that provides auditors and management with rapid, real-time, online paperless access to taxpayer data, tax documents, third-party reports, law changes, court cases and other relevant information. In its public safety group, BS has developed a data warehouse decision support system such as the one in Iowa, which helps assess the impact of new state law and law changes on prison and court resources, allowing Iowa to more accurately project defense needs for the state.

Technological Bull

While BS&S is busy in the public sector, its sibling, Bull Products & Systems, is solely dedicated to helping enterprises implement powerful, open and secure IT infrastructure solutions that help them network directly with their customers, constituents, suppliers, third parties and employees. BP&S also offers a range of infrastructure services, including architectural consulting, applications integration, and server and storage consolidation.

GETTING HIRED

Bull hopefuls can visit the firm's web site, where there are separate career portals for Austria, Belgium, France, Germany, Italy, the Netherlands, Portugal, Spain and the U.S. The firm lists open positions (updated weekly) on these sites, and provides e-mail, snail mail and fax information for sending in resumes.

Visit the Vault Consulting Career Channel at **www.vault.com/consulting** — with
insider firm profiles, message boards, the Vault Consulting Job Board and more.

VAULT CAREER LIBRARY 297

CIBER Inc.

5251 DTC Parkway, Suite 1400
Greenwood Village, CO 80111
Phone: (303) 220-0100
Fax: (303) 220-7100
www.ciber.com

LOCATIONS

Denver, CO (HQ)
More than 80 offices in 17
countries

PRACTICE AREAS

Application Development
Enterprise Integration
Outsourcing
Packaged Solutions
Training

UPPERS

• Good promotion opportunities
• Flexible travel arrangements
• Friendly atmosphere

DOWNERS

• "They can't find work"
• "Lack of loyalty to employees"
• "Arbitrary management decisions"

EMPLOYMENT CONTACT

www.ciber.com/jobs

THE BUZZ
WHAT CONSULTANTS AT OTHER FIRMS ARE SAYING

• "Solid, stable"
• "Well-managed"
• "Not diverse"
• "Callous"

THE SCOOP

Heading for the slopes

Despite sounding like a child of the Internet era, the Denver-area CIBER Inc. has maintained a long and winning career as a leading IT consulting firm. Founded in 1974, the presciently-acronymed CIBER (Consultants in Business Engineering Research) has established itself as a major player in both the private and government sectors through a combination of savvy acquisitions, in-house application development and strategic partnerships. CIBER employs around 8,000 in its 80-plus offices worldwide.

CIBER originated as a Detroit-based firm providing IT services to the automotive industry, as reflected in the "Business Engineering" portion of its title. In 1988, CIBER founder and current board chairman Bobby Stevenson moved the company to Colorado. Mac Slingerlend, an executive at CIBER since its Colorado debut, became its CEO in 1998. In 1994, CIBER went public on the Nasdaq stock exchange and was prosperous enough to graduate to the New York Stock Exchange several years later.

Acquisitive nature

CIBER's aggressive acquisition strategy has landed it on lists such as *Business 2.0*'s 2004 Fastest Growing Companies. With growth stemming from corporate downsizing in the 1990s and cash raised from its 1994 IPO, CIBER underwent a string of purchases, including C.P.U. Inc. in 1994; Spectrum Technology Group and CIBER Network Services in 1996; consulting and staffing firm Davis, Thomas & Associates in 1997; IT and project management services firm TechWare Consulting in 1997; and technology consultancy The Summit Group in 1998. CIBER completed a dozen acquisitions in 1999, and in 2000, divided its operations in two—Digiterra became its business process application integration supplier, and Neovation its Internet support service provider. The company further specialized its offerings in 2001 by dividing into three subsidiaries: DigiTerra, SAP software consultancy CIBER Solution Partners, and security consulting and services division Enspherics.

Europe and beyond

The new century found CIBER increasingly looking towards overseas expansion. In January 2003, CIBER purchased UK IT consulting firm ECsoft for $54 million, and in May 2004 further expanded into the Old Country with a $40 million acquisition of Ascent Technology Ltd. The end of 2004 found CIBER continuing its pursuit of a leading German tech consultancy, Novasoft, eventually purchasing over 93 percent of Novasoft shares. Novasoft's $78 million in annual revenues added 500 employees to the CIBER payroll and a large client list including Bayer, BASF, B&Q (UK), The Big Food Group (UK), Volkswagen, Allianz, BMW, T-Systems and Nokia.

In June 2005, CIBER acquired India-based software firm Knowledge Systems, along with its 125 employees. CIBER had been operating in India under a partnership with another company, iGate, prior to the acquisition. In a June 2005 interview with *The Denver Post*, CEO Slingerland explained that offshoring has become essentially a prerequisite for continued IT success. "If we don't offer this service to our clients, we're at a disadvantage and risk losing clients," Slingerland said. "Doing low-cost development work is critical to us maintaining our client relationships and, in fact, American jobs." Slingerland claimed that CIBER lost a valuable American Express account in the 1990s because it didn't do offshore work, a lesson he doesn't wish to repeat.

Setting "CIBERsites" elsewhere

In January 2005, CIBER announced that it had opened a center in Oklahoma City where clients could utilize American workers for software development, rather than going overseas for foreign labor in countries like India. The Oklahoma City location was the first of six "CIBERsites" the company planned to set up in second-tier U.S. cities over the following 12 to 18 months, seeking to capitalize on less costly labor and create over 1,000 new jobs. In June 2005, CIBER opened a second CIBERsite in Tampa, Fla., where the company planned to hire at least 200 local tech workers.

Uncle Sam's CIBER space

CIBER's federal practice provides information and engineering technology services and solutions to a number of national government agencies in areas such as homeland security, physical security and aerospace/intelligence. CIBER Federal had a superbly successful 2004, increasing its revenue run rate to over $162 million, an increase of approximately $80 million over the previous year, and adding more than 1,000 skilled workers in the public sector. CIBER's work in homeland security consists of supporting the Department of Homeland Security United States Citizenship and Immigration Services (USCIS) in promoting national security and transforming and improving the delivery of immigration and citizenship services. The firm also focuses on ports, utilities, oil, gas and pipeline industries to provide IT services that aid physical security domestically.

CIBER Federal's aerospace and intelligence practice supports the U.S. Northern Command (USNORTHCOM) and North American Aerospace Defense Command

(NORAD) operational and planning missions, in addition to day-to-day support of the Transportation Security Agency's mission. At U.S. Strategic Command (USTRATCOM), CIBER provides technical, analytical and operational services for the Integrated Tactical Warning/Attack Assessment (ITW/AA) and Theater Million Warning Functional Managers, supporting the integration and coordination for worldwide missile warning operators, command and control evaluation, and operational and requirements analysis.

GETTING HIRED

Dipping into the talent pool

CIBER relies on a "staff of recruiters" to conduct "initial candidate search and qualification." Insiders tell us that the company recruits "at a lot of schools with technical programs all over the U.S.," but CIBER doesn't offer internships and draws much of its talent pool from experienced applicants. The company also looks for IT professionals for its two CIBERsites, but these are generally limited to programmers.

Job seekers can fill out an application on CIBER's web site, and apply to as many as 10 jobs at a time. An insider remarks that the selection process begins when the company matches "keywords on requirements with keywords on resumes." A colleague describes the rest of the hiring procedure as such: "Candidates are required to take a technical examination or are interviewed by appropriate subject matter experts. Candidates must submit at least three references and are subject to background checks depending upon client requirements." And once the firm accepts you into its ranks, "you meet your HR person and your admin person who give you an introduction [to] what is going on—salary, what the project is all about (if you were hired for a specific one), CIBER benefits and basic administrative things."

OUR SURVEY SAYS

Everything in moderation

Sources give the company high marks for travel requirements and workload, saying they work from about 45 to 55 hours a week. One consultant adds that he only works on weekends "as needed." Travel requirements vary on a project-by-project basis. "As of the last two months I have not needed to really travel at all. But when I was working on other projects I was traveling four to five days a week," one insider claims. Despite heavy travel, at times CIBER employees manage to make time for vacation, even though some "branches have a zero bench tolerance, which has created significant turnover." As one consultant claims, working for CIBER requires facing a number of tradeoffs and that "those desiring no travel and moderate compensation, and who [possess] a wide enough skill-set could find the job enjoyable."

Solo career

CIBER offers consultants training through CIBER U, a "virtual learning environment" with "300 computer-based technical training courses, mentoring, seminars, chat rooms, expert-led forums" and other resources. Sources, though, say that a lack of guidance from above and a relatively narrow range of training options are a persistent problem. When asked about training opportunities at CIBER, one consultant says, "What training? I have pretty much been on my own to catch up with everyone else. I haven't really been trained in anything." "Training is not the greatest," a colleague adds. "I would like more training for all the different areas, from consulting to project management to sales."

Big fish, little pond

Despite any void in CIBER's training programs, employees don't find it difficult to move up in its ranks. A source explains that CIBER's corporate culture gives him "the freedom to move forward...We are not huge like Accenture, and therefore I am not competing against hundreds of other consultants." Another source calls CIBER a "very entrepreneurial environment where performance is rewarded," but says to "only consider joining CIBER if you understand their strategic direction and can live with it," making the argument that while CIBER "does have fairly robust state, federal and ERP practices," most of their business is "low-level staffing."

Extra! Extra!

Though some sources admit that "the pay is not the greatest" at their firm, CIBER "covers most benefits," according to one. This includes "401(k) match, trade stock match and discount purchase plan." A source adds that some extra perks include "a free mobile phone, overtime meals, paid kick-off in another country [and] monthly meetings with free food [and] beer." Another associate adds that "if you refer someone that is hired on to CIBER and they work for 90 days, you get a bonus."

CIBER is a "very entrepreneurial environment where performance is rewarded."

— *CIBER insider*

Visit the Vault Consulting Career Channel at **www.vault.com/consulting** — with
insider firm profiles, message boards, the Vault Consulting Job Board and more.

VAULT CAREER LIBRARY   **303**

Covansys Corporation

32605 West Twelve Mile Road
Farmington Hills, MI 48334
Phone: (248) 488-2088 or
(800) 688-2088
Fax: (248) 488-2089
www.covansys.com

LOCATIONS

Farmington Hills, MI (HQ)
27 offices worldwide

PRACTICE AREAS

Application Maintenance &
  Development
Business Process Outsourcing
Integration Services & E-Business
Offshore Outsourcing
Packaged Software for ERP

THE STATS

Employer Type: Public Company
Ticker Symbol: CVNS (Nasdaq)
President and CEO: Rajendra B.
Vattikuti
2005 Employees: 7,000
2004 Employees: 6,000
2005 Revenues: $434.1 million
2004 Revenues: $374.8 million

UPPERS

• Casual atmosphere with flexible
  work hours

DOWNERS

• Unclear promotion path

EMPLOYMENT CONTACT

www.covansys.com/careers/
welcome.htm

THE BUZZ
WHAT CONSULTANTS AT OTHER FIRMS ARE SAYING

• "Good at what they do"
• "Low-key outsourcer"
• "Old school"

THE SCOOP

Clients come back for more

With over 7,000 consultants and employees worldwide, Covansys is trying to grow fast enough to meet client need. Founded in 1985, the global technology services company specializes in industry-specific solutions, strategic outsourcing and integration services. The company offers application maintenance and development and offshore outsourcing to both public and commercial sector clients in the health care, financial services, retail and distribution, manufacturing, telecommunications and high-tech industries. Covansys prides itself on client satisfaction and claims 90 percent of its business comes from repeat customers. Covansys has 350-plus clients on its roster, including major names such as Allianz, Henry Ford Health System, Medcor Incorporated, Gap Inc., The Kroger Company, Ford Motor Company, General Motors Corporation, Lucent Technologies and Sprint. Covansys works with 47 states, the U.S. Virgin Islands, the District of Columbia and Guam. Based in Michigan, the company has offices in 27 locations worldwide.

Leadership focused on retention

Raj Vattikuti, Covansys' founder, led the company as chief executive officer until 2000, when New York-based investment firm Clayton, Dubilier & Rice—having invested $200 million in the company that year—replaced him with former IBM-er Marty Clague as president and chief operating officer.

In September 2004, a subsidiary of Fidelity National Financial, Fidelity Information Services, Inc., bought 29 percent of the firm's stock—about 8.7 million shares—for a purchase price of $95.7 million. In a five-year deal valued at $150 million, Covansys became Fidelity's primary provider of outsourced IT services and Fidelity would be allowed to raise its stake in the company to 40 percent. The deal bought out most of CD&R's stake for $180 million in cash, leaving the investment firm with just 5 percent of the company's common shares. Vattikuti returned and took control of 17 percent of the shares before replacing Clague and assuming his previous role in the firm. Upon his return, Vattikuti planned to hire more employees to put the firm "back on the growth track," especially after an organizational realignment and efforts to rein in costs in 2003 forced a stream of layoffs that same year.

The company installed some new senior management in 2005. Raj Sirohi, a 25-year industry veteran from HCL Technologies America Inc., joined the company as senior vice president of Sales and Marketing in October. G. Ravindran, known as Ravi, joined the company as senior vice president and head of Global Human Resources in

April. With 25 years of experience in training and retention, Ravi came from Bharti Televentures Limited, a mobile telecom technology service provider in Delhi, after spending time at Ernst & Young and Pepsi. At the time of Ravi's inauguration, Vattikuti stated, "We will be even better positioned to manage our rapid growth and develop training and retention programs that are critical to our continued success."

Making way for democracy

In the wake of the 2000 elections in the United States with stories of fraud, incomplete voter rolls and inefficient systems, Congress passed the Help America Vote Act in 2002. HAVA required all states to implement a centralized and interactive statewide voter registration system to be defined, maintained and administered at the state level by January 2004, though many received waivers for an extension until 2006. In 2004, Covansys signed four HAVA deals with Rhode Island, Idaho, Nevada and New Hampshire. Maine and New Jersey signed with the firm in February and March 2005, respectively, to implement voter registration systems. Covansys partnered with PCC Technology Group and Aradyme Corporation to fully implement Maine and New Jersey's systems by the end of December 2005. In total, the HAVA contracts brought in $30 million for the company.

Not going it alone

Covansys has dedicated significant time, energy and resources to establishing a network of market-leading alliance partners to provide clients with complete end-to-end business solutions. The company counts IBM, Microsoft, Informatica, Cognos, Adobe and Oracle among those in its network.

In June 2005, the firm partnered with Fuji Xerox Information Systems, a wholly-owned subsidiary of global document and imaging giant Fuji Xerox Corporation, to develop data warehousing, document management and e-commerce solutions in Japan. The work was conducted from one of its Indian offshore development centers.

Initiating in India

Covansys arrived in India in 1992 as one of the first U.S.-based IT services providers to establish offshore facilities. Deriving about a quarter of its revenues from offshoring activities, the company calls Covansys India Private Limited its "crown jewel." Covansys has four development centers throughout India, in addition to three in the U.S., making it one of the largest providers of offshore capabilities. The company provides services to both international and Indian businesses. In 2005, the firm added approximately 1,000 employees in Chennai, Mumbai and Bangalore to meet its client needs. At the end of 2005, Covansys' total headcount in India was over 4,100.

In August 2005, the company opened its latest Global Development Center in Bangalore, consolidating all of its Bangalore facilities under one roof. The new building, located in the modern business district of Bangalore, is 250,000 square feet and accommodates over 2,200 professionals. The facility is intended to accommodate "steady offshore growth," stated Raj Vattikuti at the time.

In June 2005, Covansys India acquired up to 75 percent, or 4.05 million shares, of Fortune Infotech Limited's common stock for $0.74 per share in a transaction worth approximately $3 million. While Fortune's annual revenues were less than 1 percent of Covansys' revenues, the deal allowed Covansys to expand its business process outsourcing capabilities. Combined with the 2002 acquisition of PDA Software Services, the company can now provide a full suite of BPO services. Fortune, with its Baroda and Bangalore operations and a U.S. office in Princeton, N.J., became a majority-owned subsidiary of Covansys India Limited, and its 580 employees remained with the firm. In November 2005, the company sold and transferred its PeopleSoft development center to Oracle after the database giant exercised a purchase option to acquire this facility in Bangalore.

Reaping recognition

In March 2004, the company was named to *Washington Technology* magazine's Who's Who in the State and Local Market, an annual list of leading IT companies that service the public sector, for the third consecutive year. That same year, *VARBusiness* magazine named the firm one of the top 100 solution providers in North America. Covansys also made *VarBusiness'* top 500 list of companies in 2001, 2002 and 2003, placing in the top 25 percent each year. According to the publication, Covansys displays outstanding technology performance and leadership, making it an elite IT firm.

Certification is also important to Covansys. In May 2005, three Covansys India facilities and two Covansys U.S. facilities received the British Standard Information Security Management System BS7799-2:2002 certification. The recognition comes from the international certification firm Des Norke Veritas under accreditation from UKAS. In addition, in 2002, all three of the company's wholly-owned development centers in India received ISO 9001:2000 certification and Level 5 assessment in PCMM, and in 1999, two of the three received the Level 5 assessment in SEI CMM.

Covansys cares

The company believes in sponsoring and supporting local, national and global community efforts, and actively encourages employees and their families to get involved. This culture of caring comes straight from the top. CEO Vattikuti and his wife Padma established the Vattikuti Foundation, a personal organization aimed at achieving the family's philanthropic objectives. In 2001, the foundation made several of the largest philanthropic contributions for medical care and research ever granted in the State of Michigan to Henry Ford Health System's Vattikuti Urology Institute for prostate cancer research and treatment and to Beaumont Hospital's Vattikuti Cancer Institute. According to the foundation's web site, the Urology Institute has consistently ranked among the top 30 centers in America by *U.S. News and World Report*.

Covansys employees, along with the Vattikuti Foundation and the American Indian Foundation, donated $250,000 to various charities focused on the victims of September 11 terrorist attacks and $300,000 to support tsunami relief and rehabilitation efforts in South India in 2005. Covansys India employees donated an additional $44,000, as well as their time and energy to areas affected by the tsunami. In addition, the company and the Vattikuti Foundation donated more than $59,000 to the American Red Cross for the Hurricane Katrina fund. The company also offers an annual holiday wish program allowing employees to purchase gifts for underprivileged children. In England, Covansys participated in a corporate cricket challenge that raised money to rehabilitate and mainstream underprivileged children and those with special needs.

GETTING HIRED

Search away

On Covansys' careers web pages, you can learn more about company culture, career tracks and benefits. You can also search the firm's database for jobs and set up job search engines to have openings e-mailed to you. In addition, the firm offers an online resume building application.

A source tells us the interview process consisted of "two phone interviews and one written test followed by a group discussion and face-to-face interviews."

OUR SURVEY SAYS

Casual Covansys

Covansys, insiders report, boasts a "good" work culture, with "flexible hours." In a "business casual" atmosphere, a source tells us, staffers enjoy "great exposure to multiple technologies and learning paths." Still, a source complains that there's "no promotion policy."

Sources tell us the firm offers a number of benefits, including a 401(k), a discounted employee stock purchase plan, tuition assistance and a pre-tax transportation reimbursement program.

Visit the Vault Consulting Career Channel at **www.vault.com/consulting** — with insider firm profiles, message boards, the Vault Consulting Job Board and more.

VAULT CAREER LIBRARY   309

CTG

800 Delaware Avenue
Buffalo, NY 14209-2094
Phone: (716) 882-8000
Fax: (716) 887-7464
www.ctg.com

LOCATIONS

Buffalo, NY (HQ)
39 offices worldwide

PRACTICE AREAS

Application Management Outsourcing
IT Solutions
IT Staffing

THE STATS

Employer Type: Public Company
Ticker Symbol: CTG (NYSE)
President and CEO: James R. Boldt
2005 Employees: 3,600
2004 Employees: 2,500
2005 Revenues: $294.5 million
2004 Revenues: $237.1 million

UPPERS

• Flexible work arrangements
  available
• Not overly excessive hours or
  travel

DOWNERS

• Bonuses are "occasional"
• "Marginal office facilities"

EMPLOYMENT CONTACT

Go to the Careers section of CTG's
web site to search open positions
and submit a resume
E-mail: careers@ctg.com

THE SCOOP

The formative years

Founded by former IBM employees in 1966 as Marks-Baer, Inc., Buffalo-based Computer Task Group went public in 1969 as a computer services provider for the non-tech-savvy. By the early 1980s, CTG operated in 45 North American locations and expanded into the European market, opening an office in the UK in 1986. The company quickly expanded overseas, acquiring European firm Rendeck International and the accompanying offices in Denmark, Holland and Belgium. In 1989, IBM purchased 15.3 percent of CTG, leading to a fruitful collaboration that still persists. CTG further ensconced itself with the tech juggernaut in the 1990s when it became one of eight IT firms approved to provide technical advice and services to IBM in the United States. In 1997, this partnership expanded to IBM Canada.

Boom and bust

CTG saw its profits soar during the tech boom of the 1990s, transitioning from general IT services into a consultancy for all things technological, from designing and implementing software to providing staff to run applications. In 1997, CTG revamped its client list to focus on the most lucrative of the bunch, cutting its client list in half. The strategy paid off when the company posted record revenues and profits in 1998, some $467.8 million and $24 million, respectively. In 1999, CTG expanded its reach into health care, acquiring Cincinnati-based Elumen Solutions, an IT company that specialized in working with health care providers. Elumen was renamed CTG HealthCare Solutions (CTGHS), and is now one of the firm's strongest areas. The company celebrated the beginning of the new millennium when it received ISO 9000 certification, the internationally recognized standard for superior management and efficient business practices, in June 2006.

The dot-com bubble burst resulted in several quarters of financial loss for the company, from which it has still not fully recovered. CTG declared a 27 percent drop in revenues in 2000, including a devastating 92 percent drop in fourth-quarter profits from the same period just one year prior. Profits continued to plummet, leading CTG to focus on its most lucrative sectors: health care and application management outsourcing (AMO). Individual CTG units Zenius, Exemplar and ITCapital were fused into one unit. CTG also trimmed staff and services and in October 2001 was able to announce a meager return to profitability with a net income of $200,000.

Boldting down a sense of stability

In 2001, CTG chief financial officer James R. Boldt was promoted to president and CEO. Shortly thereafter, CTG rearranged its service offerings and resources to focus on the three sectors with the greatest potential for renewed expansion in revenues and earnings: IT staffing, AMO and IT solutions. CTG launched a second vertical market focus in 2002, CTG Retail Solutions, and in 2003, formed a Life Sciences practice to capitalize on the growing profits in the booming pharmaceuticals sector.

New headcounts

The first quarter in 2005 found CTG announcing the opening of three new offices. In April, the newest office opened in San Juan, Puerto Rico, intended to service pharmaceutical companies in the area, providing CTG with a ready-made client base. Two other offices opened in early 2005 in Rochester, Minn., and Tucson, Ariz., to serve clients and operate as a recruiting base for technology workers. The company added 700 workers in the first quarter—200 more than originally planned—mainly due to a growing staffing business.

Where would we be without you?

Having been founded by former IBM-ers, CTG has maintained a close relationship with IBM. In the third quarter of 2005, IBM was by far CTG's largest customer, accounting for $27.8 million, or 37.2 percent, of consolidated revenues. IBM's business not only added to CTG profits, but to its staff, as well; in fact, a sizeable chunk of CTG's new hires for 2005 came from IBM. The company's Technical Services Agreement with IBM expires on December 31, 2007, a contract CTG is unlikely to let go.

Looking across the horizon, why not Buffalo?

As the staffing business appeared to be heating up by mid-2005, CTG shifted its focus to boosting corporate software projects, an especially profitable area of the business. Other new projects include testing software developed overseas for financial firms, a major growth area as IT companies in India draw business from U.S. clients. However, Boldt goes against conventional wisdom as he glances overseas at Indian outsourcing. Prices for "offshoring," he believes, are rising, with many clients facing costly snags attempting to manage projects across oceans. "The price gap between off-shore and second-tier [U.S.] cities is closing," Boldt told *The Buffalo News* in May 2005 from his office in second-tier Buffalo. His comment reflects the inflation and currency appreciation in India driving up costs in the country, which then impacts the numbers of IT outsourcing companies it's attracting.

Ups and downs

CTG saw its sales numbers rise to $294.5 million in 2005, a 24 percent boost from the previous year. The company also added 1,100 employees during the year, bringing the 2005 increase to some 44 percent over 2004. Most promising for CTG was the fact that solutions—the more lucrative side of technology project integration—was reviving for the first time since the dot-com crash. Additionally, business from the health care division augured well, particularly among insurers, as more and more medical records are being transferred to digital record keeping. In September 2005, CTG HealthCare Solutions announced that it would deliver health care IT services to children's health care providers. Its Children's Healthcare services will be delivered by consultants with hands-on experience in pediatrics, and is the first of several new service lines that CTGHS plans to establish for specialty markets. The company's information security business has also shown marked growth, as corporations look to protect against identity theft and credit card fraud.

The positive indicators could not have arrived at a more pressing time for CTG, which learned in August 2005 that, under a plan filed with the New York Stock Exchange, the company needed to raise its stock price dramatically over the next 16 months in order to keep its listing on the exchange. Meeting the NYSE's target means achieving a stock price of $4.48, from $3.42 in November 2005. The NYSE disallowed 4 million shares from CTG's market capitalization (19 percent of total shares) since they are held in a trust for CTG employee compensation, causing the time crunch to boost the stock price.

GETTING HIRED

Just the facts

CTG's careers link provides a basic job search engine, with no further information on what the firm looks for. But the search application does offer one unique feature: a "concept search," which allows candidates to describe what they're looking for, or even copy and paste their resume into the search box, to be matched with appropriate openings. In addition, the firm offers an online resume builder. Insiders tell us that the firm tends to lean toward experienced hires, and that its recruiters often contact candidates whose online resumes catch their eye.

Financial Insights, an IDC Company

5 Speen Street
Framingham, MA 01701
Phone: (508) 620-5533
Fax: (508) 988-6761
E-mail: sales@financial-insights.com
www.financial-insights.com

LOCATIONS

Framingham, MA (HQ)
11 offices worldwide

PRACTICE AREAS

Advisory research services
Consulting & custom research
Go-to-market services
Multiclient studies
Research reports
Spending guides

THE STATS

Employee Type: Business Unit of International Data Corporation (IDC)
COO: Michon Schenck

UPPERS

- Wide breadth of knowledge of IT application for the finance industry
- Research spans global markets with regional focus

DOWNERS

- Not as well known in Europe
- Still relatively new to the market

EMPLOYMENT CONTACT

www.financial-insights.com/FI/about/careers.jsp

THE SCOOP

Insight into Financial Insights

Financial Insights, based in Framingham, Mass., is a leading independent and global provider of continuing strategic advice, custom research and consulting services based on the significant business and technology matters of the financial services industry. Financial Insights is part of International Data Corporation (IDC)—a company that has studied trends in the IT game for more than 42 years as part of International Data Group (IDG), the world's largest IT media, research and events company—and operates throughout the world utilizing IDC's network of global facilities. IDC, the market research and advisory arm of IDG, began Financial Insights in November 2002 with the merger of Meridien Research and its IDC Financial Services Advisory unit.

Financial Insights' research primarily covers topics of strategic interest to banks, insurance companies, asset management firms, securities brokerages and diversified financial institutions around the world. Clients use the research to guide their internal investment decisions, help plan for future technology needs, benchmark themselves against competitors and stay current on solution offerings, all of which enables them to create a competitive advantage. The company compiles reports and updates concentrated on emerging technology and its application, in addition to custom research and strategic consulting services and conference hosting.

Making milestones

The firm doesn't make a lot of headlines; mostly, it sticks to publishing the results of its latest surveys and studies in the sectors it covers. But in late 2005, Financial Insights announced it had achieved a "milestone," posting its first year of full profitability, with revenue growth of 40 percent year over year in its third year of business. The firm's results for fiscal 2005, in fact, were more than 370 percent higher than the revenues posted by Meridien in its last operating year. During the year, Financial Insights expanded its client and employee rolls, expanding into Mexico and Brazil, with nearly 200 clients in 16 countries worldwide. In November 2005, the firm appointed several new senior execs, including a new director of EMEA relations in London, and new research directors in banking, risk management and insurance. The firm also expanded its risk management portfolio in Europe and Asia Pacific.

Primarily research

Financial Insights is known as a prominent provider of primary data for the financial services clients it serves. Unlike many others in the field, Financial Insights enables its clients to make technology and operational investment decisions based on hard facts and evidence rather than second-hand information or estimates. In association with IDC, Financial Insights' annual "Marco Polo" survey in Asia/Pacific reviews multi-country household data on e-banking and channel usage across important demographic segments. This data forms profiles of consumers and seeks to identify areas for potential new customer segments.

In 2004, together with *American Banker*, the leading publication to the U.S. banking market, Financial Insights created the world's first annual, fact-based ranking of financial technology providers called the "FinTech 100." Financial Insights utilizes the FinTech 100 with other proprietary data to determine which vendors, partners and service providers are "leading, lagging, or simply maintaining the status quo." The FinTech is now an annual report, with the third edition scheduled for release in November 2006.

The firm also publishes regular surveys and studies, such as annual reports on top 10 strategic IT initiatives for various regional capital markets. It also provides business insights to its target audience, publishing surveys covering consumer trends and behavior. One such survey in 2005 reported on the number of consumers who choose to switch banks following identity theft (6 percent, the firm found).

GETTING HIRED

Insight, please

Financial Insights' bare-bones Careers web page says the firm looks for candidates with relevant experience in financial services and/or technology. It posts openings as they arise, and directs interested candidates to e-mail their resumes (though the web site doesn't list a contact e-mail for recruiting). Those interested in research, sales or marketing opportunities at the firm should also visit the Careers site.

Financial Insights' research primarily covers topics of strategic interest to banks, insurance companies, asset management firms, securities brokerages and diversified financial institutions around the world.

Visit the Vault Consulting Career Channel at **www.vault.com/consulting** — with
insider firm profiles, message boards, the Vault Consulting Job Board and more.

VAULT CAREER LIBRARY   **317**

GFI Informatique

199 rue Championnet
75018 Paris, France
Phone: +33 (1) 44-85-88-88
Fax: +33 (1) 44-85-88-89
www.gfi.fr

LOCATIONS

Paris (HQ)
30 offices throughout France and
offices in 9 countries worldwide

PRACTICE AREAS

Consulting
Outsourcing
Software Applications
Systems Integration

THE STATS

Employer Type: Public Company
Ticker Symbol: GFI (Euronext Paris)
Chairman & CEO: Jacques Tordjman
2005 Employees: 7,166
2004 Employees: 6,976
2005 Revenues: €543.8 million
2004 Revenues: €516.4 million

UPPERS

- Slowly working its way up
- Flexible with regard to consultant
  needs

DOWNERS

- Stuck in Europe
- Hard to get by without French

EMPLOYMENT CONTACT

Director of Recruiting
Catherine Hankiss
E-mail: chankiss@gfi.fr
For a list of recruiting contacts in
each division, go to
www.gfi.fr/fr/recrutement/contact-
recrutement.php

THE SCOOP

Gunning for it

GFI Informatique, one of France's first IT companies, was originally founded in 1970 and has undergone a series of acquisitions and divestitures before realizing its current form. The company was formerly a part of Scicon International, SD-Scicon, and, in 1991, was acquired by the American firm Electronic Data Systems (EDS), formerly a General Motors subsidiary. Jacques Tordjman, chairman of EDS's GFI unit (and chair of GFI since 1984), repurchased the company and dubbed it GFI Informatique. Today a publicly company traded on the Paris Stock Exchange, GFI employs over 7,000 people in 13 countries worldwide, including offices in Europe, North America and Africa.

GFI undertook an ambitious acquisition strategy to build up its market share in the heady IT days at the turn of the millennium. In 1999 it purchased French IT firms Gallius and Ceacti, as well as a 70 percent share in the Milan-centered Atel Group. Early 2000 found GFI acquiring an unspecified stake in SPS & Partner, a German IT consulting firm, and a portion of Dutch firm ASN, which specializes in complex network solutions. Later in 2000, GFI added OIS and Olivetti Sanità, subsidiaries of Italian typewriters-to-computers-to-telecom company Olivetti. The new millennium saw GFI glancing beyond the horizon, as well, adding a 70 percent stake in Canadian IT consulting firm La Gestion Proben. After 2000, GFI slackened its pace a bit, with no major purchases until the 2003 acquisition of Infogen Systems, at the time the industry leader in the enterprise resource planning (ERP) market. The company announced an agreement with Conceptum in October 2004 under which GFI would gain that firm's assets relating to consulting, electronic payment and business solution integration. Most recently, GFI acquired local rivals Adelior and Actif in January 2006, in an effort to boost its growth and enhance its strategic offerings. These additions brought in around 1,000 new staff and added €75 million in revenues to the firm.

Reshaping business at GFI

An economic downturn, along with difficulties encountered by several subsidiaries, forced GFI to undergo a major strategic reassessment in 2004. Northern Europe presented severe challenges—UK, Swiss and German markets in particular—and failed to achieve prominent market shares before economic struggles hit the economy. Losses in these markets caused GFI to post a net loss for the year. In response, the firm opted to refocus its efforts on its traditional strengths, beginning

Visit the Vault Consulting Career Channel at **www.vault.com/consulting** — with insider firm profiles, message boards, the Vault Consulting Job Board and more.

VAULT CAREER LIBRARY   **319**

with its current "center of gravity" in Southern Europe, where its subsidiaries in Italy (over 1,000 employees), Spain (1,200) and Portugal (350) show the most promising forward momentum for the company's future growth. Operations in France continued to be the firm's flagship, employing 56 percent of the GFI workforce, though it brings in roughly 40 percent of sales from its operations outside France. In October 2005, GFI announced that it had sold off its UK subsidiary to communications services provider NextiraOne for an undisclosed sum.

To further streamline business, GFI renovated its operational structure to improve customer service through standardized processes and established areas of distinctive achievement. The company thus organized itself into four divisions: Industry, Retail and Services; Administration and Public Sector; Banking, Finance and Insurance; and Telecommunications and Media. The sectors accounted for 42 percent, 24 percent, 17 percent and 17 percent of GFI's total 2005 revenue, respectively. To get the job done, GFI employees are broken down into four operational groups: consulting, engineering and systems integration, software and outsourcing.

Liberté, egalité, fraternité

GFI takes its friendships very seriously, following a manifesto entitled the "Partnership Charter" that guides the company's cooperative partnerships to achieve maximum product and component integration. GFI's partners fall into three categories: manufacturers and integrators mainly involved in specific projects to enhance customer satisfaction (often flexible and temporary); editors in long-term agreements that augment GFI's ability to act as an integrator of software produced by partners; and "trade" partnerships that strive to create skills at the foundation of client businesses by joining with industry specialists. Principal partners include such luminaries as HP, IBM, Microsoft, Oracle, SAP and Sun Microsystems, among others.

GETTING HIRED

Francophones wanted

Parlez-vous francais? You'll need it if you hope to apply online for a position at GFI Informatique. The firm's English-language web page links to career information which, alas, is only available in GFI's native tongue. If you're a Francophone, you'll find an easily navigable job search engine listing positions throughout the company's locations.

According to the firm, GFI begins its hiring process with a recruiter who looks at candidates' educational and professional backgrounds. If you match the firm's needs, the recruiter will tell you about opportunities in greater detail. Soon thereafter, the firm says, those who make it past this round will meet with a manager who talks to candidates about the technical aspects of the job, as well as ongoing projects. These discussions may be followed by tests. After that, the company says, "if you meet our criteria, you will receive a quick offer." GFI assures candidates that it stays in touch throughout the process.

Flexibility is key

GFI says it manages its employees' assignments over a corporate Intranet, which allows consultants to "express their wishes" regarding the projects they take on. In addition, "certain projects will enable you to move around internationally," and staffers can transfer offices if their profile matches the needs of the location they wish to join.

Interactive Business Systems, Inc.

IBS Headquarters
2625 Butterfield Road
Oak Brook, IL 60523
Phone: (630) 571-9100
www.ibs.com

LOCATIONS

Oak Brook, IL (HQ)
12 offices in the U.S., UK and India

PRACTICE AREAS

Applications
   Application Management
    Outsourcing
   Development & Integration
   Web Solutions
Business
   Project Management Services
   Strategic Technology Planning
   Workforce Management Services
Infrastructure
   Network Security
   Network Strategies
Strategic Staffing

THE STATS

Employer Type: Private Company
Chairman and CEO: Dan Williams
2005 Employees: 776
2004 Employees: 761
2005 Revenues: $94.9 million
2004 Revenues: $93.1 million

UPPERS

- Wide breadth of industries to choose from
- Experienced colleagues

DOWNERS

- Not much name recognition
- Few opportunities abroad

EMPLOYMENT CONTACT

ibs.com/careers/default.asp

THE SCOOP

Interacts well with others

Interactive Business Systems, Inc., founded in 1981 and headquartered in the Chicago suburb of Oak Brook, Ill., has a 25-year history of providing technology solution and services to clients across a number of diverse industries. IBS clients range from mid-size to Fortune 500 enterprises in financial services, insurance, manufacturing, retail trade, transportation and distribution, pharmaceuticals, publishing, food and beverage, telecommunications, health care, utilities and energy. IBS maintains 10 offices in the U.S., with European operations in the United Kingdom and two locations in India.

An eye on health

IBS considers insurance and health care to be two areas of expertise, having developed focused services for these industries. In 2005, the firm boosted its position in these industries with several new contracts. In August, Miami Mutual Insurance Company, a property and casualty insurance carrier, debuted its new web site format, constructed by IBS. The site offers a database of downloadable documents such as bulletins, forms, manuals and rating disks and is designed to allow further functionality in later phases, including integration with Miami Mutual's core insurance system and allowing self-service functionality to be added for agents. Miami Mutual announced that it had selected IBS because of its insurance industry experience in building highly-integrated sites with back-end systems that provide real-time, functional Web tools for agents and policyholders.

In May 2005, IBS announced that it had been selected by Midwest Eye Bank—a nonprofit that provides corneal tissues transplantation—to supply software development for its core business data management system. MEB's Eye-Bank Information System collects and organizes all data related to donor screening, tissue evaluation, surgery scheduling, distribution and follow-up, and assists with MEB's federal regulatory compliance. That same month, IBS cemented a deal with ProMedica Health System to develop a proprietary I-Breathe Web System. The system will assist with patient/doctor communication, statistical reporting and pulmonary function test results through a secure patient/doctor portal.

Going for gold

In June 2005, IBS announced that it had achieved Gold Certified status in the Microsoft Partner Program with competencies in advanced infrastructure solutions and information worker productivity solutions. The certification recognizes IBS as one of Microsoft's most highly accomplished partners with proven proficiency and real-world customer recommendations in specific solution areas. "Microsoft Gold Certified Partners that have certified experience and direct training and support from Microsoft can build a positive customer experience with our technologies," said Allison Watson, VP of the Worldwide Partner Sales and Marketing Group at Microsoft, who added that IBS was awarded the honor "for demonstrating its expertise in providing customer satisfaction with Microsoft products and technology."

Clients for clients

In June 2005, IBS announced the formation of its new National Client Services division, an effort to distinguish itself in the highly competitive marketplace where clients may seek IT consultants from up to 50 providers for a single project. The NCS division maintains an extensive database of prequalified consultants and proprietary recruiting software developed to provide strategic recruitment for IBS customers. Utilizing a team of NCS recruiters and managers, IBS rapidly identifies, qualifies and presents IT candidates to its clients. If the company can't find an appropriate consultant internally, it hits job boards to search for qualified individuals. "Typically within 24 hours," said NCS director Eric Treida, "our network of recruiters can provide a client with a candidate we've already interviewed who has the right skills verified by testing, the appropriate vertical industry experience and immediate availability." IBS intends for the program to help its clients lower costs and increase efficiency and growth.

GETTING HIRED

Looking for long-termers

IBS describes its ideal employee as one with "excellent skills" who "enjoys challenges," "understands professionalism and customer service," "provides best in-class work," and boasts "business experience," a "desire to learn and grow," and a "focus on long-term employment." IBS trains its consultants in a range of Web-based technologies, such as .NET and Java/J2EE development. On the firm's web site you can search for job openings, see a list of all available jobs and submit your resume. The firm states that consultant roles can include developers, database administrators, business analysts, architects and project managers.

IBS considers insurance and health care to be two areas of expertise, having developed focused services for these industries.

Visit the Vault Consulting Career Channel at **www.vault.com/consulting** — with
insider firm profiles, message boards, the Vault Consulting Job Board and more.

VAULT CAREER LIBRARY   325

LogicaCMG

32 Hartwell Avenue
Lexington, MA 02421
Phone: (617) 476-8000
Fax: (617) 476-8010
www.logicacmg.com

LOCATIONS

Lexington, MA (U.S. HQ)
London (HQ)
More than 180 offices in 36
countries worldwide

PRACTICE AREAS

CRM
Enterprise asset management
Enterprise resource planning
HR/payroll services
IT security & outsourcing
IT skills
Open source software
Outsourcing
SAP
Security
Software engineering
Testing & quality management
Wireless enterprise solutions

THE STATS

Employer Type: Public Company
Ticker Symbol: LOG (LSE/AEX)
CEO: Dr. Martin Read
2005 Employees: 30,000
2004 Employees: 19,695
FY 2005 Revenues: €2,637.3 million
(includes Telecoms Products
revenues)
FY 2004 Revenues: €2,384.4 million

UPPERS

- "Technically challenging projects"
- "Variety of projects"
- Flexible work arrangements

DOWNERS

- "Risk aversion"
- Lack of communication from
  management
- Weak training opportunities

EMPLOYMENT CONTACT

www.logicacmg.com/careers/
index.asp

THE SCOOP

Surviving the merger

When British IT firm Logica acquired its former telecom rival—the Dutch CMG—in December 2002, the restructuring resulted in some 2,000 workers sent packing. Together, the two companies boast more than 40 years of IT experience. The merger sought to create a group focused on messaging software for mobile networks, business and IT services, outsourcing and contract programming. Today, the London-based company is the third-largest IT company in Europe with some 30,000 employees working in 36 countries across the globe. The company provides business consulting, systems integration and IT and business process outsourcing across diverse markets including telecoms, financial services, energy and utilities, industry, distribution and transport, and the public sector, and is seeking areas for expanded market growth in Europe and throughout the world.

Back in the black

In September 2003, six months after the merger, LogicaCMG announced that performances had exceeded predictions despite recording a loss for the six-month stretch. Subsequent profit warnings in 2004 and early 2005 prompted alarm that the company had deep-sixed itself by overreaching on the CMG acquisition. However, by September 2005, the firm beat market expectations with a 46 percent rise in first-half profits, primarily the result of a significant rise in companies outsourcing their IT needs. LogicaCMG CEO Martin Read declared that the group was finally beginning to see results from the mega-merger.

Many of the large contracts recently won by LogicaCMG, Read explained, including organizations such as the Ministry of Defense and the Metropolitan Police, could not have been achieved by either firm on its own. In addition, in April 2005, the firm announced that it had completed the €81 million acquisition of 60 percent controlling interest in Edinfor SA, the Portugal-based IT business of Energias de Portugal (EDP), making arrangements to purchase the remaining shares of Edinfor. With operations also in Spain and Brazil, Edinfor strengthens LogicaCMG's position in energy and utilities. As part of the transaction, LogicaCMG signed a €510 million contract with EDP to provide IT outsourcing for 10 years. By the close of 2005, overall revenues had increased nearly 11 percent to €2,637.3 million. The promising results came mainly from the company's UK and Netherlands divisions, with operations in France and Germany continuing to make a loss. Read hinted that the company was exploring options to remedy that situation.

A French connection

LogicaCMG acquired its smaller French rival Unilog SA in a €9.1 million sale in September 2005. The Paris-based Unilog, whose business focuses on building and renovating internal IT systems and training employees on the new systems, is relatively small, with a predominantly French client base. Unilog is the fourth-largest IT services company in France, trailing Atos Origin, Capgemini and IBM. Read explained that the deal would reverse his company's consistently disappointing performance in France and Germany, where the only reliable financial performance was debt. In 2004, losses in Germany grew from €14.4 million in 2003 to €23 million, while French losses in 2004 remained unchanged at €2 million. In a September 2005 interview with London's *Daily Telegraph*, Read commented, "I would put this in the same league as the merger of Logica with CMG three years ago. Customers are wanting to do business with a smaller number of big players who can support them internationally." The deal was completed in January 2006 and Unilog remains a viable force in France, recruiting staff at a rapid rate to cater to its clientele.

Space is the place

In efforts to expand mobile location technology, LogicaCMG partnered with UK firm Cambridge Positioning Systems Ltd. in the Galileo satellite program in October 2005. CPS provided its network-based Matrix location technology for the endeavor, dubbed Application of Galileo in the LBS Environment, or AGILE. The project seeks to boost sales of its Global Navigation Satellite Services to businesses and consumers across the European continent.

Global expansion

Recognizing customer demand for offshore work in countries such as India, the Czech Republic and Malaysia, LogicaCMG expanded its business outside of its traditional centers in Europe, opening a state-of-the-art campus-style facility in Bangalore, India, in 2005. The company aims to employ more than 2,000 people there by the end of 2006. Seamus Keating, LogicaCMG's financial director, notes that the firm's strategy to provide customers with "blended" services is the same that emerged in PCs and other manufacturing industries. Offering blended services involves some work conducted on a customer's premises and some done nearby, but outsourced services that don't require customer proximity will be increasingly handled in lower cost locations such as India.

Industry pundits have been divided on LogicaCMG's outsourcing strategy. Some believe that the firm has dragged its heels in shifting operations to India and that the

2,000 employees proposed to work there are but a small fraction of the firm's headcount. Others say that LogicaCMG has no reason to join the mass departure to India that so many other British firms have been swept up in, since the company remains generally well-protected from low cost challenges due to its focus on the more complicated and high-value sector of IT consulting.

The many uses of mobile messaging

LogicaCMG made a few splashes in the mobile market in 2005. In July, the firm joined with Shazam Entertainment to deliver the Music Recognition for Mobile Devices (MRMD) solution. MRMD allows mobile network operators to boost revenues from existing and new target audiences with content services such as ring tones, full music track and video downloads. MRMD's music recognition uses a process based on unique "fingerprints" that allow users to identify any track by dialing a short code and holding their mobile unit to the music source.

In November 2005, LogicaCMG and cell phone company T-Mobile announced successful tests of a new energy metering system allowing clients to monitor their electricity or gas without a meter card or key. The Instant Energy system uses a keypad linked to a utility firm's servers through a GSM telecom network, enabling utility firms to read, set up and control meters without sending engineers to the site.

GETTING HIRED

Log on

As a primarily European corporation, LogicaCMG recruits students more heavily on European campuses than in America, especially in England and France, according to several sources. "Staff go to graduate recruitment fairs and to their old university or college" to bring in new employees, one insider tells us, but the company also "tends to recruit directly using Internet sites and referrals." On its web site, U.S. job seekers can find a list of career events and job fairs where LogicaCMG representatives will be, as well as a searchable database of current openings.

Know what to expect

LogicaCMG's recruitment process includes up to four interviews, and an insider reports that "from the moment an application is received, a recruit" is invited to interview "within a week," although another source cautions that it "can take a long time" to go through the process.

Visit the Vault Consulting Career Channel at **www.vault.com/consulting** — with
insider firm profiles, message boards, the Vault Consulting Job Board and more.   V/\ULT C A R E E R
L I B R A R Y   **329**

The company's hiring process includes an "informative interview to determine a mutual match. If the first interview is OK for both parties, the actual interviews start, which include a thorough investigation of skills by a manager and an HR meeting." The "actual" interviews take one full day, "each followed by a go/no go decision among the hiring team...The day ends with a job offer and contract to be signed" by the successful candidate. One source says that the technical interview includes a "real-life exercise that depends on the job" the candidate is interviewing for, and the "results are judged by peers." One source says applicants should also expect a "possible psychometric test," though the firm notes that this is "highly unusual."

OUR SURVEY SAYS

3-D progression

LogicaCMG consultants value the "network of people" they work with, and they describe a "friendly atmosphere" of "openness and equality throughout all levels in the firm." Not all insiders have the same rosy appraisal, though, especially when it comes to the subject of promotion. The culture, they say is "pretty strict; [it's] not up-or-out, but if you fail to meet the requirements of the position, you will be demoted." Movement in the company is three-dimensional; as one of our sources tell us, "horizontal promotions are possible [and] LogicaCMG has a promotion and demotion policy in case of poor performance." Insiders ultimately say there are "good opportunities for progression, based on capability and track record" but claim that there "doesn't seem to be any logic [as] to how the company manages such selections."

Pointing fingers

Sources look to the firm's management structure as the source of some of the problems they highlight. Several report a "lack of enthusiasm" at LogicaCMG due to problems they see with how the company is managed, especially in regard to promotion. Promotion, a number of discouraged insiders tell us, is "based on cliques" and job opportunities come to those who "pander to the right people," regardless of qualifications. As a result, another source says, the company has to "eliminate layers of 'management'" in order to improve working conditions because, as things stand now, there is a sense that the company suffers from a "failure to treat staff decently."

Learning to train

Promotion qualms, combined with a "failure to provide training for career advancement or [training] related to the job" have brought another source to the conclusion that "people have reached the point where they just want to leave IT altogether because this company has put them off so much." A colleague concurs, saying that training is "nonexistent. Public offers of help [are] never delivered." The firm notes, however, that training is built into the company structure and that efforts are made to provide it upon request.

One source offers a possible road to improvement: The company can improve conditions by providing "the help it claims to offer for career guidance." Sources add that "we are doing more training now" though it's "mostly run by more senior staff towards more junior staff."

"Go above and beyond"

Insiders praise their company for its "flexibility" to create a work/life balance, but explain that consultants should "expect to go above and beyond in the hours you work" and "to commute large distances." Another source notes that consultants are "expected to work extra hours without pay" and with "no thanks and no other form of reward." Conversely, one employee tells us that "assignments can always be rejected by employees [based] on the traveling requirements."

Consultants are also frustrated with the firm's policy on compensating for travel expenses. Although LogicaCMG officially provides travel expenses, you may "have to argue over being paid for this, and certainly won't have your travel time taken into consideration." Insiders tell us that local policies, including the travel compensation policy, "can be unclear" and that the company can fix this by expanding the "car allowance, which is business-mileage linked."

Pay fair

When it comes to issues of salary, insiders have some serious advice for future employees. LogicaCMG may not always deliver on incentives it offers at hiring, sources contend: "If they like you, they will promise you whatever it takes to get you to join—don't expect them to deliver." "You'll probably be offered a nice starting salary, but you'd better like it because it probably won't change by more than 3 percent over the next five years," grumbles a colleague.

On the subject of bonuses, some sources remain heated. Some insiders appreciate LogicaCMG's benefits and bonuses but say that there is an overall "inconsistency in rewards," where there are "bonus schemes" for "selected staff" that create a need for "more equal compensation" and "more fair rewarding." Another urges the company to "separate cost-of-living pay raises from performance-based raises."

In general, though, insiders seem satisfied with the perks offered by the firm. In addition to the basic perks—medical, dental, stock purchase, 401(k), flexible spending accounts, and paid vacation and holidays—consultants get a company car, drinks on Fridays, and "the personnel organization has some interesting discounts," as well.

Looking outside the box

With respect to diversity, consultants say that LogicaCMG needs to make a more of a "commitment to hire women and minorities." And as far as hiring gays, lesbians and bisexuals, "we just don't care about it, as long as it does not hinder work," an employee states.

Insiders say the firm has "minimal" involvement in community projects; as one puts it, "evidence of this is very hard to find." The firm notes, however, that it contributed to the tsunami fund and offered employees the opportunity to donate directly from their pay. It has also been involved with projects such as Shelter in the UK.

There are "good opportunities for progression, based on capability and track record."

— *LogicaCMG employee*

Visit the Vault Consulting Career Channel at **www.vault.com/consulting** — with
insider firm profiles, message boards, the Vault Consulting Job Board and more.

VAULT CAREER LIBRARY 333

Satyam Computer Services Ltd.

8500 Leesburg Pike, Suite 202
Vienna, VA 22182
Phone: (703) 734-2100
Fax: (703) 734-2110
www.satyam.com

LOCATIONS

Vienna, VA (U.S. HQ)
Andhra Pradesh, India (HQ)
Over 53 offices worldwide

PRACTICE AREAS

Application Development &
  Maintenance Services
BPO Services
Consulting & Enterprise Business
  Solutions
Extended Engineering Solutions
Infrastructure Management Services

THE STATS

Employer Type: Public Company
Ticker Symbol: SAY (NYSE)
Chairman and Founder: Ramalinga
Raju
2005 Employees: 23,000+
2004 Employees: 16,800
2005 Revenues: $793.6 million
2004 Revenues: $553 million

UPPERS

• "You are free to say what you
  want"
• Above-average compensation

DOWNERS

• "A complex combined structure of
  centralized operations"
• Some long hours

EMPLOYMENT CONTACT

E-mail: globalhr@satyam.com

THE BUZZ
WHAT CONSULTANTS AT OTHER FIRMS ARE SAYING

• "Diverse"
• "Up-and-comer, eager"
• "Highly technical"
• "Bad local reputation"

THE SCOOP

IT from the East

Based in India, Satyam Computer Services has become a tech consulting firm to watch. Serving clients in the automotive, banking and financial services, insurance and health care, manufacturing, and what the firm lumps together as the telecom-infrastructure-media-entertainment-semiconductors industries, Satyam provides end-to-end solutions from strategy consulting to IT implementation. The firm's clients include over 155 Fortune 500 companies.

Satyam, founded in 1987, went public in 1992. The firm is a truly global enterprise, with a network spanning 53 countries in six continents. Its "development centers" employ more than 23,000 people worldwide. Services offered include Application Development and Maintenance Services, Consulting and Enterprise Business Solutions, Extended Engineering Solutions, Infrastructure Management Services and BPO services.

Catching up

Traditionally, Satyam has been seen as a runner-up among India's biggest software companies—but this is expected to change, according to a 2005 profile in *BusinessWeek*. Indeed, the firm has wowed the markets in recent years, with 2006 revenues expected to top $1 billion. In fiscal 2005, Satyam posted $794 million in revenues, up from $553 million in 2004. Satyam's founder, Ramalinga Raju, is a Harvard Business School alum. He was honored with Ernst & Young's Entrepreneur of the Year Award for Services in 1999 and was named Dataquest's IT Man of the Year in 2000, as well as CNBC's Asian Business Leader - Corporate Citizen of the Year in 2002.

Satyam describes its globalization ambitions as "relentless." Most recently, in late 2004, the firm opened a new global development center in Budapest, designed to strengthen near-shore resources for European clients. The firm has also expanded into South America with the opening of a center in Sao Paolo, and in September 2004 Satyam launched its largest global development center outside India, in Melbourne. In October 2005, Satyam announced plans to target deals worth $100 million or more, negotiating with organizations such as Pfizer, the World Bank and GlaxoSmithKline. Citing a "potential for explosive growth," Satyam execs expressed enthusiasm for breaking into the European market.

Massing the troops

Part of Satyam's growth strategy involves a solid recruitment program. The firm runs a management graduate program at its Technology Center in Hyderabad, training new recruits in marketing-related skills to help boost the company's business globally. And in November 2004, Satyam announced a plan to recruit fresh grads from local universities in Singapore, its first management graduate hiring program based outside of India. Indeed, Satyam's rapid employment uptick reflects its ambitions—the firm boosted its headcount by nearly 4,000 between 2004 and 2005.

Home-grown outsourcing

Along with competitors like Wipro, Satyam has grown powerful thanks to its home-grown approach to outsourcing, drawing from plentiful resources in its Indian home base. But Satyam's workers span the globe. In fact, Satyam calls its approach to outsourcing "RightSourcing," which is meant to indicate a flexible approach to serving clients with onsite, offshore, and offsite or near-shore delivery capabilities. Depending on clients' needs, Satyam staffers may perform work in India, the U.S., UK, UAE, Canada, Hungary, Singapore, Malaysia, China, Japan or Australia, or onsite at the customer's location.

Notable firsts

Satyam stands out for its pioneering approach to the Indian tech services market. The firm's subsidiary, Satyam Infoway, lays claim to being the first private Internet Service Provider in India, and was the first Indian Internet firm to be listed on the Nasdaq in November 1999. In fact, Satyam considers itself to be a groundbreaker in many respects. The firm claims to have established the offshore development center model for software delivery, harnessing the skills of Indian workers to serve clients abroad, particularly in the U.S. In collaboration with Carnegie Mellon University and Accenture, Satyam has developed a unique "quality hallmark," dubbed eSCM (for eSourcing Capability Model) for its IT Enabled Services offerings, the only such quality standard for the delivery of outsourced IT services. (Much of the firm's business process outsourcing is conducted through its subsidiary, Nipuna Services Limited.)

Quality is a big deal at Satyam: The firm ranks as the first company in the world to achieve ISO 9001:2000 certification (in 2001), and was one of the first 10 firms to be certified for CMM Level 5 (in 1999), both highly-regarded quality-assurance benchmarks in IT. The firm also has implemented the first PeopleSoft solution for an Indian university at Manipal Academy of Higher Education.

Big time engagements

In October 2005, Satyam inked a deal with Inco Limited, a leading Canadian mining company, for strategic IT consulting services. The firm plans to conduct a benchmark study of Inco's IT structure, identifying areas in need of improvement. Another heavy-hitting engagement came in September 2005, when the World Health Organization tapped Satyam to implement an Oracle ERP solution in offices spanning 140 countries. In June 2005, the firm won a multi-million dollar contract from polymer and fibers company INVISTA to run a global application maintenance system for at least three years. Another million-dollar deal was signed in May 2005, for an Oracle implementation at Jordan's third-largest GSM operator, Uminah Mobile Company. Other international clients include Nestle, TRW Automotive and Northrup Grumman.

Friendly relations

Satyam has built its global presence through a series of strategic acquisitions. In October 2005, the firm joined up with Ireland's IONA Technologies in a technology, marketing and sales agreement utilizing IONA's solutions in support of Service Oriented Architecture. In July 2005, the firm allied itself with The Publishing Practice Ltd. to deliver advanced content and data solutions to European and U.S. publishers. In April 2005, the firm announced its $23 million purchase of Citisoft, a specialized business and systems consulting firm operating out of London, Boston and New York, focusing on investment management consulting for clients such as Bear Stearns & Co. Satyam also enjoys alliances with a number of companies around the world. And in November 2004, the firm announced an agreement with the Indian Institute of Technology-Madras, to support research and development projects. Satyam signed on to offer practical domain expertise in manufacturing, automotive and other areas to students; in turn, the institute will offer academic resources and facilities for R&D projects.

Satyam's services have earned the company notice worldwide. In November 2004, the firm was honored with the Risk Management Award and the Solution Delivery Award at the first Global Sourcing Summit, produced by Gartner Vision Events. The awards recognize Satyam's effectiveness in managing risk and its creativity in enhancing or transforming a client's business.

A foundation of giving

The Satyam Foundation is Satyam's dedicated charitable arm, which invests in an array of projects including tsunami relief, health care, help for underprivileged children and environmental causes. Founded in 2000, the foundation, which was initially called Alambana, Sanskrit for "support," prides itself on not being a "checkbook charity organization," and instead enlists the direct involvement of Satyam associates. The firm reports that more than 20 percent of its staffers spend at least 5 percent of their time on charitable activities. The foundation also partners with local governments, NGOs and academic institutions to pursue its goals. The firm also supports the Byrraju Foundation, focused on building "progressive self-reliant rural communities" in India.

GETTING HIRED

An Indian flavor

Satyam maintains job search databases and extensive career information on its web site. The firm hires candidates around the globe, though its site reflects a particular dedication to cultivating and attracting talent in Satyam's home country of India.

A pulse on campus

The firm says it's focused on "grooming fresh talent" from university campuses worldwide, particularly management and engineering schools. Online, the firm maintains Campulse, described as a "single window" for information on campus initiatives and recruiting. Essentially an online customer relationship management tool for schools, Campulse allows academic institutions to register in order to set up recruitment dates, get information on student applications and offers, and learn more about the firm's selection process.

Think positive!

The firm, an insider says, always looks for people with "the right stuff," who are "the best in the industry." During interviews, an insider says, Satyam pays close attention to a candidate's "attitude and way of thinking." The firm prefers "positive-minded people," with a focus more on personality fit than on technical prowess, the source suggests.

OUR SURVEY SAYS

Satyam shines

Satyam's culture, an insider tells us, "all depends on where you are located." The firm's culture in India is described as "very good," though other sources agree that it varies from "country to country." Insiders like the fact that Satyam "has a very good name." "Working with Satyam is not just working; it is fun too," another source urges. "You will never feel like you are just working and life is boring." Flexibility is another hallmark of the firm, an insider suggests: "People do understand our difficulties when [we] want to change place or project."

That said, Satyam staffers are definitely dedicated to the job. Work hours, a source tells us, generally are eight hours a day, though they vary depending on project needs. A source notes that in this typical fluctuation in the work of a consultant, "sometimes we need to work 20 hours per day." As for travel, employees reportedly are put up in "best in the industry standard hotels."

Super salaries

Salaries at Satyam get high marks from staffers—the firm's compensation is the "best in [the] industry," says one insider. The firm's promotion policy, however, is "not very clear," a source reports, though promotions typically occur every two years or so. "If performance is outstanding, [you] can be promoted faster," the source adds. A colleague adds that benefits include use of a health club, a guest house, and "fun parties conducted by the company."

Visit the Vault Consulting Career Channel at www.vault.com/consulting — with
insider firm profiles, message boards, the Vault Consulting Job Board and more.

VAULT CAREER LIBRARY   339

T-Systems

701 Warrenville Road, Suite 100
Lisle, IL 60532
Phone: (630) 493-6100
Fax: (630) 493-6111
www.t-systems.com

LOCATIONS

Lisle, IL (North America HQ)
Frankfurt am Main, Germany (HQ)
Offices in over 20 countries

PRACTICE AREAS

Computing Services
Consulting
Desktop Services
E-Business Services
Network Services
Systems Integration

THE STATS

Employer Type: Subsidiary of Deutsche Telekom
Ticker Symbol: DT (NYSE)
CEO: Lothar Pauly
2005 Employees: 51,000
2004 Employees: 41,000
2005 Revenues: $16.3 billion
2004 Revenues: $13.8 billion

UPPERS

• Committed to corporate values
• Mentoring programs for women

DOWNERS

• Hierarchical corporate environment
• Limited benefits

EMPLOYMENT CONTACT

www.t-systems.com/jobs/engl

THE SCOOP

Fit to be T-ed

With 51,000 employees and offices and subsidiaries in over 20 countries, T-Systems is a leading worldwide provider of information and communications technology (ICT). The appropriately-named firm is controlled by the Deutsche Telekom Group and provides its parent company with business customer support for medium-sized and large companies, as well as for multinational corporations and public institutions. The North American branch is headquartered in Lisle, Ill., and employs some 350 people. The company's largest U.S. customers include Freightliner, Lockheed Martin and Sikorsky.

In 2005, Deutsche Telekom restructured T-Systems into two business units: T-Services Business Services (focusing on medium- and large-sized business clients) and T-Systems Enterprise Services (targeting multinational corporations and government agencies). Its customer segments contain about 60 multinational groups and major institutions in the public domain, and nearly 160,000 medium- and large-sized companies.

T-Systems claims expertise in a range of industries, including financial services and banking; telecommunications; chemicals; automotive; service sector; public sector; broadcasting; travel and transportation; education and research; insurance; aerospace and defense; health care; electrical, plant and mechanical engineering; and retail. Price competition within the telecommunications business resulted in stagnant revenue growth for T-Systems of late, as the company's 2004 revenues of $13.8 billion dropped slightly from 2003's mark of $13.9 billion, working its way up to $16.3 billion in 2005.

Blowing away the competition

T-Systems has developed a number of cutting-edge technologies in its quest for global ICT supremacy. Together with the Heinrich-Hertz Institute, T-Systems engineers succeeded in transmitting data at a rate of 160 Gbit/s on one carrier wave in installed standard fiber. This demonstration, which sends information at the equivalent of around 2.5 million ISDN channels, proved that existing networks are capable of transferring enormous amounts of data. T-Systems also runs G-Win, a communications network that contains 700 lines connecting universities and research institutions with speedy transfer rates. T-Systems runs the largest virtual hard drive in Europe for Deutsche Telekom. With a capacity of almost 100 terrabytes and rendering local hard drives obsolete, the system is accessible worldwide.

Restructuring at the core

In November 2005, T-Systems parent company Deutsche Telekom announced plans to cast off 32,000 staff members in Germany over the next three years in a restructuring plan. "On one hand, we have to cut jobs in old core markets," said Telekom CEO Kai-Uwe Ricke. "On the other, there are opportunities to create jobs in new innovative markets." Some 5,000 of those 32,000 jobs would be cut from T-Systems. Analysts regarded the T-Systems layoffs as a response to T-Systems' plans to acquire Paris-based Atos Origin SA. Such a pick-up would significantly enhance the company's ability to contend for pan-European outsourcing deals, and it is believed that a pared-down operating structure enabled by job cuts would make T-Systems a more appealing cohort. Some 300 T-Systems workers held a demonstration outside the Frankfurt headquarters in the days after the announcement, the first in a series of planned protests.

Getting strong with gedas

Outsourcing has been a primary growth strategy for the firm in the past few years. In an attempt to bolster its standing in the increasingly competitive IT outsourcing market, T-systems announced in March 2006 its acquisition of gedas AG, a Germany-based IT services provider. According to the firm, this acquisition is an "important milestone in the internationalization of the company in the global market for ICT services."

Working together with gedas—former subsidiary of Volkswagen—T-systems hopes to establish itself in the automobile industry. It has already agreed to a 2.5 million outsourcing contract with VW and hopes to capitalize on gedas' strong network of customers throughout Europe, North America, Latin America and Asia. A Gartner article commenting on the deal in February cited the acquisition as "another key example of consolidation in the IT service market," in which T-Systems has gained a set of complementary capabilities and a strong international foundation upon which it can build.

Widening its wingspan

In November 2005, T-Systems announced plans to build a new data center in Singapore, the location of the company's Asia-Pacific headquarters, that would be responsible for the "Asia South" region that stretches from India through Australia and New Zealand.

In September 2005, T-Systems set up points of service in Johannesburg and Cape Town, South Africa, to connect corporate clients to the international Sat3 cable by tapping into the worldwide network managed by Deutsche Telekom. The addition brought the size of the T-Systems global network to 150 "points of presence" delivering telecommunications to 50 countries. The company plans next to extend its network into other African countries.

Getting a foot in the sporting world

In February 2006, T-Systems received the 2006 Marketing Award of Sports. The firm was judged based on its sponsorship of a number of sailing events and implementation of high-tech solutions to market and coordinate the events. The firm has supported the South African challenger in America's Cup, as well as six German Olympic sailing teams.

T-Systems' reputation in the sporting world is spreading: Also in February, the 2006 Fifa World Cup Organizing Committee in Germany signed T-Systems to plan, set up and operate a digital radio network for all 12 Fifa stadiums. The firm will also link the soccer stadiums with the Fifa World Cup Organizing Committee headquarters in Berlin and Frankfurt, along with the International Media Center in Munich, using the TETRA (Terrestrial Trunked Radio) framework. TETRA offers wireless, tap-proof and stable communication that is independent of public networks.

Roll 'em!

The coming of digital cinema has sent shockwaves far outside the traditional markets of film production. T-Systems announced in October 2005 that it was partnering with SES ASTRA to create the first Europe-wide distribution network for digital cinema. According to the terms of the agreement, T-systems will offer a range of services, including the broadcasting, storage, administration and security of digital movies. The firm will use satellite technology to send movies to all cinemas at the same time, allowing moviegoers to view premieres of the latest films at even the smallest cinemas. It will also implement in-house, server-based cinema software, "Feature Film DC," which enables projectionists to configure movies, trailers and advertisements on a computer and distribute them to different screens within a cinema.

GETTING HIRED

A System-atic approach

On T-Systems' U.S. web site, hopeful candidates are linked to a search engine listing job openings, along with information on corporate culture and benefits. There's more detail on the firm's global web site, which links to job search engines by region and provides some hints on what T-Systems looks for in a consultant. T-Systems' "professional portfolio," the firm explains, "ranges from MBA graduates and engineers right through to computer scientists and programmers." Hallmarks of T-Systems staffers are "big ambitions" and "business flexibility," the firm adds.

The firm also offers an 18-month trainee program for recent grads, offering a chance to work on "five different project assignments in which, from day one, you will assume responsibility in day-to-day business." Applications for the program are accepted twice a year, in November and May.

One insider reports going through two interviews to get on board at T-Systems. The first interview, the source says, was a "getting to know you" meeting, including a discussion of qualifications and strengths and weaknesses, and the second was more of a "negotiation of contract details."

OUR SURVEY SAYS

T-Values

T-Systems, a source says, tends to have an "authoritarian" culture with an "uncoordinated" approach from day-to-day. There's "too much overtime," which leads to "burnout," the insider frets. But another source likes the fact that the firm's "corporate culture is stamped by 'T-Spirit,' our corporate values, [which include] respect, integrity, top excellence, innovation [and] being a partner to our customers."

While the firm's offices tend to be "dominated by male staff," the source adds, "mentoring programs are in place to encourage women starting a career in higher management." As for compensation, an insider reports that 90 percent of salary is fixed, with another 10 percent "variable based on your annual goals." There are reportedly "no additional benefits, like stock options," offered by the firm.

The firm's "corporate culture is stamped by 'T-Spirit,' our corporate values, [which include] respect, integrity, top excellence, innovation [and] being a partner to our customers."

— T-Systems consultant

Visit the Vault Consulting Career Channel at **www.vault.com/consulting** — with
insider firm profiles, message boards, the Vault Consulting Job Board and more.

VAULT CAREER LIBRARY   **345**

Technology Solutions Company

205 North Michigan Avenue
Suite 1500
Chicago, IL 60601
Phone: (312) 228-4500
Fax: (312) 228-4501
www.techsol.com

LOCATIONS

Chicago, IL (HQ)
Atlanta, GA
Herndon, VA
Minneapolis, MN
New York, NY
Stamford, CT

PRACTICE AREAS

Business Technology
Compliance
Customer Relationship Management
Enterprise Application Services
Extended Support
IT Strategy
Planning & Process Transformation
Process Adaptation & Training

THE STATS

Employer Type: Public Company
Ticker Symbol: TSCC (Nasdaq)
President & CEO: Michael R. Gorsage
2005 Employees: 168
2004 Employees: 192
2005 Revenues: $36.6 million
2004 Revenues: $32.2 million

UPPERS

• Collaborative, team-driven
  environment

DOWNERS

• Still recovering from heavy losses

EMPLOYMENT CONTACT

Recruiting Department
Phone: (312) 228-4500
E-mail: recruiting@techsol.com
Additional information available on
the Careers page of the firm's web
site

THE SCOOP

The name says it all

Founded in 1988 by a group of partners from Arthur Young & Co. (an antecedent of Big Four firm Ernst & Young), Chicago-based Technology Solutions Company focuses on specialized technology-based business solutions, as its name suggests. Since its launch, TSC has completed over 2,400 projects with almost 900 clients, including 64 of the Fortune 100. In the early 1990s, the firm began to hone in on the integrated services market, supplying implementations of cutting-edge software packages to meet market demand. The company maintains standing partnerships with numerous distinguished companies, including PeopleSoft, SAP, Apriso, Firepond and Comergent. TSC targets its consulting operations on four industries: manufacturing, health care, consumer products and retail, and retail and chain restaurants.

Seeking a solution for revenue losses

TSC suffered massive losses between 2002 and 2003, as annual revenues plummeted from $92.4 million to $45.6 million, and employee ranks dropped dramatically, from 400 to 207. Losses slowed in 2004, totaling $36.5 million at year's end. Seeking to plug the leaks, TSC appointed Michael R. Gorsage as CEO in May 2004 to replace former head Stephen B. Oresman. Gorsage brought with him over 20 years of experience in IT consulting from his former post as VP and managing director for the Customer Relationship and Business Intelligence unit of EDS. Since his appointment, the tide appears to be turning. TSC finished 2005 with revenues of $36.6 million, up from $32.2 million from the previous year.

In October 2005, TSC announced the filing of an amendment to produce a one-for-20 reverse stock split of all issued shares of the company's common stock, as well as to reduce the number of authorized shares of common stock. After the split, outstanding TSC shares numbered approximately 2.35 million and authorized shares of the company's common stock were reduced from 100 million to 20 million. "In addition to maintaining our Nasdaq National Market Listing," said Gorsage, "we believe our new capital structure will enhance our visibility among institutional investors and the sell-side community and assist in our efforts to build long-term shareholder value."

Giving voice to technology

In September 2005, TSC announced an agreement with VoiceObjects, a leader in voice application management systems (VAMS), to cooperatively develop voice-

Visit the Vault Consulting Career Channel at www.vault.com/consulting — with insider firm profiles, message boards, the Vault Consulting Job Board and more.

VAULT CAREER LIBRARY

347

driven market solutions. The partnership joined TSC's experience in consultation and solution delivery with VoiceObjects X5, a cutting-edge VAMS highlighted by scalable, carrier-grade server architecture, to deliver self-service solutions to the partnership's mutual client base.

The virtual "A-Team"

TSC refers to its consultants as the "A-Team"—consultants who are experienced, collaborative and business-benefit driven. TSC consultants average 18 years of work experience: 10 years in industry positions plus eight years of consulting experience. The company speaks of itself as a "virtual company," meaning employers are generally handled remotely, dotting the country and typically working onsite with clients, rather than at one of TSC's offices. The firm organizes teams that range from five to 25 consultants who work on projects that can last from a few months to a few years.

GETTING HIRED

Searching for seasoned staffers

Want to be a part of the A-Team? TSC says it hires candidates from a host of different backgrounds. The firm's mission is to find staffers with seasoned skills, a collaborative work style and a "business-benefit driven viewpoint." Candidates also are required to have a high level of industry or technology expertise; be able to think and act proactively; work well both in teams and with little to no direction; display high energy and enthusiasm; and be focused on client satisfaction.

As you might have guessed, TSC generally recruits candidates with some experience—the firm says the majority of its consultants have a decade or more of consulting positions. TSC typically recruits for client officers; vice presidents; project, solution or technical managers; solution or technical leads; functional or technical analysts; and associate consultants. The firm outlines and describes these positions in detail on its web site.

A way in

TSC also hires for the associate consultant position, designed for recent undergrads or master's degree holders looking to get a foot in the door. Associates, who come from business, engineering and computer science programs at top schools, participate in a 12-month training program during which they shadow more experienced consultants. The firm notes that associates do more than just observe: They play a key role in hands-on project work.

The firm explains that its consultants live in locations across the country, typically traveling to the client site each week. New hires immediately begin working in small teams, a hallmark of TSC's hands-on approach. TSC wannabes can find a link on the firm's Web site to job openings listed on Monster.com.

Visit the Vault Consulting Career Channel at **www.vault.com/consulting** — with insider firm profiles, message boards, the Vault Consulting Job Board and more.

V/\ULT CAREER LIBRARY

349

Telcordia Technologies

One Telcordia Drive
Piscataway, NJ 08854-4157
Phone: (800) 521-2673
www.telcordia.com

LOCATIONS

Piscataway, NJ (HQ)
More than 30 offices worldwide

PRACTICE AREAS

Consulting Services
Generic Requirements
Network Element Provider Services
Network Solutions
Product Support
Software Training
Transaction Services

THE STATS

Employer Type: Private Company
CEO: Daniel J. Carroll Jr.
2005 Employees: 3,200
2004 Employees: 3,284

UPPERS

- Flexible hours, telecommuting encouraged
- Diverse

DOWNERS

- All telecom all the time
- Recovering from downturn

EMPLOYMENT CONTACT

www.telcordia.com/careers
E-mail: jobs@telcordia.com

THE BUZZ
WHAT CONSULTANTS AT OTHER FIRMS ARE SAYING

- "Experts in the telecom field"
- "Strong technically"
- "Some good staff; not consistent"
- "Expensive"

THE SCOOP

Telecom calling

The telecommunications industry has evolved at a dizzying pace over the last decade, and Telcordia Technologies has been part of the revolution. Providing services and products in virtually every area of telecom, the firm is responsible for 80 percent of today's U.S. telecom network and 85 percent of toll-free traffic, and has been expanding rapidly abroad. In fact, the firm can take credit for much of the underlying software and applications for today's communications networks.

Telcordia provides both consulting services and products designed to help telecom providers boost revenues, enhance their services and streamline their infrastructures. The firm's customers include not only the communications industry's heaviest hitters—including cable operators, wireless service companies, voice networks and IP networks—but also government agencies (including NASA and the FBI) and global enterprises. Telcordia today serves customers at more than 800 commercial and government sites worldwide and employs approximately 3,200 employees.

Ringing a bell

Founded in 1984 as Bellcore (Bell Communications Research Inc.), a research laboratory for the seven Bell telephone companies that were created with AT&T's divestiture, the firm got the Telcordia name in 1997 when it was acquired by Science Applications International Corporation (SAIC). By 2002, the firm needed to expand its services and innovate in order to survive in a hard-hit telecommunications market. Matt Desch, an industry vet who served as president of Nortel's highly successful Global Service Providers division, was brought on board as CEO in July 2002.

It's Elementive

Desch helmed the development of Telcordia's "Elementive" strategy, introduced in July 2003. The modularized Elementive portfolio emphasizes flexibility, adaptability, efficiency and speed, and combines a variety of initiatives, including new software, an expanded partner network and innovation in the wireless market. The new portfolio led to new contracts with clients such as Tata Teleservices, Ltd, and Swisscom Mobile.

Passing the phone

In July 2004, SAIC announced its plans to sell Telcordia, and in March 2005, the deal was sealed when Telcordia was purchased by Providence Equity Partners and

Visit the Vault Consulting Career Channel at **www.vault.com/consulting** — with insider firm profiles, message boards, the Vault Consulting Job Board and more.

VAULT CAREER LIBRARY   **351**

Warburg Pincus for $1.35 billion in cash. According to CEO Desch, the investment firms "have the resources available to enable us to reach our full potential, capitalize on our market-leading intellectual capital and secure a global leadership position."

Along with Telcordia, Providence also acquired the firm's many subsidiaries. These include Granite Systems, a provider of service management software; InterConnect Communications, a management consulting firm specializing in telecoms out of Chepstow, Wales; and Mesa Solutions, which handles systems integration for electric, gas and telecom concerns.

In September 2005, the firm announced the appointment of Daniel J. Carroll Jr. as its new president and CEO. Carroll formerly served as COO of the Business Communications Services Division at Lucent Technologies.

Transcontinental telecom

As the newest incarnation of Telcordia settles in, the company has continued to expand its presence worldwide. The firm set up a Brazilian-based entity, Telcordia Technologies Telecomunicacoes do Brasil Ltda., with offices in Rio de Janeiro and Sao Paulo, and has teamed with many of Europe's largest carriers and government organizations, including Greece's national telecom office, Telecom Italia, Saudi Telecom and British Telecom. In the Asia-Pacific region, Telcordia has partnered with Taiwan's Industrial Technology Research Institute to open an Applied Research Center focused on developing a next-generation Open Network Service Platform. Recent international engagements include a September 2005 $20 million contract to help leading Indian wireless firm Tata Teleservices support its long-term evolution of prepaid and postpaid convergent solutions; a July 2005 agreement to provide Lithuania's communications authority with a number portability solution; and the selection in May 2005 of Telcordia's Granite Service Resource Management solution by a subsidiary of China Mobile.

The latest technologies

The firm has gotten more heavily involved with voice over internet protocol (VoIP) technologies, forecasting that the number of VoIP subscribers worldwide will grow from 9.5 million in 2005 to 97 million in 2009. In September 2005, Telcordia introduced the Telcordia® VoIP Routing Registry, a new service that enables cross-carrier VoIP calling. In February 2006, the firm received the 2006 Frost & Sullivan Award for Product Innovation for the Routing Registry, solidifying its reputation as a leading innovator in IP communications.

The firm also publishes research in its *Telcordia Digest of Technical Information*, a monthly publication for the telecom industry. The *Digest* is available on Telcordia's web site in PDF format.

GETTING HIRED

Telcordia calling

On Telcordia's web site, you can call up job openings by location and job title, submit a resume, and learn more about benefits and training at the firm. The firm also provides information for students on college recruiting and internship opportunities. In 2005, Telcordia held recruiting events at Morgan State in Baltimore; NJIT in Newark; Penn State; Princeton; Rochester Institute of Technology; Rutgers University; and Stevens Institute of Technology in Hoboken.

Paid summer internships at Telcordia run from the end of May through early August. The firm accepts applications through the first week of March. Undergrad and graduate students with computer science, computer engineering, electrical engineering or systems engineering majors with at least a 3.5 GPA are invited to apply. In addition to hands-on experience, the firm offers interns partially subsidized housing at Rutgers University.

Co-ops are another way to get hands-on experience at Telcordia. These paid, full-time positions are open to undergrads and grads in their last semester, with the same majors and GPA requirements as those for interns. Sessions run from January through May and June through December.

Just the facts, ma'am

An insider who managed to break in at Telcordia tells us that the hiring process consisted of two interviews, one with a manager and one with a future co-worker. "The manager interview focused on my school experiences, explained some of what the job entailed, and then asked very basic questions about items listed on the resume, with some drill-down for topics of interest (such as database classes or compilers)," the source says. "The co-worker interview asked more detailed questions about programming languages, classroom experiences [and] algorithm design. Nothing really out of the ordinary."

OUR SURVEY SAYS

Telcordia, reborn

Telcordia, insiders suggest, is a firm "in a state of flux." As one source explains, "From a management perspective, it has been a revolving door. We have gone through four or five CEOs in the past five years." All this change has had a noticeable effect on culture, a colleague notes—though that's not entirely a bad thing. Whereas in the past (pre- bubble burst), the firm had "lots of money to put towards projects"; these days, the source says, "with limited people (the corporate communications organization went from more than 130 people to approximately 30) there is better rationale for doing projects. Being more strategic is critical. Being a team player and delegating is essential. There is little room (and even less tolerance) for those who don't perform well or significantly contribute."

In short, the insider says, "the corporate culture is transforming," shifting more toward marketing and sales rather than strict research and development. "The executive team realizes that having the best (newest, fastest, neatest) products on the market is important but gaining buzz in the market and executing strong product and corporate marketing programs is a critical step in driving interest and, ultimately, securing sales."

Meanwhile, a colleague notes, Telcordia's new push to outsource some tasks is "making it difficult for the average programmer to stay employed. The business staffing model is to keep a lead developer, system engineer and tester onsite, with the rest of the development occurring off shore."

Casual days

For average Telcordians, "The work environment is sub-business casual," says a source, as "employees typically dress in jeans and t-shirts" and "management tends to wear slacks and dress shirts." "Diversity is huge here," says another insider, adding, "it's truly a global company and boundaries of age, sex and ethnicity don't exist."

As for hours, a source tells us, they are "pretty flexible, but there is a lot of process-fat involved in doing day-to-day tasks." A colleague agrees, "Hours are the typical 9 to 5-ish, but a tremendous amount of flexibility is allowed. It's more about getting the work done than getting it done during normal working hours. Telecommuting is encouraged."

Back to bonuses

Telcordia insiders suffered during the economic downturn, with "massive layoffs," a "lack of raises" and, "for salaried employees, a sub-par bonus." These days, consultants usually receive some bonus "based on level," along with "limited stock options." An insider tells us that "Telcordia does offer a tuition reimbursement program, and has been affiliated with Stevens Institute of Technology, as well as Columbia University, for undergraduate and graduate degrees."

Sources suggest that the firm is on the upswing. According to an insider, "Opportunities for advancement are improving a bit as the company continues to recover from the bubble burst." The source adds that the "future looks brighter as hiring has ensued again for the first time in quite a while."

TIAX LLC

15 Acorn Park
Cambridge, MA 02140
Phone: (617) 498-5000
www.tiaxllc.com

LOCATIONS

Cambridge, MA (HQ)
Cupertino, CA

PRACTICE AREAS

Creating Technology Platforms
Defining Technology Opportunities
Developing Products
Maximizing Technology & IP Value
Optimizing Applications

THE STATS

Employer Type: Private Company
President & CEO: Kenan Sahin
2005 Employees: 250
2004 Employees: 250

UPPERS

- Exceptional colleagues
- Get to work on cutting-edge projects
- Opportunities for advancement

DOWNERS

- Highly selective
- Most interesting work goes to advanced-degree holders
- Profit-sharing "not profitable"

EMPLOYMENT CONTACT

David Benoit
Phone: (617) 498-6414
E-mail: benoit.david@tiaxllc.com
www.tiaxllc.com/careers/index.php

THE SCOOP

TIAX-achusetts

Unlike most IT firms, Cambridge-based TIAX LLC can trace its roots back to the 19th century. TIAX's pedigree goes back to 1886, when Arthur D. Little helped found Griffin & Little, the firm that would eventually adopt Little's name as its own. Even then, the company was involved in scientific projects such as the creation of nonflammable motion picture film for Kodak and the material that would be used to invent fiberglass.

These projects were funded by Arthur D. Little's technology and innovation division, which the consulting firm placed on the market in May 2002. Former MIT professor and software billionaire Kenan Sahin shelled out $16.5 million for the division and the 250 staffers who came with it. Sahin quickly renamed the company, opting for a flashy acronym—TIAX, or "technology and innovation applications, to the power of X." Today, the firm provides R&D services to customers in a variety of industries, including applicances and building systems; automotive and transportation; chemicals and materials; consumer products; energy and power; food and food service; health care; and various public sector clients. The firm concentrates on five aspects of innovation: creating technology platforms, product development, optimizing applications, defining technology applications, and maximizing technology and IP value. TIAX's engineers, technologists and scientists are formed into multidisciplinary teams that link different approaches and combine technical knowledge with industry experience. As such, the firm is making headway in its field, being selected in 2003 by the World Economic Forum as a Technology Pioneer and maintaining ISO 9001 certification with over 50 research and development labs.

Clearing the air

In July 2005, TIAX was awarded a new contract from the Gateway Cities Clean Air Program (GCCAP) to continue overseeing the replacement of heavy-duty trucks in the Los Angeles area with lower-emission vehicles. The company has been involved with the project since 2002. The new contract means that TIAX will continue to arbitrate deals between the GCCAP and truck owners to ensure that they grant requirements and adhere to the program's guidelines. The company will also "retrofit" devices on trucks to reduce diesel exhaust emission levels and attach global positioning systems that allow TIAX to monitor each truck's activities and obtain a better understanding of where emissions are being successfully reduced.

Travel safely

Also in July, TIAX began work on two projects to design safer seats and worktables for the U.S. Department of Transportation. The projects are part of a five-year contract the company received in 2004 from the Volpe National Systems Transportation Center to improve the crash-worthiness of rail equipment. TIAX is hard at work creating a workstation table that can absorb the impact of passengers who may collide with it in the event of a crash, and the product is intended to allow a way out from behind the table, in addition to minimizing head, chest, abdomen and leg injuries. The safer seats are designed to reduce injuries, keep occupants compartmentalized and remain attached to the railcar. These projects are the most recent in TIAX's 10-year relationship with the Volpe Center.

Building a better spacesuit

In August 2005, the first phase of TIAX's contract with NASA got underway, as the company began work on a variety of products and structures, from space suits to landing pads to inflatable habitats. TIAX's mission is to develop intelligent and flexible materials that can monitor their own condition, diagnose punctures and self-repair. Also in development are materials that can fight off corrosive materials, generate and store power, prevent oxygen loss and fend off radiation. The intention is for these materials to be used not only in space suits and landing pads, but also in air lock chambers used during docking and the balloon-parachute hybrids—ballutes—that slow spacecraft reentry into the atmosphere. The product that stirs the most excitement within the company is inflatable habitats the size of a three-car garage that can orbit in space or rest upon rugged terrain on the moon or Mars and house up to 10 astronauts.

Linking academia and the market

In August 2005, TIAX CEO Kenan Sahin announced that TIAX would be opening an Innovation Implementation Center at the University of Massachusetts Amherst to initiate a culture of "upstream implementation" in academic research labs. "Upstream is high-value added and requires a lot of cerebral power," Sahin said at the time, explaining that products could be developed at the center and then licensed to low-cost producers elsewhere. "Academics are superb at starting things, lousy in finishing them." The center is intended to breed a corps of "implementation engineers" who excel in finding commercial applications for the types of innovation Sahin believes are progressing at unprecedented rates. To wit, the UMass center will develop implementation textbooks, run clinics and provide the services of TIAX consultants experienced in matching ideas with markets. "While innovation is important, it's the implementation of innovation that creates value," Sahin said. "We have a huge backlog of innovation, and we keep adding to it."

GETTING HIRED

Top-tier at TIAX

TIAX lists job openings on its web site, but provides a snail mail address to which resumes for these positions must be sent. The firm is heavily into campus recruiting, drawing candidates from top-shelf schools, including the Ivies and especially MIT, sources suggest.

Ready for recruitment

TIAX says it looks for "outstanding scientists, engineers, and industry experts with BS, MS and PhD degrees at all career stages." The firm seeks out "innovative, creative thinkers" who are "the best in their field." It also helps if you're practical, resourceful, a risk-taker, a problem solver, a self starter and a team player.

Those hoping to join the firm with a BS can expect to work on a variety of demanding projects, the firm says. Preferred backgrounds are in mechanical, chemical or electrical studies, as well as industrial engineering, computer science, physics and natural sciences. These same qualifications apply to MS and PhD holders, but these candidates should also come armed with a "solid track record of accomplishments" and "seek a high level of responsibility." The firm accepts resumes and cover letters from hopeful campus recruits e-mailed to benoit.david@tiaxllc.com.

OUR SURVEY SAYS

Really nice, really smart

TIAX boasts a staff full of "really nice people" who are "really, really smart," insiders tell us. Consultants work on "lots of interesting and diverse projects," says a source, and the firm is full of "great people and intellectually challenging work based on a novel approach to developing new technology for commercialization," a colleague says. But one insider grumbles that "there is a serious disconnect between the scientific culture and the blind adherence to its founder and chairman's psychobabble."

The firm offers opportunities to get ahead, sources suggest. "TIAX has a very flat structure, but anyone can progress. Some former support staff now work in technical positions, for example," says a consultant. However, a source notes, "Sometimes people who do not have advanced degrees do not get to do interesting work." The firm reportedly offers profit-sharing of up to 25 percent, but it's "not profitable at present," an insider says. Consultants typically work about 45 to 50 hours per week.

"TIAX has a very flat structure, but anyone can progress. Some former support staff now work in technical positions, for example."

— *TIAX source*

Visit the Vault Consulting Career Channel at **www.vault.com/consulting** — with
insider firm profiles, message boards, the Vault Consulting Job Board and more.

VAULT CAREER LIBRARY   361

Xansa

420 Thames Valley Park Drive
Thames Valley Park
Reading, United Kingdom
RG6 1PU
Phone: +44 (0)8702 416181
Fax: +44 (0)8702 426282
www.xansa.com

LOCATIONS

Reading, UK (HQ)
12 offices throughout the UK and
India

PRACTICE AREAS

Business & Technology Consulting
Business Process Outsourcing
Finance & Accounting Outsourcing
IT Outsourcing
IT Services
    Applications Management
    Full LifeCycle
    ERP
On- and Offshore Delivery

THE STATS

Employer Type: Public Company
Ticker Symbol: XAN (London Stock Exchange)
CEO: Alistair Cox
2005 Employees: 6,847
2004 Employees: 5,189
2005 Revenues: $717.8 million
2004 Revenues: $744.2 million

UPPERS

- Flexible hours
- "Employee-friendly" culture

DOWNERS

- "Interoffice politics is high"
- "Bureaucratic"

EMPLOYMENT CONTACT

www.xansa.com/careers

THE SCOOP

IT from X to A

With clients in the banking, government, pharmaceutical, retail, utilities and public sector industries across Asia and Europe, UK-headquartered Xansa is one of Europe's leading IT firms. The company specializes in large-scale projects and develops systems that control functions such as accounting, billing, customer services, online banking, purchasing and sales. Xansa counts a number of leading blue-chip clients in its customer ranks, including Barclaycard, AXA, National Health Services (NHS), BT, Thames Water, MyTravel and Prudential. The firm, which employs over 6,000 employees in the United Kingdom and India, has a well established integrated UK and India delivery model and continues to grow its numbers in India. Xansa completed a massive restructuring campaign in the last two years, selling subsidiaries in Belgium and the Netherlands in 2003.

Pioneering history

Xansa's history includes a true rarity—a female founder. Utilizing the "teleworking notion that allowed women to combine work and motherhood, Dame Stephanie "Steve" Shirley founded Freelance Programmers in 1962 with less than $100 and an all-female staff of telecommuters. Soon thereafter, Shirley adopted the pseudonym of Steve Shirley to combat gender discrimination in business. The early focus of Freelance Programmers's all-female, work-at-home programming team was on developing and manufacturing applications software for contract clients like esteemed chocolatier Mars, one of its first customers. (It didn't hire its first male employee until the mid-1970s). The company changed its name to F International in 1971, then F.I. Group in 1988. By 1987, the firm's annual revenues topped $16 million and Shirley ceded the chief executive role to Hilary Cropper. In 1996, Cropper took the company public, collecting some $25 million for the firm, and led an employee buyout in 2001. By 1999, she was the highest-paid woman in Britain, earning over $30 million. With the acquisitions of IT consulting firms Druid Group and Synergy International Consulting in 2000 and 2001, Xansa began to expand beyond its application development ancestry.

Shirley retired as company president in 1993 and was recognized in October 2004 with the British Computer Society's Lifetime Achievement Award. Xansa is currently headed by Alistair Cox, the company's first male CEO, who joined the firm in 2002 from Lafarge. Cropper stepped down as chairman in 2003 due to ill health, and passed away a year later. During her tenure, the company's annual revenues grew from $12 million to over $890 million.

Sitting Indian style

Xansa pioneered onshoring and offshoring in the UK and was one of the first IT companies in India, where it has maintained a presence since 1989. The firm acquired IIS Infotech, an Indian software developer, in 1997, and began an aggressive expansion strategy in India in 2002 that included building two new facilities. Xansa currently has operations in three cities in India. Its facility in Chennai handles the insurance segment and parts of the finance and accounting services. The Noida center operates in retail, utilities and parts of the banking sector, while the Pune center is engaged in banking, telecom, and finance and accounting services. In October 2005, Xansa picked up the BPO project of the year award at the National Outsourcing Association Awards for its work with MyTravel's finance and accounting processes, in a seven-year outsourcing contract signed in April 2004.

Xansa's financial returns demonstrate the dangers of shifting to an offshore delivery model. While the company's net profits grew to $15.1 million in 2005, it endured a 3.5 percent drop in revenue to $717.8 million. The company attributed the fall to the transition of private sector work from the UK to Indian delivery centers. In 2005, revenue from Indian operations grew 45 percent to $98.8 million. Xansa's Indian workforce grew to 2,815—approximately 50 percent of its total staff—a number the company plans to approach 4,000 by the end of 2006. In October 2005, Xansa announced plans to increase total headcount in India to 10,000 over the next three years.

By December 2005, CEO Alistair Cox declared that Xansa had reached a "tipping point" in its three-pronged strategy—to grow the business, particularly in the public sector; to raise profit margins by offshoring more work to India; and to win new clients and develop the joint venture with Britain's National Health Service.

Gunning for government

Despite its strong presence in India, Xansa derives the majority of its revenue from the UK. In 2005, UK operations turnover increased 3.5 percent to $655.3 million, while operating profits rose 29.3 percent to $37.6 million. That same year, sales in the firm's government business unit alone saw revenue growth of 31 percent. That growth was in part due to the addition of a number of new clients, including the Metropolitan Police, the Foreign and Commonwealth Office and the city councils of Peterborough and Cornwall. Xansa's finance and accounting joint venture with the

UK Department of Health, NHS Shared Business Services—originally announced in November 2004—performed ahead of expectations over the same period. The partnership, which benefits NHS organizations through cost savings, reduced capital expenditure and "best in class" services, and enabled some $390 million to be reinvested into front-line patient care. By the end of 2005, 100 of the 663 NHS trusts were either using the venture's services or about to transfer their operations over to NHS Shared Business Services.

Director of government consultancy Simon Coles plans to sustain the momentum by adding about 50 senior consultants to the team in 2006. In a February 2006 interview with *Consulting Times*, Coles said he wants to bring on more sales-savvy consultants. The firm aims to attract hires who are not just good consultants, but "entrepreneurial people that want to develop the business as well."

Need for speed

In October 2005, Xansa announced a partnership with Renault, a Formula One race team, to provide offshore analysis in real time during races and test runs. Cox explained that Xansa's analysis would enable Renault team members to fine-tune their vehicles, including the engine, suspension and even aerodynamics, in real time. Twelve Xansa engineers at the plant in Noida and several onsite team members had already started work on the project. The analysis was expected to compute nearly 2 million instructions every second and send back instructions to engineers or mechanics at the race site. Xansa envisions this sort of high-volume analysis extending beyond Formula One to other segments such as engineering and data analysis for the financial services industry.

GETTING HIRED

India or UK?

On its web site, Xansa lists job openings at its UK and Indian locations. The firm also provides information on submitting resumes for each location—Indian applicants are advised to e-mail relevant contacts in Chennai, Pune and Noida, while UK applicants are instructed to contact jobs.uk@xansa.com. CVs received at the firm's UK offices are held for six months, after which applicants should resubmit them, Xansa says.

The firm's hiring process, says an insider, is "quite streamlined." At the "first level," resumes are screened, followed by an interview with HR, two technical interviews,

Visit the Vault Consulting Career Channel at **www.vault.com/consulting** — with insider firm profiles, message boards, the Vault Consulting Job Board and more.

V/\ULT CAREER LIBRARY 365

"and sometimes online tests." All this is followed by a last round with a manager, and "sometimes there could be a client interview as well."

OUR SURVEY SAYS

From can-do to "caring"

Xansa is an "employee-friendly and caring organization," where the work hours are "easy," a source says. "It gives you space to put your ideas to work." Still, the firm's culture continues to recover from its period of major changes. One insider who was with Druid before the merger complains that the culture has "transformed from a can-do to a bureaucratic and unimaginative civil service style."

When it comes to compensation, the "pay rewards are competitive," a consultant tells us, but "the bonus schemes haven't paid out in years (so you should discount them) and some questions have been raised by others over the pension scheme, which is not administered with enormous clarity." The firm explains that it has moved from a final salary to money purchase scheme, adding that it has recently been planning to address the final salary scheme deficit, which is now common to most final salary schemes.

APPENDIX

Index of Firms

Alphabetical list of firms

Accenture 66
Affiliated Computer Services, Inc. .254
Ajilon Consulting 262
Alliance Consulting Group 270
Appian Corporation 276
Aquent .282
Atos Origin 288
BearingPoint 114
Booz Allen Hamilton 22
BT 248
Bull 294
Capgemini 96
CGI Group Inc. 218
CIBER Inc. .298
Cisco Systems, Inc. 58
Computer Sciences Corporation . . .130
Covansys Corporation 304
CTG 310
Deloitte Consulting LLP 36
DiamondCluster International Inc. .168
EDS 140
Financial Insights, an IDC Company .314
Fujitsu Consulting 236
Getronics NV 206
GFI Informatique 318
HP Services 104
IBM Global Services 44
Infosys Technologies Ltd. 198
Interactive Business Systems, Inc. . .322
Keane 180
Lockheed Martin Corporation 80
LogicaCMG 326
Oracle Consulting 90
PA Consulting Group 242
Perot Systems 188
Sapient 160
Satyam Computer Services Ltd. . . .334
T-Systems .340

Tata Consultancy Services 226
Technology Solutions Company . . .346
Telcordia Technologies 350
TIAX LLC .356
Unisys 150
Wipro Ltd. 212
Xansa 362

Firms with non-U.S. headquarters

Atos Origin 288
BT 248
Bull 294
Capgemini 96
CGI Group Inc. 218
Getronics NV 206
GFI Informatique 318
Infosys Technologies Ltd. 198
LogicaCMG 326
PA Consulting Group 242
Satyam Computer Services Ltd. . . .334
T-Systems .340
Tata Consultancy Services 226
Wipro Ltd. 212
Xansa 362

Firms with U.S. headquarters

Affiliated Computer Services, Inc. .254
Ajilon Consulting 262
Alliance Consulting Group 270
Appian Corporation 276
Aquent 282
BearingPoint 114
Booz Allen Hamilton 22
CIBER Inc. .298

Cisco Systems, Inc. 58
Computer Sciences Corporation . . .130
Covansys Corporation 304
CTG 310
Deloitte Consulting LLP 36
DiamondCluster International Inc. .168
EDS 140
Financial Insights, an IDC Company .314
Fujitsu Consulting 236
HP Services 104
IBM Global Services 44
Interactive Business Systems, Inc. . .322
Keane 180
Lockheed Martin Corporation 80
Oracle Consulting 90
Perot Systems 188
Sapient 160
Technology Solutions Company . . .346
Telcordia Technologies 350
TIAX LLC 356
Unisys 150

Lockheed Martin Corporation 80
LogicaCMG 326
Oracle Consulting 90
Perot Systems 188
Sapient 160
Satyam Computer Services Ltd. . . .334
Tata Consultancy Services 226
Technology Solutions Company . . .346
Unisys 150
Wipro Ltd. 212
Xansa 362

Private firms

Appian Corporation 276
Aquent 282
Booz Allen Hamilton 22
Interactive Business Systems, Inc. . .322
PA Consulting Group 242
Telcordia Technologies 350
TIAX LLC 356

Publicly traded firms

Accenture .66
Affiliated Computer Services, Inc. .254
Atos Origin 288
BearingPoint 114
Bull 294
Capgemini 96
CGI Group Inc. 218
CIBER Inc. 298
Cisco Systems, Inc. 58
Computer Sciences Corporation . . .130
Covansys Corporation 304
CTG 310
DiamondCluster International Inc. .168
EDS 140
Getronics NV 206
GFI Informatique 318
HP Services 104
Infosys Technologies Ltd. 198
Keane 180

Firms that are subsidiaries of larger companies

Ajilon Consulting 262
Alliance Consulting Group 270
BT 248
Deloitte Consulting LLP 36
Financial Insights, an IDC Company .314
Fujitsu Consulting 236
IBM Global Services 44
T-Systems 340

Visit the Vault Consulting Career Channel at **www.vault.com/consulting** — with
insider firm profiles, message boards, the Vault Consulting Job Board and more.

V/\ULT CAREER LIBRARY   **369**

How many consulting job boards have you visited lately?

(Thought so.)

Use the Internet's most targeted job search tools for consulting professionals.

Vault Consulting Job Board

The most comprehensive and convenient job board for consulting professionals. Target your search by area of consulting, function, and experience level, and find the job openings that you want. No surfing required.

VaultMatch Resume Database

Vault takes match-making to the next level: post your resume and customize your search by area of consulting, experience and more. We'll match job listings with your interests and criteria and e-mail them directly to your inbox.

About the Editor

Naomi Newman is the Consulting Editor at Vault. She graduated with a BA in American Studies from Barnard College, with a concentration in Economics.